A Hitch
in Time

A Hitch in Time

Reflections Ready for Reconsideration

Christopher Hitchens

TWELVE

New York   Boston

Twelve
Hachette Book Group
1290 Avenue of the Americas, New York, NY 10104
twelvebooks.com
twitter.com/twelvebooks

Originally published in the UK in 2021 by Atlantic Books

First U.S. Edition: January 2024

Twelve is an imprint of Grand Central Publishing. The Twelve name and logo are trademarks of Hachette Book Group, Inc.

The publisher is not responsible for websites (or their content) that are not owned by the publisher.

The Hachette Speakers Bureau provides a wide range of authors for speaking events. To find out more, go to hachettespeakersbureau.com or email HachetteSpeakers@hbgusa.com.

Twelve books may be purchased in bulk for business, educational, or promotional use. For information, please contact your local bookseller or the Hachette Book Group Special Markets Department at special.markets@hbgusa.com.

All articles were previously published in the London Review of Books

Library of Congress Cataloging-in-Publication Data has been applied for.

ISBNs: 978-1-5387-5765-9 (hardcover), 978-1-5387-5767-3 (ebook)

Printed in the United States of America

LSC-C

Printing 1, 2023

CONTENTS

Contents

Foreword
James Wolcott

I RECALL vividly my first beholding of the Christopher Hitchens Experience, one of those epiphany moments that drops into your lap unbidden. The occasion was *Vanity Fair*'s holiday party for staff and contributors, the venue that year being Joe's Pub, a restaurant and performance space. Magazine holiday parties traditionally tended to be brisk, collegiate affairs held in the office after a regular workday, consisting of a judiciously sipped drink or two, a few flurries of flirtation here and there, and a bit of "face time" with the editor in chief before a discreet getaway, the streets thronged with other early evacuees desperately trying to flag a taxi in those pre-Uber times. Not *Vanity Fair*'s. *Vanity Fair* holiday parties, like the magazine itself in those ad-flush days, laid on the bezazz. They were what parties were meant to be, beehive buzzfests building in noise and body English until the floorboards seemed to bounce. Spilled drinks, shards of laughter, impetuous doings in the bathrooms. And this party was even more boisterous than its predecessors. One editorial assistant had to be lofted and carried out like a fallen comrade. The whole evening had a theatrical oomph as a DJ kept everything in throbby motion. All that was missing was a disco ball.

And then, on the Joe's Pub stage, like an Avengers' portal opening from another dimension, materialized editor Graydon

Carter and star columnist Christopher Hitchens, embracing the tribal spirit and grooving away to the thudding beat. Others were on stage as well, but all eyes still capable of focusing trained on the dynamic duo. They weren't dancing with each other so much as at each other, loosely mirroring each other like friendly tugboats, and at one point Hitchens whipped off his jacket with toreador flair to whooping cries of encouragement. He undid a button of his white shirt or perhaps it popped on its own and chugged toward Carter, attempting to bump bellies. Graydon retreated a few steps, protecting his front. It was one thing for the editor in chief to electric boogaloo, but bumping bellies was a bridge too far. Decorum must be maintained even in the midst of bacchanal. Yet Hitchens persisted, his belly declining to take no for an answer, this sweaty pagan spectacle unfolding before our eyes until it looked as if he might strip off his shirt entirely and cast it aside like a Chippendales dancer. "My God," I thought, "the legends are true. Dionysus rides again!" Then the portal resealed and the vision dissolved, or maybe the music just stopped, and into the night we trooped, with much to talk about the next day.

For years Hitchens and I shared Vanity Fair's front of the book as monthly columnists, nobly pulling our load. Our shoulder-rubbing adjacency in print led to occasions of misidentity. More than once I was complimented on a coruscating piece that had been Hitchens's handiwork. "That was ballsy of you to get water-boarded," a stranger on the bus leaned over to confide one afternoon, leaning back after I informed him, "That wasn't me, that was Hitchens." Similarly, I was once consoled on the Brazilian bikini wax I had so

sportingly undergone for the purposes of participatory journalism. Again, Hitchens. Despite our sharing the same real
estate in VF's glossy pages and being mistaken for each other
by random civilians, we had almost no personal overlap or
exchanges, apart from the seasonal holiday bacchanals or the
occasional book party. He was based in Washington, DC, his
residence the nearest thing the Potomac had to a brainy salon
(it was also the site of *Vanity Fair's* gala White House Correspondents' Dinner after-party, whose guests one year included Salman Rushdie, Olivia Wilde and Tucker Carlson); I called
Manhattan home. He was peripatetic, a roving correspondent who filed reports from the Middle East and even North
Korea; me, not. We stayed in our separate lanes, his lane far
more spacious and trafficked than mine. Unlike so many others, then, I have no picnic basket of personal anecdotes to un-
pack, no intimate exchanges. In conversation with others I
never referred to him as Christopher or Hitch; that would
have presumed a familiarity I didn't possess.

Had we been able or inclined to spend time in each other's
company, I would have been at a disadvantage, my capacity
for alcohol being far below that of the average debutante's.
One drink and I begin to stare out at sea, looking for white
sails. Many others did their valiant, futile best to keep up
with his industrial quota. After Hitchens's much mourned
death in 2011, the last stanza in his grueling, unflinching,
heroic battle with esophageal cancer (documented in his
posthumous memoir, *Mortality*), one personal tribute after another related how the subject and mentor spent hours talking and drinking into blue midnight, the narrator reduced to
a woozy heap as Hitchens padded off to his keyboard and

batted out a ream of copy that was witty, informed, sardonic and rounded off, as glistening and pristine as a Richard Avedon contact sheet. No matter how high the evening's intake, one pavilion of Hitchens's brain remained brightly lit and open for business.

In the autumnal fullness of time, Hitchens's prodigious amount of alcoholic input and journalistic output, the lubricated churn of his powerhouse intellect and his unflagging stamina, the barnstorming pace of all those panels, speeches, debates, and TV appearances, seemed to defy the laws of human biology. How did he not implode? Plus, he smoked. The premier action shot of Hitchens at the crest of his public notoriety would show him steaming up to the auditorium lectern with a glass in one hand and a cigarette in the other, the last of the living-large, two-fisted provocateurs, ready to conquer ideological foes and hecklers alike as a lick of hair flopped over his forehead like Elvis Presley. He could be droll one moment, cauterizing the next, thunder-rumbling as he reached a peroration, an old-school duelist and rhetorician like we ain't got much of in Amurrica. In his adopted country (he became a U.S. citizen in 2007), Hitchens's methodical glee in flustering everyone's preened feathers provided welcome relief from the fraternal order of technocratic weenies, Beltway insiders, meritocratic humbugs and conventional-wisdom recyclers who plagued us then (and are even more prevalent today—another swamp Trump failed to drain), but his roguish image often overshadowed the actual writing, especially with the rise of social media, which tends to caricature everything and everyone into a meme or a jokey GIF, catering to the twitchy eyeballs of the attention-deficited and sleep-deprived.

So revisiting this selection of pieces from the *London Review of Books*, none of which has been anthologized before in his other essay collections, is restorative: an extended spa treatment that stretches tired brains and unkinks the habitual responses where Hitchens is concerned. Tonic too are the fencing matches in the letters printed after a few of the pieces. In one exchange he makes mincemeat of the historian Arthur Schlesinger Jr. over the schmaltz that was Camelot. Writers weren't reluctant to rumble then. For some, the punchy effect may be almost prelapsarian. The reviews run from the year 1983 until, significantly, 2002, a key demarcation line in the Hitchens chronology. That was the year Hitchens resigned as a columnist on the *Nation* (where he had alternated with fellow expat Alexander Cockburn), over the magazine's opposition to the proposed invasion of Iraq, which Hitchens full-throatedly championed, to the anger and dismay of his dovish comrades and disciples (in 2003, Hitchens and his book-length tribute to Orwell were on the receiving end of an air-land-and-sea assault by Stefan Collini in the LRB entitled "'No Bullshit' Bullshit," indicative of how bitter the breach had been). Hitchens's war stance amounted to quite a pivot from his past. Here he is in the second piece in this collection, a diary about the (first) Gulf War: "There were a thousand ways for a superpower to avert war with a mediocre local despotism without losing face. But the syllogisms of power don't correspond very exactly to reason." George Packer, author of *The Assassins' Gate: America in Iraq*, later attempted to account for this abrupt turn from militant gadfly to taloned hawk:

> He was, by his own lights and that of his admirers, a thoroughgoing contrarian. (One of his lesser-known books was called

Letters to a Young Contrarian.) And nothing could be more contrarian, in the early years of the last decade, than for a hero of the left to embrace George W. Bush. It breathed new life into Hitchens, his persona and his prose.

A snootful of dragon fire, more like. The evening sky crimsoned from all the bridges he burned. Before the decade was over Hitchens would break with former friends and allies such as Cockburn, Harold Pinter, Edward Said and his eminence Gore Vidal (the review of *Palimpsest* in these pages emanates a fond regard that would be dashed during their bitter divorce), while annexing a new audience and further expanding his army of admirers and detractors with the rousing success of his Menckenesque diatribe *God Is Not Great* (2007), which elevated him into perhaps the most formidable gladiator for what was then called the New Atheism. His bestselling memoir *Hitch-22* (2010) further bronzed his foxy, avuncular status as public entertainer/public intellectual. Everything would have been fine if only, if only. But blood is a difficult stain to remove, and the tragic debacle that resulted from the botched occupation of Iraq, coupled with Hitchens's chummy relationship with some of the chief architects of that horror (particularly Bush's deputy secretary of defense, Paul Wolfowitz), continues to discolor the legacy of Hitchens 2.0. This mottled legacy will give biographers (at least one biography is in the works) and memoirists much to mull over and grapple with, so let us leave them to their mulling and grappling while we crack open this jewelry case.

When it comes to English prose, Hitchens wrote as he spoke, an offhand eloquence that seemed to roll off the wrists, conscripting the listener-reader into his confidences to the melodic clink of ice cubes in the clubby background. His classic, roguish, cant-defoliating English style, an inheritance from Hazlitt and similar bravehearts, is fortified by an armory of deep reading and lucid recall, wide acquaintanceship (which translates over time into an abundance of sources), and a close proximity to many of the major players of the day as they promenaded across the stage or, in the case of his friend Salman Rushdie, hid for their lives. In a diary published after the fifth anniversary of the fatwa against the novelist over *The Satanic Verses*, the following parenthetical surfaces like a soap bubble:

> (In a rather mad piece in the *New Yorker*, Cynthia Ozick compared Rushdie to "a little Israel," surrounded as he was by ravening Muslim wolves, and also remarked on the evident expansion of his waistline since the last time she saw him in public. Ms. Ozick, as it happens, is rather keen on the expansion of the Israeli midriff as it extends over the once slimline waist to engross the Occupied Territories. So the comparison was a doubly tactless one...)

In "On Spanking," Hitchens recalls the blushing thrill of being disciplined by Margaret Thatcher for being a saucy boy (a smack across the bottom with "a rolled-up parliamentary order paper," presumably no copy of the *Spectator* being nearer to hand) as the springboard to a larger inquiry into the upper class's craving for bent-over supplication:

> In the great rolling growl that used to sweep Tory Party Conferences at any mention of the birch, there could be detected a thwarted yearning to have everybody under control again: back in school, with its weird hierarchy of privileges and sufferings; back in the ranks of the regiment where a good color sergeant could keep them in order; back in the workhouse and under the

whip of the beadle. If this means a population that is somewhat infantilized and humiliated, well how else can you expect to get people to wait in the rain to see a royal princess break a bottle of cider over the bows of a nuclear submarine?

Now there are newer, easier, less inclement ways to infantilize a nation, but enough about *Love Island*.

For writers attuned to the follies of their day, every fleeting encounter presents a possible frisson. That Princess Margaret, for example, she sure got around:

> If you were a commoner of average social mobility in London in the 1960s, 1970s and 1980s, there was a better than average chance that you would have met her in some club or at some party, or even on the pavement outside. Martin Amis remembers her showing up at the end of a dinner, on the arm of Nicholas Soames, and seating herself at the piano to sing "My Old Man's a Dustman" (to which, of course, the only answer was "No he ain't").

In a review of a biography of Diana Mosley, one of the most over-doted-on ivory swans in the unsavory annals of the 20th century, Hitchens asides:

> I once spent some time with Sir Oswald Mosley, in a television green room. He chatted amiably enough, reminiscing away and turning on the charm, and recalling...that the most disconcerting disruption of any of his speeches took place in Oxford, when some pinko students simply opened newspapers in the front row of the hall and read them calmly throughout his rantings. Then he got on the set, adjusted his mike, set his jaw and delivered (this was 1972) a hideous attack on the arrival of Ugandan Asian refugees.

Off came the mask of gentility, out jutted the gargoyle.

Never a writer to shirk a challenge, no matter how much tedium it threatened, Hitchens manages to perform feats of levitation on the seemingly inert bulk of a biography of the former prime minister Harold Wilson, and does his valiant best to cut through the thick, overcooked spinach of pseudo-historical, mytho-hooga-booga of Cold War spy lore, arriving with a fed-up frustration with these "endless quasi-disclosures and planted rigamaroles." New to me, the magisterial essay on Michael Ignatieff's biography of Isaiah Berlin is like moving into an ivy-draped mansion, tastefully apportioned and strewn with mirrors that begin to give you the willies. Nothing written on the author of *Russian Thinkers*, *Against the Current* and the worn-to-nub distinction between *The Hedgehog and the Fox* has so painstakingly delineated the performative nature of Berlin's bony, beleaguered donnish toga-modeling: "the combined ingratiation and self-pity no less than the assumed and bogus late Roman stoicism." The veneration of Berlin into the supreme stately ambassador for the life of the mind obscured the Lionel Trilling-ish qualms, equivocations and vacillations eating away inside the polymath. Hitchens:

> I propose that Berlin was somewhat haunted, all of his life, by the need to please and conciliate others; a need which in some people is base but which also happened to engage his most attractive and ebullient talents. I further propose that he sometimes felt or saw the need to be courageous, but usually—oh dear—at just the same moment that he remembered an urgent appointment elsewhere.

The torrential commentary and interview palaver that gushed from Berlin's spout produced an impressive din that sounded swell but didn't add up to much. "If it is fair to say, as

Ignatieff does, that Berlin never coined an epigram or apho-rism, it is also fair to add that he never broke any really original ground in the field of ideas. He was a skilled ventriloquist for other thinkers." Yet the essay isn't a hit job, tipping a marble bust from its plinth for a satisfactory crash. It's a true re-valuation, an antidote to the hagiographical aura that still persists.

Hagiography will never attach to Hitchens, no matter how much hero worship he still inspires from fellow thespians of the written word (see Martin Amis's valedictory *Inside Story*, an ode to male friendship where the voice seemed to crack). Hitchens generated buffetings of turbulence his entire career and the air of contention has yet to subside. This is for the best. Few things sink a reputation in posterity as irretrievably as a well-formed consensus that functions like embalming fluid, leaving behind a waxy, respectable relic, and there's no danger of that with Hitchens. Even in death he remains uncontainable.

A Hitch
in Time

The Wrong Stuff
On Tom Wolfe
1983

H ERE, for a start, are some nuggets of the old and the new New Journalism. What do they have in common?

By now, 1967, with more than a hundred combat missions behind him, Dowd existed in a mental atmosphere that was very nearly mystical. Pilots who had survived that many games of high-low over North Vietnam were like the preacher in *Moby-Dick* who ascends to the pulpit on a rope ladder and then pulls the ladder up behind him.

"The Truest Sport: Jousting with Sam and Charlie"

It is entirely possible that in the long run historians will regard the entire New Left experience as not so much a political as a religious episode wrapped in semi-military gear and guerrilla talk.

"The 'Me' Decade and the Third Great Awakening"

The reception of Gropius and his confrères was like a certain stock scene from the jungle movies of that period. Bruce Cabot and Myrna Loy make a crash landing in the jungle and crawl out of the wreckage in their Abercrombie & Fitch white safari blouses and tan gabardine jodhpurs and stagger into a clearing. They are surrounded by savages with bones through their noses—who immediately bow down and prostrate themselves and commence a strange moaning chant:

The White Gods!
Come from the skies at last!

From Bauhaus to Our House

In the margin of the first extract, one might simply write: no they weren't. In the margin of the second: no it isn't. After the third: no it wasn't. But that would be much too literal. What those three paragraphs have in common are the three things that go to make up the Tom Wolfe effect. One, a glibness that is designed for speed-reading. Two, a facility with rapidly cross-cut images and references: a show of learning. Three, a strongly marked conservatism. It is the third of these features, Wolfe's subliminal advertising for the New Right, that has had the least attention. But in this collection of his favorite journalism the artifice and the foppery are not sufficient to conceal it.*

Wolfe had the excellent idea, way back when, of being in the 1960s but not quite of them. His idea of participation was to appear, but to appear detached. The formula caught and held a whole imitative school of lycanthropic scribblers, who could mock and jeer at the antics of the period without being so square as to be left out of the party altogether. The summit of this style—its glass of fashion and its mold of form— was attained by Wolfe himself when he attended Leonard Bernstein's never-to-be-forgotten cocktail party for the Black Panthers. "Radical chic" has passed so far into the Anglo-American argot that it may be futile, thirteen years later, to attempt to expose it. For one thing, it was so nearly right.

---

* *The Purple Decades: A Reader* by Tom Wolfe (Cape, 1983).

Everybody knew somebody who answered or fitted the description. For another, the older and cleverer phrase—limousine liberal—had gone out with Adlai Stevenson and needed a retread. To take up *Radical Chic* now (excerpted in this volume) and to turn its pages is to undergo a disturbing experience compounded of déjà vu and disappointment. Was there really a time when Park Avenue bled for the American black—even for his most egregious and posturing spokesmen? And did Wolfe really finish off the 1960s by holding up the Bernsteins to ridicule and contempt? Finally, was he just having fun? The answers to these questions supply the key to the Wolfe code.

Yes, there was a time when Park Avenue bled for blacks, for Vietnamese, for grape-pickers and draft-evaders and the rest of it. That time is long past. Today, the ruling style is overwhelmingly narcissistic or outright conservative or both. The national tone is set more by Nancy Reagan's lavish White House, and by the "new opulence" of the private jets massed at Washington National Airport. It is also set, some might argue, by the distribution of surplus cheese to lines of unemployed people of all colors. These days, Tom Wolfe is a guest at the White House, sometimes making up a table with the William F. Buckleys. Any magazine editor in America would pay any sum for an article by him on the absurdities of such evenings. But he seems oddly reluctant to abuse hospitality from that quarter. Yes, Wolfe changed the way people thought about the 1960s. He made people feel embarrassed about their "emotional" and spasmodic reactions to war and revolution. It might be clearer to say that he made them feel self-conscious about their lapses into commitment. And self-consciousness, often of the most exorbitant kind, has been the thing ever since.

Was Wolfe just having fun at the expense of the smart set? He certainly worked hard at coining his phrase. The words "Radical Chic" appear eight times, capitalized, in the first nine pages. The effect-producing stuff about Manhattan celebrities works only if you know them. What Wolfe did, really, was not so much a social or stylistic satire as a political hatchet-job. Take, for example, his long and incongruous exegesis of Seymour Martin Lipset, who was then attempting to open a fissure between American blacks and American Jews. The uneasy context of Black Panthers at the Bernsteins made this general theory, for Wolfe, easy of illustration. So when Otto Preminger raised some awkward Middle Eastern question with the Panther leader Don Cox, Wolfe was onto it like a lynx:

> Most people in the room don't know what the hell Preminger is driving at, but Leon Quat and the little gray man know right away. They're trying to wedge into the argument. The hell with that little number, that Israel and Al Fatah and UAR and MiGs and USSR and Zionist imperialist number—not in this room you don't.

That was very perceptive: the ideological equivalent of what Wolfe elsewhere terms "status radar." But, to most of his readers, his political shrewdness was irrelevant or went unnoticed. *Radical Chic* seemed like a good laugh at the expense of a traditional target: the well-heeled reformer otherwise known as the salon socialist, parlor pink, Bollinger Bolshevik, or more candidly and less attractively, as the do-gooder.

In a thoughtful and spirited article, Garry Wills once analyzed the selfish commonplaces which underlie the antido-gooder school. He was in a strong position to do so, having been a star at William F. Buckley's *National Review* even while it was heaping praise on Tom Wolfe (as it still does). Wrote Wills:

> It takes a very dull or skewed acquaintance with our history to think that elite interest in reform arose at last (and only then as an aberration) when a composer-conductor got interested in restive blacks awash in the streets of his own town. He did, after all, compose the song "New York, New York"—why should interest in the "colored" part of the city's population arise from nothing but *nostalgie de la boue*. Is Mr. Wolfe saying that blacks and Puerto Ricans and Chicanos are *boue*?

He added: "Capitalists revolutionized our society. Having started that process, the sorcerer's apprentices cannot call it off overnight or blame the whole thing on cocktail parties for Cesar Chavez." That suggestive judgment would come as more of a surprise to his lazy fans than it would to Wolfe. He, at least, knows what he's on about. As the 1980s advance, he is more and more frank about his convictions. These are: that the United States was stabbed in the back over Vietnam ("The Truest Sport"); that welfare deliberately encouraged ghetto insurrection ("Mau-Mauing the Flak-Catchers"); that elitist designers are responsible for the failings of modern architecture (*From Bauhaus to Our House*); that men of action have been fettered too long by wet liberals (*The Right Stuff*, "The Truest Sport," passim). He once told me that his favorite journalist was Taki Theodoracopulos, best-known in America for his essay "Ugly Women," which argues (surprise) that feminism is a neurotic disorder of the ill-favored.

Ah, but does Wolfe *write* like a dream? Depends. He certainly has a gifted ear for American speech. He can even catch it without directly quoting it, as in this piece from *The Pump House Gang*:

> The Mac Meda Destruction Company is...an underground society that started in La Jolla about three years ago. Nobody can remember exactly how; they have arguments about it. Anyhow, it is mainly something to *bug* people with and organize huge beer orgies with...They have Mac Meda Destruction Company decals. They stick them on phone booths, on cars, any place. Some mommy-hubby will come out of the shopping plaza and walk up to his Mustang, which is supposed to make him a hell of a tiger now, and he'll see a sticker on the side of it saying, "Mac Meda Destruction Company," and for about two days or something he'll think the sky is going to fall in.

Others have their own preferred pieces. But there are two objections to the view of Wolfe as merely an elegant and sardonic chronicler of manners. The first arises simply from reading him for several chapters at a stretch. After a cloying interlude, his use of affectation becomes tiresome. The italics, the exclamation marks, the arch Capital Letters, the repetition of anecdotes and of keywords ("lollygagging" must appear dozens of times): all these begin to pall. Second, we have the testimony of somebody called Joe David Bellamy. Mr. Bellamy appears, presumably with Wolfe's warm approval, as the writer of an introduction to this anthology. Here he is in full spate:

> Temperamentally, Tom Wolfe is, from first to last, with every word and deed, a *comic* writer with an exuberant sense of humor, a baroque sensibility, and an irresistible inclination toward hyperbole. His antecedents are primarily literary—not journalistic, and not political, except in the largest sense. All

6

these years, Tom Wolfe has been writing Comedy with a capital C, Comedy like that of Henry Fielding and Jane Austen and Joseph Addison, like that of Thackeray and Shaw and Mark Twain. Like these writers, Tom Wolfe might be described as a brooding humanistic presence. There is a decided moral edge to his humor. Wolfe never tells us what to believe exactly; rather, he shows us examples of good and (most often) bad form. He has always proffered these humanistic and moral perspectives on his subjects.

Well! One wonders briefly what Wolfe would say if anyone else got himself promoted in this fashion. "Not political, except in the largest sense." Hah! Oh yeah? And as for the Comedy with a capital C . . .

It's not that Wolfe cannot write really memorably. This passage, for example, has stuck in my mind ever since I first read it:

> The traffic jam at the Phun Cat ferry, going south to the Ho Chi Minh trail, was so enormous that they couldn't have budged even if they thought Dowd was going to open up on them. They craned their heads back and stared up at him. He was down so low, it was as if he could have chucked them under their chins. Several old geezers, in the inevitable pantaloons, looked up without even taking their hands off the drafts of the wagons they were pulling. It was as if they were harnessed to them.

And then:

> For two days they softened the place up, working on the flak sites and SAM sites in the most methodical way. On the third day they massed the bomb strike itself. They tore the place apart. They ripped open its gullet. They put it out of the transport business.

Now it's not as if, in "the largest sense," Wolfe knows anything *about* Vietnam (he says of the year 1963 that it was a year "when the possibility of an American war in Vietnam was not even talked about"). But he followed the lurid, almost pornographic passage above with a bitter attack on the *New York Times* for eroding domestic morale in the face of the foe. It seems to me, therefore, that he is at best inconsistent in his attack on the politicization of writing that occurred (according to him and others) in the 1960s. He is simply, as was once said of the old German ruling establishment, blind in the right eye. He devotes a whole section of "The 'Me' Decade" to a critique of pseudo-religious cults, blaming them all on the mushy permissiveness of the hippies and the Guevara left. You would never suppose that two of the most virulent sects, the Mormons and the Moonies, still provide muscle and money to the New Right of which Wolfe recently announced himself a charter member.

Peel away the hidden agenda of his prejudices, and the residue is precariously thin. A freakish trip with Ken Kesey, an idolatrous profile of the bootlegger and stock-car racer Junior Johnson, and various other bits of slumming. These are American ephemera, and good American ephemera, but it's clear from the packaging and introduction of this collection that Wolfe wants to be taken more seriously than that. He wants to be thought of as an anthropologist, almost as an authority—which is why I have concentrated so much on his social and political hard core.

In *Radical Chic* Wolfe remarked that "moderate" black politicians could be detected by their habit of wearing suits three times too large for them. He must have thought this to be clever (like the old Vietnamese "geezers" in their "inevitable pantaloons") because he made the observation several times. The other day, there took place in Washington (where I live) a meeting of moderate black politicians. I didn't especially notice their dress, but I did notice that when one of their leaders made a speech about the hopes of the vanished 1960s, they wept. They were crying. Crying for the 1960s! For the resources that were meant for them, and which went on Vietnam. For the moral energy that has become so dissipated and introverted. Perhaps this is why Wolfe has started to lose his cutting edge. I suspect that he is running short of targets. His latest book, *From Bauhaus to Our House*, was a flop by his standards: people are not ready to believe that modern building and its disgraces are to be blamed on an imported conspiracy of pointy-heads. Indeed, the pointy-heads are out these days. Blacks and the poor are scarcely fashionable. Progressive talk is at a discount. The official line is that Vietnam was a war well worth fighting. In the crass, *natural* wealth of Reaganite Republicanism, Wolfe cannot find the snigger potential he found in Leonard Bernstein's naive philanthropy. He now has the America he always wanted, and I hope it stays fine for him.

Diary
Operation Desert Storm
1991

THE GREEKS had a saying that "the iron draws the hand toward it," which encapsulates, as well as anything can, the idea that weapons and armies are made to be used. And the Romans had a maxim that if you wish peace you must prepare for war. Oddly enough, even strict observance of this rule is not always enough to guarantee peace. But if you happen to want a war, preparing for it is a very good way to get it. And, among the privileges of being a superpower, the right and the ability to make a local quarrel into a global one ranks very high. Local quarrel? Here is what the United States ambassador to Iraq, Ms. April Glaspie, told Saddam Hussein on 25 July last:

> We have no opinion on the Arab-Arab conflicts, like your border disagreement with Kuwait. I was in the American Embassy in Kuwait during the late 1960s. The instruction we had during this period was that we should express no opinion on this issue, and that the issue is not associated with America. James Baker has directed our official spokesmen to emphasize this instruction.

Even as the latest in "smart" technology grinds and punctures the Iraqi military, this amazingly explicit enticement to Saddam is still being debated. Did the United States intend to keep Iraq sweet by giving it a strategic morsel of Kuwait and access to the sea? Or did it intend to remind its Gulf clients that only American umbrellas could protect them from Iraqi rain? Or did it perhaps intend both? Those who think this too cynical might care to remember that Washington incited Iran to destabilize Iraq in 1973, and Iraq to invade Iran in 1980, and sold arms on the quiet to both sides throughout. As Lord Copper once put it, "the *Beast* stands for strong mutually antagonistic governments everywhere. Self-sufficiency at home, self-assertion abroad."

Considerations of this kind tend to be forgotten once war begins, but one day the swift evolution from Desert Shield through Imminent Thunder to Desert Storm will make a great feast for an analytical historian. For now, everything in Washington has narrowed to a saying of John Kennedy's, uttered after the Bay of Pigs, to the effect that "success has many fathers—failure is an orphan."

The debate in Congress, which was very protracted and in some ways very intense, was in reality extremely limited. The partisans of the administration said, "If not now, when?" and their opponents replied: "Why not later?" The partisans of the administration said there would be fewer body bags if Saddam was hit at once, and their opponents replied feebly that all body bags were bad news. Only Senator Mark Hatfield, the Republican from Oregon, refused either choice and voted against both resolutions. In his speech announcing the immediate exercise of the powers Congress had conferred on him, Bush oddly borrowed a phrase from Tom Paine and said: "These are the times that try men's souls." This line actually introduces Paine's masterly pamphlet "The Crisis," and goes on to talk scornfully of "summer soldiers and sunshine patriots."

In the present crisis, with the hawks talking of war only on terms of massive and overwhelming superiority, and the doves nervously assenting on condition that not too many Americans are hurt, almost everyone either is a summer soldier or a sunshine patriot.

This is true even of the surprisingly large peace movement, which has spoken throughout in strictly isolationist terms. True, there was some revulsion at the choice of 15 January for the deadline, because it is the officially celebrated birthday of Martin Luther King and many felt that Bush either knew this and did not care or, worse still, had not noticed. But, except for a fistful of Trotskyists, all those attending the rally in Lafayette Park last weekend were complaining of the financial cost of the war and implying that the problems of the Middle East were none of their concern. I found myself reacting badly to the moral complacency of this. Given the history and extent of U.S. engagement with the region, some regard for it seems obligatory for American citizens. However ill it may sound when proceeding from the lips of George Bush, internationalism has a clear advantage in rhetoric and principle over the language of America First. The irony has been that, in order to make their respective cases, both factions have had to exaggerate the military strength and capacity of Iraq: Bush in order to scare people with his fatuous Hitler analogy, and the peace camp in order to scare people with the prospect of heavy losses. Therefore, as I write, American liberals are coming to the guilty realization that unless Saddam Hussein shows some corking battlefield form pretty soon, they are going to look both silly and alarmist. Surely this cannot have been what they intended?

Conor Cruise O'Brien once told me that when he took the Irish chair in the United Nations, Ireland having joined rather late, he found his delegation seated alphabetically next to Israel. The Dublin delegates were overwhelmed by the warm hospitality displayed by their Jewish neighbors, who were almost embarrassing in their effusiveness. Only after a while did they realize that before Ireland's accession Israel had been sitting next to Iraq. Then came the grim day when O'Brien and his Israeli counterpart, Gideon Rafael, watched their mutual friend Adlai Stevenson trudge through a mendacious speech about that same Bay of Pigs. He knew he was lying, they knew he was lying, he knew they knew that he knew. As a consequence, he would sometimes lift his eyes to where they sat, as if in mute appeal for them to realize that he hadn't written the damn speech. And as a secondary consequence, he muffed his lines. Concluding the administration's case against Castro for his "crimes against man," he repressed a sigh and turned to his "crimes against God." Glancing up again to where his friends sat, he grotesquely misread: "Fidel Castro has circumcised the liberties of the Cuban churches." Rafael turned to O'Brien with a classic shrug and muttered: "I knew *we'd* get blamed for this sooner or later."

The line between self-pity and self-mockery in that case was very well drawn. Better than it is today, at any rate. It has been doubly unedifying to see Bush pretending that he has never met an Israeli in his life, and the Israelis pretending that a war between America and Iraq has nothing to do with them unless they are attacked. The element of denial here is what lies behind the refusal to consider "linkage." In a region so thoroughly and multiply imbricated, linkage is no more than an everyday term for common sense. Obviously, a solution to the Palestine question would help compose most of the regional disputes. No less obviously, the United States was committed to this view of the matter well before it gave Saddam Hussein the green light to invade Kuwait. Nor does his exorbitant interpretation of that green light make a settlement of the Palestinian question, or the suddenly discovered problem of nuclear proliferation, for that matter, any less urgent. Yet Bush's refusal to consider an international conference is in itself a negative "linkage," because it predicates a future discussion of peace on a current conduct of war instead of the other way round.

One linkage that is scarcely ever mentioned here is the adamantine link that binds John Major, via the Desert Rats, to Desert Storm. It is easy to find news of the French, the Kuwaitis and other participants in Bush's international brigade—or is it General Schwarzkopf's, since Bush, in a chilling moment, announced that he would leave the conduct of the war to the military? Of the poor Brits, we hear barely a squeak. It was the same when Major came to Camp David just before Christmas—he could as well have been traveling incognito. I think myself that Mrs. Thatcher grew so sensitive to the cry of "Reagan's poodle" that she never failed to give tone and color and visibility to the favors she undertook for Washington, even if she was bound to perform them anyway. She also very seldom neglected to ask for something in return. Major is more like a traditional Labour prime minister (or opposition leader) eagerly assuring the Americans that they can count on him no matter what. That of course is just what they then proceed to do. Had I the ear of Mr. Major I would urge him to be a touch more theatrical in his declarations, with possibly the teeniest bit of reservation tossed in. There's more joy in heaven that way, and a touch more respect too.

The night before the bombers left their Saudi and Turkish airfields, I was faxed the following appeal, which didn't make it into any American newspaper. Addressed to Perez de Cuellar (or Pair of Quaaludes, as he is known in Washington), it called for an international conference on the Baltic states *and* an extension of "the deadline for UN Resolution No. 678 of 29 November 1990, relating to the Persian Gulf crisis." Signed by the presidents of the republics of Lithuania, Latvia and Estonia, and by Boris Yeltsin on behalf of the Russian Federation, it ended very simply by saying: "We hope we will be understood." Here is another linkage which George Bush can scarcely affect not to comprehend, though it seems he took no notice at the time. Perhaps it would have been harder to dismiss such an appeal as a call for "appeasement." It was as a consequence of Munich, after all, that the fate of the Baltic republics was sealed in the first place. Concentration on the Suez-Hungary precedent of 1956 may obscure the fact that an opportunity exists now that did not exist then. The Soviet Union has colossal oil resources, which it needs technical help to exploit and develop. If the United States were not so obsessed by its imperial control of Arab oil, it could be evolving a longer-range policy of enriching both former Cold War antagonists by investing in and purchasing Russian oil and, as part of the bargain, insisting on respect for majority rule in the Baltic. More than one chance has therefore been missed by giving another wrench to the spiral of resentment and dependence in the Middle East, while awarding a freer hand to the Soviet military-industrial complex. "Only connect" is still a better motto than "no linkage."

Talking of links means talking about Cable News Network, Ted Turner's amazing practice of his "one world" principles via an Atlanta, Georgia, satellite company (in 1990, he issued an instruction that his newscasters refer to "international" rather than "foreign" news). Until Saddam's ruffians cut off the line, Peter Arnett, the intrepid New Zealander who must now be the world's senior war correspondent, was providing actuality from Baghdad. I once met Arnett and was fascinated to learn that it had been he, interviewing the American officer in charge of the Ben Tre region of Vietnam in 1968, who had been unironically told that "we had to destroy the town in order to save it." One of the greatest unforced wartime scoops, this line is bound to recur in consciousness as one watches America yet again trying out new weaponry.

Unlike Vietnam, Iraq is neither ethnically nor politically homogeneous. If its infrastructure and psyche are badly torn, it has the recognized potential of becoming another Lebanon, with Sunni, Shia and Kurd making up for lost time. As with Lebanon also, neighboring countries might interest themselves in the turmoil. Syria would undoubtedly do so, newly emboldened by its vast subvention for opportunistically joining Desert Storm. Iran would be unlikely to resist the chance to break the stalemate of 1988. And from Turkey come irredentist calls for a move on the Iraqi oilfields around Kirkuk and Mosul. (Saddam is right about the "colonial" border with Kuwait, but all the borders of Iraq are colonial if it comes to that, and liable not to be respected in their turn.) The Turks might remember that Kemal Ataturk did not want the Kirkuk and Mosul fields when the borders were first being drawn. Possession of oil was tempting, he said, but it was also tempting to outside powers, and the country which had it might lose its independence and its soul. What a curse the stuff is, and how wretchedly distributed. Arab nationalists are rightly fond of recalling the glories of Arab civilization, but these glories predate the discovery of the region's greatest resource.

Not that the region was free of curses and plagues in earlier times. I was more than usually depressed to see that, the night before unleashing Desert Storm, George Bush had a prayer meeting with Billy Graham in the White House. Every time that a conflict impends in any formerly biblical land, this elderly nuisance starts driveling about the last days and the end of time, and the Christian Broadcasting Network (which still feeds an astonishing number of American homes despite Ted Turner's Trojan exertions) starts to run the Book of Ezekiel in prime time. It's always been a source of perplexity to these already perplexed characters that, however interpreted, none of the ancient prophecies ever mentions the United States or anything that could remotely be construed as prefiguring it. That's why it was unfair of me to mention the *Beast* at the outset. But perhaps Bush's locutions contain a clue. While everybody else refers to the real Beast—the Baghdad and Babylon beast—as *Saddam*, the president doggedly calls him Sodom.

We appear to live in a time when things that were once unthinkable come to seem inevitable. I have believed in the certainty of a Gulf war ever since last November, when I stood on the tarmac at Dhahran in Saudi Arabia and heard Bush tell his troops that he, like the peaceniks, wanted them home soon, but thought the quickest way home lay through Iraq and Kuwait: all empires learn that it is very unwise to make false promises to the soldiery, and Bush certainly kept this one. But I am to this day unsure of the motivation. There were a thousand ways for a superpower to avert war with a mediocre local despotism without losing face. But the syllogisms of power don't correspond very exactly to reason. It now emerges that there had to be an assault in mid-January because the weather was about to turn nasty, the pilgrimage season was about to begin, the cost of maintaining idle forces was too high and, as the Boston Globe put it in a story on the budget in January, "administration economists admit their projections assume a quick, clean finish to the Persian Gulf crisis, probably by March, and concede that if anything else happens the country's economic troubles will deepen."

Oh, Lionel!
On P. G. Wodehouse
1992

WE KNOW from his immense correspondence that P. G. Wodehouse was at once omnivorous and discriminating in his reading (garbage in; synthesis out—a good maxim for any young reader-for-pleasure setting out on life's road). He cited authors as various as Lion Feuchtwanger and Rudyard Kipling, and didn't bluff about a book he hadn't read. And we know that he was excessively fond of the theater. But he never alluded to the author of these ensuing lines, which come from Act I, Scene i of an imperishable stage moment, when the young master is discovered by his manservant while trying out the piano:

ALGERNON: Did you hear what I was playing, Lane?
LANE: I didn't think it polite to listen, sir.

This bit of business, with a line being perfectly lobbed and beautifully returned over the social net, inaugurates a play in which: 1. The butler always has the last, crisp word. 2. Young men stutter cretinously when left alone with the adored object. 3. Country houses ("How many bedrooms? Well, that point can be cleared up afterward") are an essential retreat from the cares of Mayfair and Piccadilly. 4. Aunts are mythical monsters ("Never met such a Gorgon...I don't really know what a Gorgon is like, but I am quite sure that Lady Bracknell is one"). 5. Preposterous rural churchmen are on hand to supply authenticity ("My sermon on the meaning of manna in the wilderness can be adapted to almost any occasion"). 6. Ridiculous matrimonial entanglements are resolved by absurd accidents of genealogy and dowry, leading to a massed chorus of happy endings.

Oscar Wilde doesn't get so much as a walk-on part in Barry Phelps's hearty, upbeat, point-missing celebration of the man he rather tryingly calls "The Master."* This further omission helps to materialize Alexander Cockburn's surmise that "Wodehouse's almost pathological prudery in sexual matters, a reticence sublimated in the jocular male partnerships employed in his fiction and the loyal epistolary male friendships of his life, caused him to shy away in extreme nervousness from mention of Wilde." Phelps touches on this recoil himself, recording Wodehouse's distaste for Beverley Nichols as an interviewer and quoting a letter from Wodehouse to Bill Townend, saying: "Can you imagine giving lunch to celebrate the publication of a book? With the other authors, mostly fairies, twittering all over the place, screaming 'Oh, Lionel!' " This may make George Orwell seem rather naive for having made the otherwise useful observation that "how closely Wodehouse sticks to conventional morality can be seen from the fact that nowhere in his books is there anything in the nature of a sex joke. This is an enormous sacrifice for a farcical writer to make. Not only are there no dirty jokes, but there are hardly any compromising situations." It's the idea of

---

* *P. G. Wodehouse: Man and Myth* by Barry Phelps (Constable, 1992).

"sacrifice" here that seems, on consideration, to be the disputable one.

In this oddly sorted book of facts and reminiscences, Phelps does occasionally contrive to sharpen the outlines of our existing profile of PGW. It's melancholy but unsurprising, and oddly reassuring in view of the foregoing, to discover that Wodehouse's sexlessness arose from a frightful case of the mumps in early youth. So that at least his passivity was not the outcome of any repression or trauma. It enabled, in some fashion, an essential part of him to remain childlike. While this is no psychohistory (no mumps doesn't necessarily equal no Gussie Fink-Nottle) it does help us in considering a possible connection between the knowing and the innocent in modern English comic writing. To take another coincidence which, likewise ignored by Phelps, was pounceable on as I came across it: "Wodehouse also helped C. Aubrey Smith, later Sir Aubrey and a Sussex and England cricketer when Plum was at Dulwich, to found the Hollywood Cricket Club...The club became the social center for the British colony in Los Angeles." That was in 1931, more than a decade before *The Loved One* and Sir Ambrose and the tragicomedy of Anglo-American manners. (And one might also mention the "Bide-awee" pet shelter to which the Wodehouses donated a small fortune, to say nothing of the cemetery in which they buried six Long Island pets.) Anglo-American cultural tensions, as it happens, didn't trouble PGW overmuch. He developed a pretty thoroughgoing indifference to England and the English, of a sort which mocks his more roast-beef retinue of affected acolytes. He displayed none of the condescension with which Waugh, for example, approached Anglo-American locutions, and he never scorned to lard his discourse with terms like "rannygazoo," "hornswoggle" and "put on dog."

Phelps earns his keep by faithfully tracking these entries (many of which went straight from novelty to redundancy to antiquity and are only preserved by "Plum" having taken notice of them) and other taxonomies and lexicographies:

> Wodehouse invented many phrases, such as "down to earth," which are now so much part of the English language that we assume they are of ancient provenance instead of being only a few decades old. Other examples are "to have a dash at something," "dirty work at the crossroads," "foggy between the ears," "loony bin" and that splendid back-formation "gruntled" . . . The OED refers to his work 1255 times!

Here is a twinge, conveyed among other things by that last exclamation mark, both of what is compelling and of what is exhausting in Wodehouse idolatry. None of the above hits is a real chartbuster except perhaps "gruntled" ("He spoke with a certain what-is-it in his voice, and I could see that, if not actually disgruntled, he was far from being gruntled"), which is drawn from *The Code of the Woosters* yet which Phelps sources as—gawd-'elp-us—a find by Gyles Brandreth and further sources as—gawd-'elp-us again—Pelham Books. The atmosphere of a jolly buff's reunion, complete with painful Drones impersonations and ritual bread-throwing, lies heavy about this work.

As Phelps puts it in his no-nonsense style, having discovered that Wodehouse once spoke well of a Tom Sharpe effort, "that The Master should commend such bawdy black humor is superficially surprising, given his dislike for anything raunchy, but he must have appreciated that he had met another comic master who could also make the language dance to his bidding." Well, I mean to say, really. This dance business seems to be on the Phelps brain, since later he avers, or asserts:

> If your criteria for great literature require Sturm und Drang with penetrating insights into the human predicament then Wodehouse is not great literature. If those criteria include total mastery of written English, the ability to make it dance to your bidding with a poetic beauty and to any job desired and to give joy to readers across the entire spectrum, then Wodehouse is great literature.

Golly. So the good end happily and the bad unhappily, because that is what Fiction means and anything else would be too brainy. If Phelps thinks that there is no Sturm und Drang in Bertie's confrontation with Sir Roderick Spode and the Black Shorts, he must be a hard man to please. Or perhaps an easy one: he refers twice to a master short story writer called O'Henry and says of Agatha Christie that she is among those "whose mastery of plot is unbettered and whose use of language to achieve their aims is total."

There's a reactionary growl underlying all this good clean fun interpretation. Phelps believes that Wodehouse said the last word on socialism in one of his Psmith juvenilia stories: "It's a great scheme . . . You work for the equal distribution of property and start by collaring all you can and sitting on it." He also defines this as "satire." But much more satirical, surely, is Wodehouse in the fine maturity of Right Ho, Jeeves, where Aunt Dahlia speaks woundingly of the fabulously wealthy Uncle Tom as having "just had a demand from the income-tax people for an additional fifty-eight pounds, one and threepence, and all he's been talking about since I got back has been ruin and the sinister trend of socialistic legislation and what will become of us all."

Wodehouse was here being, among other things, self-satirizing. He was, all through his life, absolutely obsessed with money and with the necessity of preserving it from the clutches of the Revenue. This theme permeates his letters and took up much of his time with agents, lawyers and accountants, long surviving his access to prosperity. As is so often the case, the consciousness arose from penury in boyhood and from the crushing disappointment of the cancellation of his Oxford entrance due to a sudden crisis in the family funds. These were all vested in India.

> What made the blow even worse was being withdrawn from the scholarship exam at the last moment. In the face he showed the world young Wodehouse accepted the decision with good grace and clothed it in humor, writing of the rupee—in which Ernest's pension was paid—jumping up and down and throwing fits. "Watch the rupee" was, he claimed, the cry in the Wodehouse household and expenditure had to be regulated in the light of what mood it happened to be in at any moment.

Perhaps this supplies another reason for Wodehouse's possible repression of *The Importance of Being Earnest*. Does not Miss Prism say to her pupil: "Cecily, you will read your Political Economy in my absence. The chapter on the Fall of the Rupee you may omit. It is somewhat too sensational. Even these metallic problems have their melodramatic side." (The play was first performed in 1895: Wodehouse's Oxford misfortune occurred in 1899.)

Phelps strains for effect by writing as if there were a vast anti-Wodehouse consensus, split into two factions. The first faction, one might be led to believe, cannot forgive him for his "unpatriotic" wartime broadcasts from Berlin. The second faction cannot abide his elitist focus on butlers and wastrels. Thus we are given yet another vindication of Plum for his evident innocence about the broadcasts, and then a story (which I must say was new to me) about Wodehouse being sponsored for his knighthood by the superannuated trade-union bureaucrat Walter Citrine. (Phelps spoils this by foolishly going for unironic paradox and describing the fuddled old carthorse as "a red-in-tooth-and-claw socialist.")

The fact is that there are only a few mysteries and controversies left. One of these—a very minor one—Phelps proposes to solve by instructing us that Jeeves (first name Reginald, as was revealed by Bertie in a moment of almost unpardonable familiarity) took his name from Percy Jeeves, a Warwickshire fast bowler felled in Flanders in 1916. A second enigma, and one that I should very much like to see cleared up, concerns Wodehouse's motive in giving the name Roderick to both Bertie's chief male nemeses—Glossop and Spode. Evelyn Waugh hung the name Cruttwell on several posturing idiots in his early fiction, and apparently by this means induced a nervous prostration in an Oxford figure of the same name on whom he sought revenge. The Eulalie business teaches us that Wodehouse well kenned the power of humiliating nomenclature. But I still have no Roderick data on which to base a solid speculation.

This is all footnoting. Between Wodehouse and Wilde there is an enormous gulf apparently fixed. Both died in exile, having been meanly treated by a culture that prides itself above all on having a broad and keen sense of humor. Both were vilely baited by the pseudo-lions of a cowardly establishment. Both were tougher eggs than they looked, and both thought the class system an absolute scream. It would be encouraging to think that an unacknowledged, latent tie existed between the louche Irishman and the reticent minor public schoolboy, because only by brooding on such connections can we hope to save the idea of English humor from the drawing-room and saloon-bar conscription that is eternally levied on it by bland, Loamshire wits like Mr. Phelps.

Mary, Mary
On J. Edgar Hoover
1993

WHO CAN FORGET the moment in Chapter Six of *Greenmantle* when Richard Hannay penetrates the inner apartments of Colonel Ulrich von Stumm and, with a thrill of horror, realizes that there is something distinctly rum about the chief of Prussian intelligence:

> Everywhere on little tables and in cabinets was a profusion of knick-knacks, and there was some beautiful embroidery framed on screens. At first sight you would have said that it was a woman's room.
>
> But it wasn't. I soon saw the difference. There had never been a woman's hand in that place. It was the room of a man who had a passion for frippery, who had a perverted taste for soft delicate things. *It was the complement to his bluff brutality.* I began to see the queer other side to my host, that evil side which gossip had spoken of as not unknown in the German army. [Italics mine.]

On page 222 of Anthony Summers's vastly enjoyable and revealing book,* we find J. Edgar Hoover's lovely home in

---

* *Official and Confidential: The Secret Life of J. Edgar Hoover* by Anthony Summers (Gollancz, 1993).

Rock Creek Park being done up at taxpayers' expense, complete with "hand-crafted fruit bowl" and "a heated toilet seat, invented in the FBI laboratory. When he decided it was either a quarter of an inch too high or too low, it had to be redone." One girlish employee recalled: "he really liked pretty flowers. That was a good thing to give him. I personally or my group made sure that we gave him azaleas. That was his favorite."

Most of the above comes from an official audit into directorial corruption—conducted many years too late, as such audits always are. And then we have the freelance testimony of Susan Rosenstiel, wife of the mobbed-up "businessman" and swinger Lewis Rosenstiel, one of Hoover's many and sweaty connections to the high life of organized crime. At a session with Roy Cohn in the Plaza Hotel in 1958, the director of the FBI was allegedly

> wearing a fluffy black dress, very fluffy, with flounces, and lace stockings and high heels, and a black curly wig. He had make-up on, and false eyelashes. It was a very short skirt, and he was sitting there in the living room of the suite with his legs crossed. Roy introduced him to me as "Mary" and he replied, "Good evening," like the first time I'd met him.

Mrs. Rosenstiel, who has what I'd call an unusually good memory for apparel, possessed that keen sense of self-preservation that the more emotional Dick Hannay lacked. "I certainly didn't address him the way I had at other times, as Mr. Hoover." I should just about think *not*.

A year later, Mrs. Rosenstiel, still a martyr to her hubby's specialized tastes, was commanded to another Plaza soirée (I understand that the Plaza has brushed up its act since being taken over by Donald Trump), and this time Roy Cohn again produced "Mary," but in a more daring outfit. "He had a red dress on, and a black feather boa around his neck. He was dressed like an old flapper." This was too much for Mrs. Rosenstiel, who fell out with her husband over the business and only saw Hoover once more, when he visited her country estate in the company of Cardinal Spellman. On this occasion the old flapper was attired as for the office, clearly knowing when he was licked. You couldn't hope to out-dress old Frankie-Frank Spellman, one of the great bitch drag queens of this or any other age.

Nobody should grudge the frumpish Hoover a fling or two, or indeed a flounce, though probably with his figure and complexion the stockings were a mistake. (Didn't he have one kind friend who could have whispered *something* tactful?) As John Updike has put it in a very thoughtful fashion commentary on the whole unfortunate business:

> Ike, for instance, dear Ike with his infallible instincts, would never have let himself be caught in lace stockings, even though he did have the legs for them. I remember, within a month of St. Laurent's 1958 collection for Dior, Ike coming out in a stunning cobalt-blue wool trapeze, with white open-backed heels and a false chignon. That very day, if memory serves, he had sent five thousand marines to Lebanon, and not a hair out of place.

Dear Ike. This distinction may be a helpful one. Though Eisenhower might have been a moral coward on matters such as McCarthyism and segregation, he often expressed himself in private as a prisoner of public opinion and regarded colleagues like Nixon, for example, as distasteful political necessities. His mind was broader than his circle, and he had an instinctive aversion to crooks. With Hoover, the case is rather different, not to say opposite: public austerity and private squalor—a neat Galbraithian inversion. He wanted a Neronian life for himself; a subsidized world of jowly luxury and excess. And he demanded a Prussian and Spartan existence for everyone else. In the year before his first recorded beano at the Plaza, he brayed a stentorian national call for the repression of pornography and for a "new generation of young people with clean minds and healthy bodies living in a better, cleaner America." His exacting standards for FBI recruits—mandatory blond hair, blue eyes and slender waists—were of the Frederick the Great variety. And if you suspect what that may have meant for black agents, Jewish agents, female agents, Hispanic agents, let alone for avowedly homosexual agents, you suspect right. Hoover believed in niggers, kikes, wops, spies and fags to the end of his days. He never left the United States except for day-trips to Canada and Mexico. The only "foreigners" to whom he showed any warmth at all were Mafiosi.

At one level, this is an old story about denial and doubling. I keep an idle watch on new congressmen in Washington, and also on the electronic moralists of the airwaves. No sooner do they start bawling about sodomy and degeneracy than I contentedly set my timepiece. Soon enough, Congressman Snort will be found on all fours in the Capitol men's room, his every negotiable crevice and orifice crammed with delinquent members; the Reverend Jim-Bob Vermin will be entrapped with an expired Visa card in some drear motel, where he has paid well over the odds to be peed on by an Apache transvestite.

Thou rascal beadle, hold thy bloody hand!
Why dost thou lash that whore? Strip thine own back;

Thou hotly lust'st to use her in that kind
For which thou whipp'st her.

Bend a few genders in that stave, and you have Hoover to the life. But how much greater a lie his life was than the career of the run-of-the-mill closet hypocrite. Fooling yourself is one thing. Fooling and bullying half a dozen presidents, both Houses of Congress and the entire print and television racket, and getting away with it, is quite another. Such a feat is not to be explained merely by reference to sub-Freudian categories. One must touch the more ramified ganglia of American Cold War morality, and also of American nervousness about the multicultural.

Hoover's record and personality can be read as a sort of mirror obverse of what is tiresomely called the politically correct. He was not, for instance, just afraid and ashamed of being queer (seeking therapy and counseling from the Washington expert Dr. Marshall Ruffin as early as the 1940s, before he became ashamed of that too). He was also terrified of being black. Gore Vidal has a distinct recollection of a tarbrush rumor about Hoover's family that extended back at least to the Depression. "People said he came from a family that had 'passed.' It was the word they used for people of black origin who, after generations of interbreeding, have enough white blood to pass themselves off as white." As well as exploding when the occasional gossip made a crack about his mincing gait, Hoover must have winced at the sly references to his crinkly hair and darker than usual skin. This in turn might go some way to explaining his psychopathic, prurient hatred for Martin Luther King. Hoover was compulsive in his taping and bugging of King's highly virile private life, and in his campaign to use the tapes for blackmail. He officiated in the twisted plan to send King these recordings, with threatening notes, in an effort to induce suicide. This, too, is a twice-told tale, though I did not know until I read Summers that the FBI had an "alternative" black leader they wished to emplace by these means. It was Samuel Pierce, later to be Ronald Reagan's ultra-corrupt secretary for housing and urban development, greeted by the sinister cretin Reagan on one occasion with the salute (to the only black member of his own cabinet): "And how are things in *your* city, Mr. Mayor?"

One way of looking at the whole record of American empire, and of American Cold War fanaticism, is to see it at least in part as a device for entrenching WASPery and nativism, with the attendant pseudo-Protestant ethical baggage. Hoover's resistible rise is certainly a parable for such a theory. In his teens at school he proposed and won the debating society motion that "Cuba should be annexed to the United States." He also spoke sternly in favor of capital punishment and against the enfranchisement of women, citing biblical authority in both cases. The First World War, with its chauvinistic orgy of attacks on un-American and hyphenated immigrants, found him as the model of the sunshine soldier— going to Cadet Corps parades and cotillions while carefully avoiding service at the front and stressing preparedness at home. By 1917, with the country's first Red Scare getting into its stride, young J. Edgar was an enthusiastic snooper, chasing down aliens and subversives as if they were the same thing. (He recommended internment, on one occasion that now seems significant, for a German-American who publicly called President Woodrow Wilson "a cocksucker and a thief.") Soon fully enrolled in the FBI's predecessor Bureau of Information, Hoover was well placed when Attorney General Palmer launched his crusade of postwar repression and deportation. He took personal credit for the expulsion of Emma Goldman and Alexander Berkman, adding (in what was then perhaps only a tic rather than a full-fledged disorder) that Goldman's private love letters made "spicy reading." Always there was the connection—sometimes latent and sometimes blatant—between the defense of America's ethnic purity, its political orthodoxy and its sexual continence.

Who shall tell the habits of the heart? We don't know why it is that such a triptych has so great an attraction for sadists, molesters and the libidinally challenged, but we do know that it is so. It is not unlike—indeed, it may be a version of—the symbiotic fascination of the cop and the criminal. At any rate, there were lousy foreigners and crooks and terrorists and people of low moral character of whom it can be fairly said that Hoover couldn't get enough. As the historian Albert Fried once phrased it, "intelligent gangsters from Al Capone to Moe Dalitz and Meyer Lansky have always been fierce, voluble defenders of the capitalist faith, and to that extent they were and are J. Edgar Hoover's ideological kinsmen." Thus, though women couldn't develop the moral fiber to be cops (couldn't fire a gun, apart from anything else), and blacks were shiftless and thick, and Mexicans needed only to be feared "if they came at you with a knife," wide-shouldered mobsters were great, whether they came from Calabria or the shtetl. Between Prohibition and McCarthyism (the two last stands of modern American Protestant and nativist bigotry, even though

"Tailgunner Joe" was a populist Catholic as well as a raging queen) Hoover stuck to this conviction, if one can call it that. There is perhaps an aspect of the Manichean here. It had been announced officially that in the battle against the Red Antichrist and his (her?) mongrel allies, anything was permitted. Did you say "anything"? Well, then ...

This also elucidates the appalling record of Congress and the press. Summers rightly stresses the element of straight-out blackmail in Hoover's approach. Even Senator Karl Mundt, a dinosaur Republican and tireless witch-hunter, could no longer live with his public endorsement of Hoover and privily told his aide Henry Eakins that "Hoover is the most dangerous man in the United States. He has misused his office. There are things I know that Hoover has done to congressmen and senators, things that should never have happened. He has things on them." But this only appears to be a paradox. Of course it would be people like Mundt, and people like the demented James Jesus Angleton, who guessed the truth about Hoover and fought filthy, frightened, secret turf wars with him. Angleton, indeed, was the surreptitious circulator of the photograph that purportedly showed Hoover administering a languorous blow-job. This back-stabbing (if that's the word I'm fumbling for) is the hallmark of secret police rivalries in banana republics and people's democracies; the sort of thing that eventually caught up with Yagoda and Yezhov and even Beria. What! Moral equivalence! How dare one compare Stalinism with the American way, however imperfect. My point is that the United States, though never threatened by any internal or external foe, managed to have itself a prolonged racial and political inquisition, and that the man chiefly responsible died full of rank and honor, and still has a large Washington police bureau named after him. It's a poor compensation that a few journalists and academics, many of them not even Americans, have got at the truth twenty years too late.

I said no external or internal enemies, but I suppose I meant no communist ones. "If it were not for me," Hoover told the assistant secretary of security at the State Department in 1963, "there would not even be a Communist Party of the United States. Because I've financed the Communist Party, in order to know what they are doing." Everybody knew this who wanted to know, but Congress could be blackmailed in general as well as one by one, and the atmosphere of siege and *Kulturkampf* was one which few dared to try and dispel. That Hoover knew the threat was bogus, yet employed it as the ticket to his own rich and dark entitlements, was another thing that everyone "knew" but nobody dared say. Neoconservative fellow-travelers to the contrary, that's how democracies perish.

Under the deceptive rubric of the Cold War, in which not even its sternest proponents really believed, a war was nonetheless being fought. Here is how it was declared by McCarthy's chief lieutenant, Congressman John Rankin, at a time when Hoover was slipping secret files in McCarthy's direction. My citation comes from Dalton Trumbo's "Honor Bright and All That Jazz," and concerns the so-called Hollywood Ten:

> They sent this petition to Congress, and I want to read you some of these names. One of the names is June Havoc. We found out that her real name is June Hovick. Another one was Danny Kaye,

and we found out his real name was David Daniel Kaminsky...
There is one who calls himself Edward G. Robinson. His real
name is Emanuel Goldenberg. There is another one here who
calls himself Melvyn Douglas whose name is Melvyn Hessel-
berg. There are others too numerous to mention. They are at-
tacking the Committee for doing its duty to protect this country
and save the American people from the horrible fate the Communists have meted out to *the unfortunate Christian people of Europe.*
[Emphasis in original.]

That was in the 1940s. In the 1950s and early 1960s, the
FBI didn't care as much about communists as it did about
uppity niggers. In the late 1960s and early 1970s, it was campus
dissent and the androgynous cut of young people's hair. In
the 1980s, Salvadoran and Guatemalan immigrants and their
defenders, and of course all people with Arab-sounding names,
were the targets of choice. At all times, it was "the arts" and
the cultural radicals (Richard Nixon warned his daughter to
keep away from "the arts, you know, Jewish and left-wing")
that inflamed the police mentality. By the late 1980s the
worst attorney general in history, Edwin Meese, was bringing things full circle with a campaign against pornography.
Hoover's fan Pat Buchanan, deprived of a Leninist foe he'd
always known to be spurious, opted for a cultural war instead
at the 1992 Republican Convention. The wider society has
meanwhile been bullied and frightened into endorsing a "war
on drugs" that will make Prohibition seem tame in its impli-
cations for liberty and its vast opportunities for authoritarian
corruption.

In his rather wonderful essay "The Culture of Complaint,"
Robert Hughes addresses the radical counterpart of this

"culture war" and marvels that after the 1989 revolution "the world changes more deeply, widely, thrillingly than at any moment since 1917, perhaps since 1848, and the American academic left keeps fretting about how phallocentricity is inscribed in Dickens's portrait of Little Nell." A shrewd thrust all right, and a good counterpoint. However, it is true that the rise of "in your face" sexual and racial movements *does* have something to do with the end of the Cold War, and a student of the Hoover period need not be unduly startled by the fact. It isn't very long since "family values" meant accoutring a docile society to combat socialism and miscegenation. (In a hilarious moment of misapprehension, the American Mothers Committee once named J. Edgar Hoover in its Best Fathers of the Year roll of honor.) One of the few women to keep a dinner date with Hoover was Lela Rogers, the mother of Ginger and the founder of MPAPAI— the Motion Picture Alliance for the Preservation of American Ideals. I'm not saying that one ought to *prefer* Lesbian Puerto Rican Sisters for Sodomizing the Unborn, but I think that one needs to know more about the one before satirizing the other.

As Summers's book shows, the word "repression" was intended to mean exactly what it said. It involved depths of self-hatred and sexual misery that are only now being properly charted, and by shaming and intimidating the political class it choked off many means of "normal" redress. The carnival of narcissistic enthusiasms that now furrows so many brows is a tribute, however oblique and perverse, to a chaotic pluralism which, absent the influence of men like Hoover, Nixon, McCarthy, Joseph Kennedy and Roy Cohn, would have reached and passed maturity long ago. The current ridiculous fuss over the rights of homosexuals in the armed forces demonstrates, as conclusively as does Hoover's joyless cross-dressing, the truth that blatant is better than latent and always was.

Say What You Will About Harold
On Harold Wilson
1993

S INCE it can be properly said that nothing in Harold Wilson's political career became him like the leaving of it, there is some justice in the fact that he is now best remembered for one photograph and for one action. The photograph shows him next to the Duke of Grafton while assuming his stall at Windsor as a Knight of the Garter, and the action was the compiling (would that be the word?) of a resignation honors list that rewarded those who—oh, dash it, I don't know—shall we say *made* money rather than earned it? Anyway, in the photograph Wilson looks like nothing so much as a grinning monkey on a stick, and in the matter of the honors list he achieved the near impossible feat of discrediting the discredited and making a laughing stock out of something already rather disagreeably risible. So I suppose that one can spare about ten milliseconds of sympathy for those, suggestively calling themselves "revisionist," who have attempted to sweeten Harold Wilson's memory. (I mean our memory of him; not his memory of us, which has notoriously faded.)

For the sake of contrast, one might mention the limerick which Clement Attlee once wrote about himself:

Few thought he was even a starter
There were many who thought themselves smarter
But he ended PM
CH and OM
An Earl and a Knight of the Garter.

Who can doubt that this rhyme was intended partly at the expense of its own author? Attlee was more of a child of privilege than Wilson, and belonged firmly on his party's conservative wing, but he was a brave soldier and a principled man on the whole, and his first ministry saw the inauguration of National Health, the belated grant of independence for India, the reform of the electoral system and some small inroad on privatized folly in basic service industries. Would anyone from Pimlott to McKibbin to Howard to Ziegler care to mention one—even one—attainment of the Wilson period that could bear comparison?

Lord Melbourne's over-used but pungent observation about the Order of the Garter, that he liked it because there was "no damned merit in it," is very necessary for any consideration or reconsideration of the Wilson phenomenon. If he represented anything at all, he stood for the idea of meritocracy. In British terms, and especially in British Labour terms, this has long meant a demonstrated willingness to fawn on the crown, the Lords, the Foreign Office, the "intelligence" services, the chiefs of staff and the Inns of Court, while manifesting a pugnacious plain-man's dislike of "intellectuals," especially if these can be represented as public school, Oxbridge or parlor-pink intellectuals. It's a tried and tested applause line, and it hasn't failed yet. While I myself was in the process of unlearning a few illusions about Mr. Wilson, I remember, I noticed his frequently retrieved memory of the public school Marxists he had despised (while at Oxford), and also his man-of-the-people Uriah Heep admission that "I never got beyond that whacking great footnote on the second page of *Das Kapital*." I turned (not for the first time in my life, since I had had the benefit of a public school education) to the second page of that arduous but seminal work. There *is* no footnote on page two. In this it is unlike Wilson's ingratiating Oxford entry for the Gladstone Memorial Essay Prize, which was entitled "The State and the Railways in Great Britain 1823–63" and which contained four hundred of them.

At what point, I wonder, could anyone have seen it coming? The advance, I mean to say, of a mediocre but ruthless man without qualities? Philip Ziegler's book charts the boy Wilson's ghastly youth, replete with team spirit, sycophancy, Scout's honor and a craving to please elders and authority.* There it all is, if you can stomach the reading of it. (It used to be expressed in another photograph, of infant Harold and his dad outside Number Ten.) The humdrum Chapel morality; the Nonconformist self-righteousness; the passive-aggressive display—when the antagonist was insecure enough—of a home-spun Yorkshire chauvinism. I did not know, until I plowed through Ziegler's lusterless narrative, that the undergraduate Wilson had had a flirtation with Moral Re-Armament—surely the most dank and dingy of all the pietistic movements to have borne the "Oxford" prefix, and sinister to be going on with, but the discovery didn't surprise me. When Harold Wilson chose professional Lib-Lab politics as his career path,

---

* *Wilson: The Authorised Life* by Philip Ziegler (Weidenfeld, 1993).

the main loss was suffered by the world of husky, insincere lay preachers and by the dire counselors of the nation's Wolf Cubs and Scouts. (No shock to find that Wilson's chief pride in that milieu consisted in the putting-down of beastliness.)

For some reason or other, perhaps connected with the narcotic idea of his being the authorized biographer, Ziegler chronicles the rise of a consummate liar and phoney while invariably letting his "objective" prejudice obscure his view of the facts. An early point at which Wilson might have been unmasked—as someone provincial rather than regional, someone evasive rather than subtle, someone populist rather than democratic—came in 1948. In that year, Wilson made a speech in Birmingham claiming that when he was at school "more than half the children in my class never had any boots or shoes to their feet." He did not mind leaving the impression that he himself had been in the unshod or clogged half, if half it was. We know for a fact that he was much fussed over as a lad, and that his school was by no means of the poorest. But in describing the ensuing row over Wilson's veracity, Ziegler misses trick after trick. He cannot support Wilson's bogus claim, which was quite famous at the time. Nor can he say what is obvious—that a politician who starts manufacturing a deprived past for himself is a dangerous and disordered animal with very watchable symptoms (Nixon and Clinton both leap to mind). He doesn't even record Iain Macleod's withering and unanswered observation—"If Harold Wilson ever went barefoot to school, it was because he was too big for his boots." Is this the writer who gave us sprightly books on Diana Cooper and, indeed, Lord Melbourne? For shame!

Of course, many millions of Britons had been shoeless and worse when Wilson was growing up, or at any rate growing, and there came a time in the life of the Attlee government when the newly instated welfare provisions (are they still patronizingly called a "safety net," as if they covered the vicissitudes of deck tennis?) were to be sacrificed to the Moloch of rearmament. It's been debated for decades whether Wilson resigned on this matter, along with Aneurin Bevan and John Freeman, because of the principle of National Health, or because of the more ancient principle of reculer pour mieux sauter. And it's hard to blur this choice, but Ziegler has a clumsy try at the task. Prescription charges, on the one hand, Gaitskell's Korean War budget, on the other; Bevan determined to resign anyway, the Attlee government facing electoral defeat; prizes to be won on the National Executive and the backbenches for respectable opposition—who would doubt that Wilson was figuring his options of opposition? Ziegler would. In leaden phrases he instructs us:

> It is possible to construct two plausible scenarios: the first featuring Wilson as a gallant young idealist sacrificing his job and risking his future for the sake of a principle and in support of a cherished leader; the second portraying him as a cynical schemer, calculating the course of action that promised him greatest advantage in the long term and inflicting grave damage on his party in the pursuit of his individual ambitions.

One thing must be said at once. Even those who are so careless as to write about "plausible scenarios" would still find it flat out impossible to describe the first of those as plausible in the least. Does this leave us necessarily with the second of the straw men? Not if we accord to Ziegler, who sets out to split the difference:

> Wilson did look before he leapt; he did make calculations about his political future; but equally he did feel strongly about the burden of defense and the health charges; he did admire and feel loyalty to Aneurin Bevan, one of the few politicians admitted by Mary to the family home as a friend; above all, he was taking a serious and avoidable risk.

This isn't good biography, good psychohistory, good political analysis or even good journalism ("equally," for heaven's sake). Elsewhere in the book Ziegler makes painfully plain that Mary Wilson's humane and decent views on public affairs were invariably treated by her husband with cold contempt. Elsewhere in the book, also, we learn that within a very short time of his resignation, which occurred in April 1951, "Wilson had become 'a deviationist from the Bevan line,' Carol Johnson, the secretary of the PLP, declared as early as December 1951 ... By January 1952 Wilson was sounding out Bevan and Crossman about a proposal that he should go back on the front bench." Clear? Another way of making the same point is to cite Freeman, who resigned with Bevan and Wilson and who said: "If there were a word 'aprincipled,' as there is 'amoral,' it would describe Wilson perfectly." (Freeman, as well as having been a co-resigner, a beneficiary of future Labour governments and a late defector to the right, nonetheless holds the un-Wilsonian distinction of being one of the few men in public life who are known to have refused a peerage.)

As it falls out, there is no way of charting Wilson's subsequent political backing and filling *except* as an essay in opportunism, and with no great relish or skill Ziegler gets us through the years 1951 to 1964. One must be candid and say that minutes of trade-union gatherings in Margate are not quite his thing, and that he must often have wished for some more Samgrass-like commission in a great house or archive like that of the Mountbattens. One must also be candid and say that one doesn't blame him. His sense of fairness may well arise from his sense of being out of his depth, however, and it hit me on page 250, where Ziegler writes: "It was the seamen's strike which threw the government off course." By then we are at 1966, with the full disgrace of the July deflationary measures and the headlong rout of all the promises made by Wilson, Callaghan and Jenkins, to say nothing of Crosland and Healey, and come to that, Castle and Peart. Anyway, those of us who still remember Wilson's crushing of a revolt by underpaid and exploited seafarers, and his later lame excuses for the collapse of the currency, recall that he himself said: "We were blown off course by the seamen's strike." So it seems that Ziegler has subliminally surrendered to much of the contemporary Wilsonian alibi, including the inept nautical metaphor.

The Labour government which Wilson led, or over which he presided, was immolated morally by its support for a war of atrocity and aggression in Vietnam, and immolated politically by its fetishization of an impossible and illusory position for sterling. The innumerable other corruptions and failures and betrayals all stemmed from these two calamities, which were, as even Ziegler grants, essentially one and the same. The price exacted by Lyndon Johnson for support of sterling was that British Labour lent its vanishing prestige to his Indochina adventure. This was and remains a worse historical humiliation even than Suez—because it was more protracted, and because it involved the exertion of financial blackmail, not to get Britain out of a sordid colonial entanglement, but to embroil it in one more deeply. Ziegler actually phrases this rather briskly, but again as if he were retained as Wilson's attorney or spin-doctor:

> Worse still, these problems were interrelated: if he made no concessions to the left wing over the deterrent they would be more likely to revolt on Vietnam: *if he did not do as the American president wanted over Vietnam the run on sterling might become a stampede.* To give the Rhodesian negotiations the calm and concentrated attention which they deserved against such a tempestuous background was beyond the powers of any except the superhuman. [Italics mine.]

I want very much to come back to Rhodesia in a moment, but notice for now that even when he puts things as Wilson and Marcia Falkender might wish them put, Ziegler acknowledges what was hysterically denied at the time—namely, the *connectedness* of the foreign and domestic capitulations.

Despite his lenient style, Ziegler possesses one great advantage over Ben Pimlott's even lengthier retouching. He has dwelt in the stacks of the LBJ library in Austin, Texas, and has discovered slightly to his own shock that all of Wilson's Vietnam diplomacy was a deliberate fraud. This fraud could be termed great if it had not turned out to be so paltry. In one of his excursions into pure delusion (it was at about this time that he declared that Britain's "frontiers are on the Himalayas") Wilson posed as a broker between Kosygin and Johnson, and moreover as a broker who had found a formula for peace. "Peace is within our grasp," as he put it, always citing Ambassador "Chet" Cooper, who was the point-man for the White House in these supposed talks. In the LBJ archives, old "Chet" is quoted as saying: "He didn't have peace within his grasp, he was always overly optimistic about it...The U.S. administration regarded Wilson at best as marginal, at worst as a nuisance, and did not bother to keep him informed, even when he thought he was negotiating on their behalf." Or, as LBJ said when he heard that Wilson had called an election: "I suppose I'll have that little creep camping on my doorstep again." It's consoling, in a way, to discover that those who waged the Vietnam War found Wilson almost as contempt-ible and fantasy-sodden and solipsistic as did those who op-posed it. Not until Clinton's recent exposure of John Major's blubberings about Bosnia, perhaps, has one felt such an authentic thrill of "special relationship" humiliation. And if that seems to be setting the standard pretty high, then please to remember who first set it.

Wilson's willing annexation by national security ortho-doxy at home and abroad meant that he took the unsupported word of the CIA types about Vietnam, and of the MI5 types about the British Labour movement. In the case of the sea-men's union, according to Ziegler:

> The briefings were not recorded, and conducted in great secrecy—the only time that the door between the offices of Marcia Williams and the prime minister was locked was when the representatives of MI5 or MI6 were visiting—but Wilson found the evidence conclusive. After the strike had dragged on for six disastrous weeks he denounced the union leaders in the House. A "tightly knit group of politically motivated men," he said, were hoodwinking the seamen and holding the country

to ransom for their own nefarious ends. The far left were naturally outraged.

Skipping over Ziegler's dull consensus prose here—disastrous for whom and dragged out by what?—one may note two things. First, it was not just the "far left" that found itself shocked. Not even Heath could bring himself to repeat or support Wilson's vulgar charges. Second, this was Wilson's own deliberate aggrandizement of the very same political force—the unleashed and promiscuous secret police—which he was later to blame for all his own troubles. The same James Jesus Angleton for whom he had done so many favors over Vietnam, and the same MI5 and MI6 whom he had encouraged via the good offices of the bad George Wigg, were to find him unsound in spite of (or perhaps also partly because of?) his gruesome eagerness to please. None of Wilson's exculpatory recent biographers has troubled to minute this irony, if indeed it is one.

There came a time, late in the life of Wilsonism, when you would hear his hacks and flacks begin their sentences with, "Say what you will about Harold, but..." and then would follow some piece of half-baked sentimentality. A common offering was that our Harold could not—perhaps for Christian reasons—abide racism. Not such a big claim on its face. Do you know any morally serious person of whom it could usefully be said that "at least he has no racial prejudice"? But both Pimlott and Ziegler are curiously addicted to this point. And they give the same pair of examples. It's true that Wilson once attacked the Tory victor in Smethwick in 1964 for letting his canvassers say that if you wanted "a nigger neighbor, vote

Labour." And it's true that he became annoyed when Ian Smith kept Joshua Nkomo and Ndabaningi Sithole in a boiling police van, without food or water, while they waited to be produced for a meeting with Wilson himself.

The two stories, however, have one other thing in common. In both instances, Wilson's own person was being inconvenienced or insulted. In the case of Smethwick, he had been robbed of the parliamentary presence of the tenth-rate Patrick Gordon Walker, whom he wished to make foreign secretary in preference to the even more hideous George Brown, and was thus subjected to the vast annoyance of a by-election, which he went on to mishandle badly. In the case of the brutish conduct of Smith, Wilson was being made to look a fool. He was also being tested as to whether there was any outrage committed by the Rhodesian Front that would shake his far from "superhuman" commitment to inaction and inanition. One had not to wait long for an answer. By 1968 Wilson and Callaghan had deprived British passport-holders in Kenya of their rights in a racist panic measure described by the *Times* as the most unprincipled in living memory, and well before that Messrs Nkomo and Sithole had been returned to their detention in the bush, while Wilson chartered frigates on which to shake paws with Ian Smith. By the close of his regime, Labour was one of the few governments in the world that was deliberately breaking the arms embargo on South Africa.

Isaiah Berlin once said of a person I shall not identify (except to say that his surname rhymes with Heine) that he was "that very rare thing—a completely genuine charlatan." British political biography does not readily allow for this concept, and it's easy to see why. If by any chance it is true that Harold Wilson was an empty, nihilistic and vainglorious crook, then where does that leave Nuffield College and MORI and the whole apparatus of moderation and maturity? If he was a con man, you can hear them muttering (I have heard them muttering), then logically that means we were conned. The natural resistance offered to this unwelcome conclusion is of course the precise reason so few con men are ever caught. The victims are embarrassed at the thought of testifying to their own gullibility. Yet, when they try and witness to the contrary, they do an even neater job of work.

In our sad times, the image of the perfect phoney is very often an aspect of the social-democratic political style. A classic social democrat is one who must continue to please his constituents while laboring to reassure the powers that be. ("There are two things to dislike about Harold Wilson," it used to be said. "His face.") The resulting practice of theatrical— no, *operatic*—dissimulation was best caught by Isaac Deutscher in his study of the Scandinavian social democrat and all-purpose political conjuror and thug Trygve Lie. Yet there are honorable contrasts, such as Willy Brandt. In the whole of Brandt's memoirs, the name Wilson is mentioned twice and then with a very pallid politeness. But when Wilson's career began, it could still be said that British reformist socialism counted for something in the world.

The fact that this is no longer true is a fact that has yet to be definitely registered, either by its remaining adherents or by those who are the gatekeepers and umpires of moderate and statesmanlike standards. Before Wilson, it is true that there was Ramsay MacDonald and all the rest of it. But before

Wilson it was not so candidly admitted that the point of being in politics was to be in politics, nor that the point of being in power was to be in power. Not until the genial, vacuous, canny pipe-smoker came our way could it be said that Labour might lose an election and nobody with a tincture of radicalism *or* realism be other than stoic about the fact.

During one of the 1974 general elections I took a ride off the quite nice John Smith, who guided me around his Lanarkshire constituency. In the course of the tour I predicted a poor outcome, because Harold Wilson was presenting himself as an alternative prime minister rather than a leader of the opposition. After a pause which I may have misinterpreted, Smith slowly replied: "That might just be a very exact criticism." That Smith has now so little to bargain with is due to the fact that so many electors are far beyond disillusionment. If Baron Wilson of Rievaulx did a service, it was to make certain that the Labour Party, and some enduring illusions about the political calling, became properly divorced. What he put asunder, no one will ever put together again.

Diary
The Salman Rushdie Acid Test
1994

I N ALL the stultifying discussion of Prince Charles's fitness to grasp the orb and scepter of kingship, there is one qualification that is almost never canvassed. I refer to his ability to give the annual Christmas broadcast to the Commonwealth. No light matter this—it was a dreaded annual penance for his grandfather—and made no lighter by his presumptive inability to end the chat by saying: "My wife and I..." But never mind. He is in every other respect ideally suited to the task; even better at discharging blank or false-alarm fusillades than he is at receiving them.

I can attest to this, having recently read "Islam and the West," the text of a short address given by the prince to the Oxford Centre for Islamic Studies, a body of which he serves as patron. (Royal seals are not wanting in King Charles I's old royalist military HQ: the other two patrons are the House of Saud and the sultan of Brunei, the latter best known for his under-the-table donation of a few off-the-record millions to the cause of the Nicaraguan Contras.) Anyway, in his speechlet to the Sheldonian version of a multicultural audience, HRH got off some real ripe ones, such as the following: "We live today in one world, forged by instant communications, by television, by the exchange of information on a scale undreamed of by our grandparents. The world economy functions as an interdependent entity. Problems of society, the quality of life and the environment, are global in their causes and effects."

I remember that his mum used to be fond of saying that modern science had given us great opportunities, both for good *and* ill, until somebody broke her of it. But, veering back to the Islamic theme, Charles did manage one shrewd point. He announced, correctly as far as I know, that "Cordoba in the tenth century was by far the most civilized city in Europe." Dilating a bit on its splendors of learning and research and inquiry, he singled out Averroes and Avenzoar, though suggesting that their work was solely in the field of medicine. Still, I always warm to an Averroes fan. In Cordoba once, I made a special trip to the Averroes memorial, which on its plinth gives the full name of Averroes Ibn Rushd. And I know something about this name that the heir to the throne seemingly does not.

A few decades ago, in what is now Pakistan, a certain enlightened Muslim father decided, on what might be called Ataturkist principles, that his family should take a surname instead of the more customary patronymic. And, seeking to make his own *hommage* to the Cordoban synthesis of religious toleration and high learning, and to Averroes in particular, this man decided on the family name Rushdie. His eldest son, Salman, has since managed to keep the name, and himself, alive. He's also written rather eloquently about religious and cultural fusion in medieval Andalusia. But this famous name was not mentioned, even in passing, in a speech on "Islam and the West" given by Rushdie's liege-apparent. Did the monies of Riyadh and Brunei furnish more than a few richly worked Qurans for the Oxford Centre? Did they also ensure a "non-controversial" address from a monarchy whose sworn historic duty is the defense of the realm and its subjects?

As Julian Barnes has recently pointed out, the same curious omission occurs in the memoirs of Baroness Thatcher. Never jollier than when seconding Good Queen Bess at Tilbury, and repudiating any foreigner who durst trespass on the rights of English subjects and dependents, be they never so remote or obscure, the old girl was utterly silent on the open suborning of murder for gain by a foreign prelate who sought to spill blood in England itself. So that's how our fearless leaders behave when the ammunition is live, or when they think it is.

The same ignoble reticence is also to be met with lower down, or sideways, or elsewhere, among those who concern themselves with "sensitivity" and the multicultural. It is impossible to be sufficiently irritated by such people. Not only do they, first, associate the entire monotheism of Islam with one edict or ukase issued by a moribund fanatic. That on its own would be insulting enough to serious Muslims. They also insist on representing the difference as one between "Islam" and "the West." Ignorance here coexists only too well with a sort of cultural masochism or self-hatred, where no robust critique of any other religion is possible lest it remind us of the "colonial."

Yet within weeks of the original fatwa (now just past its fifth infamous anniversary), and increasingly over the past year or two, the whole grand implication of the Rushdie case disclosed itself as a contest, at once bitter and subtle, *within* Islam. The most salient instance of this is the recent publication, in Paris, of a volume entitled *Pour Rushdie*. Almost two dozen of the leading novelists, poets and essayists of the Arab and Muslim world offer, within the pages of this book, their reasons for sympathizing with Rushdie and their reasons for regarding his own case as, in some important way, their own. Naguib Mahfouz, the Egyptian Nobel laureate, is probably the best-known of these authors, but many of the leading Palestinian, Algerian and Tunisian voices were heard also. A separate petition, inscribed by 57 of the leading artists, writers and scientists of Iran, and requiring even more fiber from the signers, puts the same point in a different way. To take a side against Rushdie, or to be neutral and evasive about him in the name of some vaguely sensitive ecumenical conscience, is to stand against those who try to incubate a Reformation in the Muslim world.

The political level is cruder, as usual, but still quite an acute register of maturing differences. Yasser Arafat, for example, has given an interview—to an Irish paper—which defends Rushdie in ringing tones. Clearly, this is not unrelated to his own confrontation with the grim Hamas forces and with their Iranian paymasters. In Washington recently, I had the chance to introduce Rushdie to the editor of *Oslobodjenje* (*Liberation*), the indomitable daily newspaper of Sarajevo. The editor told him that *Oslobodjenje* had published a special multi-page feature on the Rushdie affair, and identified closely with his position (as he does with theirs). Again, there was an evident allegorical connection between Bosnia's attempt to uphold a secular, pluralist Islamic culture—this time against

Christian medievalism—and the ayatollah's attempt to define Islam as a theocratic uniformity. (In a rather mad piece in the *New Yorker*, Cynthia Ozick compared Rushdie to a "little Israel," surrounded as he was by ravening Muslim wolves, and also remarked on the evident expansion of his waistline since the last time she saw him in public. Ms. Ozick, as it happens, is rather keen on the expansion of the Israeli midriff as it extends over the once slimline waist to engross the Occupied Territories. So the comparison was a doubly tactless one. There can be little doubt that if Salman were unlucky enough, on top of everything else, to be a small, embattled country, he would be Bosnia-Herzegovina.)

It's been remarked before, by keener minds than my own, that almost all great moments in the history of censorship and free expression have turned on the question of blasphemy. There's a question of proportion here, and I'm sure that Rushdie himself would blush and wriggle at the implied comparison with Socrates, Jesus Christ, Galileo, Luther, Spinoza and Tyndale. Still, a phrase keeps recurring to my mind. It comes, bizarrely, from Paul Newman in *The Verdict*, as he mutters anxiously outside the courtroom: "There are no other cases. This is the case." By this he plainly means to convey, not that there are no other disputes or dramas or miscarriages of justice, but that this one has become the unavoidable one, or the defining one. The acid test. The test case. The crux. In our time, those of us who unavoidably missed the opportunity to discover where we might have stood on earlier occasions of sheep-goat separation have now been offered the chance in a rather direct fashion. Paradoxically, perhaps, it is the minds of certain "Oriental" scholars and dissidents which have been swifter to recognize this than many of their self-constrained "Western" counterparts.

Easily the best essay on the matter has been written by the Syrian critic Sadik al-Azm, who in 1967 had his own bad moment with the local mullahs. Appearing in *Die Welt des Islams* XXXI (1991), if you want to look it up, "The Importance of Being Earnest About Salman Rushdie" is the most tough-minded and skillfully written defense of the author to have flowed from any pen. Rightly enough, though he does not neglect the political dimension, al-Azm thinks of this as principally a literary matter:

> If by universal consent Nobel laureate Naguib Mahfouz is the Arab Balzac, then I am inclined to think that Salman Rushdie may very well turn out to be the Muslim James Joyce. It seems to me that the same cultural forces, historical processes and social oppositions that made the emergence of an Arab Balzac probable have also made the emergence of a Muslim Joyce possible.

Some of the arising comparisons are relatively simple ones. Both Joyce and Rushdie write about being priest-ridden. Both come from countries dismembered by the British Empire. Both exiled themselves to metropoles like Paris and London. Both kept in touch with their respective homelands nonetheless. But it is when he attends to the language that al-Azm excels:

> Joyce's heightened sensitivity to the fact that he was writing about Ireland in a language other than his own, thus enriching the oppressors' literary treasury, is to be detected in Rushdie's art too. Both *Ulysses* and *The Satanic Verses* are, in the strong sense of the term, multilingual works exhibiting much heteroglossia

(to use Bakhtin's term) and copious interlingual play on words, double entendre, puns and slang usages.

Authors who have the nerve to try something revolutionary are often somewhat cocky, and often somewhat disliked for it. After tedious and cynical delay had overtaken the publication of *Dubliners*, Joyce wrote to his publisher in 1906: "I seriously believe that you will retard the course of civilization in Ireland by preventing the Irish people from having one good look at themselves in my nicely polished looking-glass." The words recall Wilde on the rage of Caliban. They also take one's breath away. As some of our better-bred reactionaries are fond of saying about Rushdie: "Oo does 'e think 'e is?" But this kind of high confidence in the value and importance of literature seems as justified in Rushdie's case as it now does in Joyce's; justified not only by Khomeini's unfavorable review but by the warm and receptive reviews accorded by every Arab, Muslim and Persian author worthy of the name. Recently I read an article about the murder campaign being mounted in Algeria against secular writers, none of whom now dares to sleep in the same house twice running. They said, often anonymously, that they thought about Rushdie all the time.

As this argument broadens and deepens (a bad punch-up in Turkey the other day; an intensifying contest in Egypt; a recent fatwa calling for the head of a feminist fiction-writer in Bangladesh), one has to revisit some of the boring old arguments. "He knew what he was doing," wiseacres used to say darkly about Rushdie. "And he tried to get out of it," say some pristine radicals, recalling the sad episode of the attempted settlement involving the dubious forces of the Regent's Park mosque. Neither point seems to have any weight any more, if indeed it ever did. Of course Rushdie could have guessed that there would be an argument, perhaps even a bitterly Joycean one, about profanity. And since when should a writer be unaware of his implicit intentions? If anything, though, Rushdie underestimated the ripeness of his moment—an underestimate he had in common with all Muslim intellectuals who are now living through the Reformation and Counter-Reformation struggle in their own world.

As to the attempted composition or patching-up of matters, about which I admit I felt somewhat let down at the time, it appears to me in retrospect as an absolutely necessary stage in the evolution of this argument. Rushdie is a writer of fiction, not a political tribune or a martyr in embryo. He also has the right and the duty of self-preservation. Given the ghost of a chance to let this cup pass him by, he took it (the chance), as anyone might have done. But having found the proffered option to be false, he has made prodigious efforts to identify himself with people he has never met, and has not shirked the responsibility he did not seek. Without that one hesitation, I submit, he would not be the essentially reluctant witness that he is, a conjecture where reluctance is one proof of integrity.

Yet there is a monograph to be written on the variations of anti-Rushdie pathology. At one moment, one hears that his security costs the taxpayer too much. At another, that he has recently been spotted at, say, a wedding, evidently enjoying himself, so to speak at the taxpayers' expense. Yet again, one is liable to be told that he is, by his mere existence, endangering or compromising British or Western interests overseas.

For quite a time, he was even accused of jeopardizing the safety of the hostages in Beirut if he said a word on his own behalf. Now that he is Khomeini's last hostage, the official and unofficial point-missers will have to come up with a fresh excuse for their blasé, postmodern cynicism; a mode where nothing really matters any more than anything else.

I had a recent TV debate with Pat Buchanan, whose acknowledged heroes are General Franco, Cardinal Spellman and Joe McCarthy. Mr. Buchanan identifies with the ayatollah on matters of blasphemy (as do the Vatican, the See of Canterbury and the rabbinate). He attacked me for justifying Clinton's reception of Rushdie, the ground for the attack being that Rushdie wasn't an American. I ought to have replied, but didn't think of it in time, that Rushdie is not Czech but has been welcomed by Havel, is not Irish but has been received by Mary Robinson, is not Portuguese but has been the guest of Mario Soares, and is neither Arab nor Persian but has become the emblem of those Arabs and Persians who refuse the definition of their culture as monochromatically orthodox. Not a life badly spent, if you can think of it like that. Wherever you are, Salman, cheer up. Take heart. You may not have volunteered for them, but on a good writing day you could even think of the last five years as having been well spent.

Diary
Spanking
1994

SOMETIME in the late autumn of 1977, I went to a book party that was held in the Rosebery Room of the House of Lords. Why I went I can't think—the volume was some piece of unreadable bufferdom extruded by Lord Butler, who as "Rab" had never in his life done anything to live down the Greek Street sobriquet "flabby-faced old coward." He himself was vaguely present, moving about the carpet like a terrible tortoise. A sprinkling of hacks and politicos completed the scene, which was identical to a score of similar gatherings except in point of its grand setting. And then there was a sort of sensation at the door and in came Margaret Thatcher. Rab's shell crackled and contracted a little, as he tried to look flattered by the attention of his new leader: she whose whole purpose it was to cram Butskellism as harshly as possible into the wpb of history.

And I? Reader, I was *bewitched*. A dull pre-dinner drink-stop had been entirely transformed. You may have forgotten, but the regnant left-liberal idiocy of the period had it that Thatcher was a shrill, suburban and narrow housewife, the outcome of a spasm of folly among the Tory backbenchers. Unsound, unelectable, extreme... shouldn't be long now before the voters remind us that politics, as Rab had once so originally said, is the art of the possible. Having observed her arresting qualities of domination at the previous Conservative Party Conference, I had been ridiculed for writing, in the *New Statesman*, that she was a great fanged and clawed feline, replete with sex and spite, her tawny whiskers flecked with cream past, cream present and cream to come (I exaggerate only slightly). And I wondered to myself. Had she read my paragraph? Surely, if you're leader of the Tory Party and the (then) leading journal of socialist opinion says that you're a bit of a bombshell, you get to hear about it? Would she recall the byline? Peregrine Worsthorne sportingly offered to introduce us. I eased my way over to her side. Worsthorne did his stuff, saying that he and I had just returned from a most interesting trip to Rhodesia. And here also was a good test, because Thatcher had attacked the two-party consensus on the Smith-Muzorewa deal, suggesting that if elected she would lift sanctions on Salisbury.

At once we were in an argument. Of Joshua Nkomo I remember her saying: "I think Joshua is absolutely *sweet*." That was the least of our disagreements. On one point of fact, too abstruse to detail here, I was right (as it happens) and she was wrong. But she *would not* concede this and so, rather than be a bore, I gave her the point and made a slight bow of acknowledgment. She pierced me with a glance. "Bow lower," she commanded. With what I thought was an insouciant look, I bowed a little lower. "No, no—*much* lower!" A silence had fallen over our group. I stooped lower, with an odd sense of having lost all independent volition. Having arranged matters to her entire satisfaction, she produced from behind her back a rolled-up parliamentary order paper and struck—no, she thwacked—me on the behind. I reattained the perpendicular with some difficulty. "Naughty boy," she sang out over her shoulder as she flounced away. Nothing that happened to the country in the next dozen years surprised me in the least.

Actually, I was surprised by a few things. (After all, within a year or so of being elected she had steered Zimbabwe to independence under an elected majority government, something that no Labour government had summoned the nerve to do in more than a decade of dithering and funk.) But whenever I read of the humiliation of some over-mighty cabinet colleague—Geoffrey Howe, say, or Jim Prior or John Moore or Francis Pym—I could picture the scene only too well:

> I can do no better at this stage than describe my own punishment chamber, which I call the Lady Chapel.
>
> This is not blasphemy on my part. It is a chapel to the Lady (the Lady I serve) in her aspect as Aphrodite Philomastrix. It is a room dedicated to the use of the birch-rod so closely associated with her, the rod she plucked from the air with which to chastise her son, and so bestowed on human kind another primary tool—like Fire—with which to master our destiny.

The introduction to this reprinted classic informs us that it was first privately published in 1924, seized by the zealous constabulary in the autumn of that year, and made the subject of a show trial with Mr. Justice Ticehurst, later Lord Justice Woodhelves, presiding. All known copies were sentenced to be burned, and the defendant printers awarded stiff and condign prison terms. We now believe that the author of the supple and muscular prose instanced above was Alice Kerr-Sutherland, a no-nonsense governess who in the early years of the century had abandoned her errant but legitimate little charges to pursue the high road of madamhood. Her flagellation brothel in St. James's was a place of resort for the gentry and nobility and, before the walls of Holloway jail closed around his befurred Venus, it was to Alice that George, Marquess of Milford Haven and elder brother of Mountbatten, was in thrall.

The absorbing fact about this gruelingly detailed and thorough manual is its utter want of anything that might be called prurience. Even the illustrations (lovingly etched by "A Former Pupil") are innocuous to a degree; mere putti rendered in a sort of arch Pre-Raphaelite pastiche and consisting of sexless buttocks and downcast eyes. The point of all the exercises, inflictions and routines here described is very simple— to show who is boss:

> There being a natural level of formality in a caning, this tone should be maintained both before and after the punishment proper, wherever it is inflicted and under whatever conditions of dress. At the very least I make a caned offender write an imposition. On occasions—when the trousers have been taken down for example—I send him shuffling to the corner to further shame and isolation, with his garments about his ankles and his hands on his head.

As the editors so sapiently remark, in an introduction that bears all the marks of some hard thinking: "The Mother Country version of the Discipline oeuvre is resonant with memories from school and home: the swishy cane, the maternal slipper, the smell of chalk-dust and fear, bending over, bare bottoms, and so on." Attempting to write about the subliminal character and appeal of Thatcherism, I would make little references to the enduring persistence of this trope (concentrated among, but not confined to, the public school classes). I would make reference to Geoffrey Howe, quivering in the headmistress's study. To satirize a famous editorial in the old *Daily Telegraph*, headed "The Smack of Firm Government," I penned a *New Statesman* editorial entitled "The Smack of a Firm Governess." And there was "sado-monetarist" and all the rest of it. People would smile as if one was, of course, joking. But it was noticeable all the same that the joke was one that few people failed to get. If I were Geoffrey Howe, leafing through this guide, I wonder how I would feel on confronting this sentence: "I am a firm believer in punishing before witnesses whenever the behavior warrants it, since nothing is more shaming to a big chap than to have his trousers taken down and his bottom whipped in public."

Banned and burned as it may have been, this book must have enjoyed something of a secret life among clubmen, martinets and discipline-fanciers. I noticed that, in her chapter thoughtfully entitled "The Birch," and exhaustively and profusely illustrated with different styles, intensities and postures, Ms. Kerr-Sutherland had this to say about judicial birching, of the kind that used to be so popular in British magistrates' courts:

At present a judicial birching is inflicted in private by policemen. One (or more) holds down the boy across a table, while another officer applies the birch...I have long believed that delinquent boys, sentenced to be whipped, should receive their punishment in public, immediately, and at the hands of a strong *woman* police constable. [Italics in original].

I knew that I had read this, or something like it, before. On your behalf, gentle reader, I went back to Ian Gibson's classic study, *The English Vice: Beating, Sex and Shame in Victorian England and After*. In a riotous House of Commons debate on the cat and the birch in February 1953, there was the following intervention from Captain C. Waterhouse, Conservative Member for Leicester Southeast and later a leader of the Suez Group—ancestor of the Monday Club and thus indirect progenitor of one strand of Thatcherism: "We should allow magistrates, if necessary, to order the cane or to send the culprits back to school to be caned. If a policeman should be too strong, put a stout policewoman on the job." Gibson comments that he has seen flagellant porn mags in which this wish is gratified, but the actual prompt may well have come to the gallant captain from the riveting work under review.

Gibson also detailed the work, around that very parliamentary debate, of Eric A. Wildman and his National Society for the Retention of Corporal Punishment. Wildman's own illiterate seminal work, entitled *Juvenile Justice*, proclaimed the following:

> We are doing everything in our power, but so much depends upon the support we can command. With us is allied the Corpun Educational Organisation which exists to provide teachers, educational authorities and parents with carefully selected and manufactured instruments of correction. Already there are 10,000 "satisfied customers." Corpun also runs a unique literary service publishing the personal experiences of those entrusted with the care of the young of administering corporal correction and providing them with a media for the frank expression of opinion.

Corpun's "unique literary service" actually consisted of pamphlets, often with introductions by eager clergymen and titles like *A Girl's Beating: Punishment Postures*, which landed him in court, despite his claim to be upholding "old-fashioned discipline." (Another interesting literary footprint occurs to me here. The only other place I have seen the word "corpun" in print is in the *Letters* of Philip Larkin. As a neologism, it is as ugly as any one could contrive, but as a salacious expression and—apparently—as a piece of authentic Englishry, it was very close to his core.)

The key phrase in Captain Waterhouse's distraught peroration above is surely the one in which he calls for the victims to be sent "back to school to be caned." In the great rolling growl that used to sweep Tory Party Conferences at any mention of the birch, there could be detected a thwarted yearning to have everybody under *control* again: back in school, with its weird hierarchy of privileges and sufferings; back in the ranks of the regiment where a good color sergeant could keep them in order; back in the workhouse and under the whip of the beadle. If this means a population that is somewhat infantilized and humiliated, well how else can you expect to get people to wait in the rain to see a royal princess break a bottle of cider over the bows of a nuclear submarine? And be glad, nay proud, to get soaked if she were late ("Gawd bless yer, mam!" as the Ealing Studios used to put it). Kerr-Sutherland had a keen instinct here. "From time to time throughout this Guide I have referred, obliquely, to 'infantile punishments.' What are these? Briefly, they are punishments designed to force an apparent reversion to infancy—babyhood—on the part of the culprit." As she states, in her character-building fashion,

> oddly enough—or perhaps not oddly at all—I have found over the years that the type of offender most likely to benefit from

such an ordeal is also the type most likely to accept it with humility. (Often these are the artistic or musical cases.) To them I promise that the credit they gain from submitting with courage to the flogging, far outweighs that which they lose from being petticoated and birched in public—unlikely though it might seem at the time. I also point out that they will be the center of attention in a very old and beautiful ceremony. For some reason, this often appears to carry considerable weight.

One can imagine. And one either understands what la Kerr-Sutherland is driving at, or one does not. It might seem childish to look down from the gallery in the House of Commons and play the old game of guessing which law-and-order and family-values chap is sitting on the green leather bench secretly wearing rubber knickers, or nappies, or lace-trimmed split-crotch lingerie under his pinstripes. But only a political establishment suffering acutely from arrested development could make the game so well worth playing, and so rich in disclosure and reward.

(Caricatures of the English vice as being also a Tory vice may be about to show symptoms of redundancy. In the old days, men who wanted to be caned or spanked, by women or men, seemed to coalesce around Conservative Party embarrassments. There was the testimony of the gorgeous, pouting Vickie Barrett at the Profumo/Ward hearings, about her five-quid-a-stroke sessions of plying the rattan. More recently, there was of course the *flagellatrice* who had managed to rent herself space in Norman Lamont's capacious, not to say elastic, basement. However, I note that the winsome Tony Blair, who is not about to be outdone on any sector of the law-and-order front, has recently stood up before the whole school and bared his reminiscences. On a recent edition of *Panorama*, he told a pro-corpun couple he met on some stricken doorstep in Southampton that: "I'm actually someone who received the cane when I was in school. It probably did me no harm." He drew instant endorsement from Sir Rhodes Boyson, the Wackford-whiskered fallabout who used to speak for the Tories on education. Sir Rhodes, if one can call him that with a straight face, also testified that caning had done him no harm. Why do people invariably make this claim; usually before anyone has asked them? Anyway, Blair's standard disclosure is interesting chiefly because for the first time in history the Labour Party is led by a public schoolboy while the Tory Party is not. We had already guessed, I fancy, that on all painful questions he was better at taking it than dishing it out.)

In the days when those who lusted for the private lash also controlled the lord chamberlain's theater censorship office, so as to deny any desublimated sexual portrayals to the rest of us, Laurence Olivier wrote a magnificent essay which demonstrated that he had, from early youth, grasped by instinct what lay behind the beating business. He was writing in defense of Edward Bond's censored play *Saved*:

> The first time a schoolmaster ordered me to take my trousers down I knew it was not from any doubt that he could punish me efficiently enough with them up. The theater is concerned, whether in the deepest tragedy or the lightest comedy, with the teaching of the human heart the knowledge of itself, and sometimes, when it is necessary, with the study, understanding and recognition of that most dreaded and dangerous eccentricity in the human design, the tripartite conspiracy between the sexual, the excretory and the cruel.

It is at the precise apex of this triangle (or if you insist, at all three of its precise apexes) that Kerr-Sutherland operates. It is the meticulous codification and ritual of each castigation that makes such a brisk pamphlet seem many times longer than it actually is. Here, she demonstrates how to break and reset the armature of a living personality:

> To put it bluntly, after bowel movements all human beings must thoroughly clean themselves—there is no need to go into details; we all know what I am saying. However, some boys, either because of laziness or because they have not been properly trained when they were very small, are—let us say—lax in this matter. The evidence for this can be found by an *ad hoc* inspection...Any resistance should be punished by smacking, public scrubbing, and rubber knickers or napkins until further notice.

Any *resistance*. Oh *Matron*...The desired end result, and the one that is depressingly often achieved, is a kind of fawning gratitude. "Never did *me* any harm...schools these days no idea of discipline...short sharp shock the only answer." Kerr-Sutherland probably made no idle boast when, after detailing her dirty underwear program (and completing Olivier's triptych by describing her lavishly sadistic treatment for the maximum offense of self-abuse), she closed on this note: "Time and again a former pupil comes to see me, to reminisce or perhaps for another purpose. Boys who have passed through my hands have gone on to win the highest awards their country can bestow, for gallantry, self-sacrifice and leadership—I do not need to say any more."

She didn't need to say any more because she and her clientele imagined that they shared an exciting secret. The labor of exposing the secret is well worthwhile, because it reminds us, when the hearty cry of "Back to Basics" is heard, of the occluded roots of this inverted nostalgia. It shows us precisely what the fuck it's all about, or about what fuck it all is.

Who Runs Britain?

Police Espionage

1994

I N THE 1930S Wal Hannington, the communist organizer of the National Unemployed Workers' Movement, was leaving a committee meeting when an unknown comrade came up and pressed a letter "to be read later" into his hand. Hannington soon removed the envelope from his pocket, opened it idly, and was astonished to find himself summoned to a secret meeting where all kinds of mayhem and sedition were on the agenda. The note was couched in terms that suggested the discussion would come as no surprise to him. He threw the letter away. Very shortly afterward, he was stopped by the police ("Just a routine inquiry, sir") and given a very thorough search indeed. The investigating officers seemed to be looking for something in particular, and moreover to be disappointed at not finding it.

Of course, you may object, this story is too elaborate. Too conspiratorial. If the rozzers want to do an old-fashioned fit-up, they can simply produce the letter from one of their own pockets, hand it to the suspect so as to get some fingerprints, and then say: "Well, well, well, what do we have here?" But where, really, is the fun in that? For one thing, it means that the victim of the plant knows everything. He is not compelled to wonder which of his colleagues and brothers is the fink or the nark. For another—and call me an old sentimentalist if you will—it runs the slight risk of offending the professional pride of one of the cops involved. A real framing must allow for conscience if it is to allow for deniability. And since deniability has deposed accountability as a principle of our unwritten constitution, elegance in framing has become an art as well as a science.

The first consideration—the sowing of distrust and suspicion—is of especial salience when dealing with workers and trade unionists. The success of a hard-fought strike, particularly in times of unemployment and declining wages, depends on the chemistry of solidarity. People really will treat one another as brothers and sisters (how one can hear the contented chortles at that old rhetoric) if they can be brought to believe that an injury to one is an injury to all. But, as we have known ever since the Judas myth, if a band of brothers can be made to start asking who is the clever-clogs insider, then the crowing of the occasional cock will be the least of it. J. Edgar Hoover used to say that FBI informers on the left didn't have to be everywhere, just as long as they were thought to be everywhere. Leo Huberman's classic book *The Labour Spy Racket* detailed the brilliance of this insight as it applied to the union-busters and paid informants of the heroic period of American industrial organization. The stool-pigeon and the provocateur act as a vicious solvent on the very notion of fraternity, which is why Jack London once famously wrote that it was only when the Creator had perfected the snake, the rat and the toad that he began work on designing the scab.

In an Edward Thompsonian echo, Seumas Milne reminds us of the British tradition of police espionage by quoting from the constitution of the London Corresponding Society, drawn up in 1795: "Extreme zeal is often a cloak of treachery."* Since well before the time of Pitt, the authorities have been adept at suborning treachery, arranging for outrage and for outrages, commissioning forgers and blackmailers and recruiting degraded lumpen elements into politics.

It is the argument of Seumas Milne, in this important (perhaps very important) book, that the breaking of the coal-miners' union over the past decade was the outcome of a concerted secret police campaign that deserves to be classed with the Cato Street "conspiracy," the Zinoviev letter and the defamation/destabilization of Parnell and Casement. Clever readers of a certain type may object that Arthur Scargill and Peter Heathfield made rods for their own backs, dug their own graves, committed various sins of hubris and all the rest of it. Milne himself takes an honest and open line in favor of the NUM's all-out strategy for the defense of the coalfields and the union, which he regards as being virtually identical. But his unashamed—indeed almost uncritical—political stand has the same effect as all honest prose, in dispensing with needless ambiguities and in forcing attention on the chosen subject. He, at least, has no hidden agenda. And he possesses reportorial skills and tenacities which, if he can slow down his prose style just a trifle, will one day make him what he seems least to care about being—a famous and admired journalist.

---

* *The Enemy Within: MI5, Maxwell and the Scargill Affair* by Seumas Milne (Verso, 1994).

Early in 1974, I went up to Grimethorpe colliery on a hunch. The Yorkshire area of the miners' union had for decades been one of the safest baronies of the bovine, block-vote Labour Party right wing. But, in the aftershock of a local colliery disaster, a tough-minded and fluent union compensation agent named Arthur Scargill had made a bit of a name for himself. In union elections that were faintly premonitory of the coming confrontation with the Heath government, he and a colleague named Owen Briscoe had swept the poll and begun to take over the district. After spending some quality time down the pit and taking the odd sounding at the club, I thought I realized that even the highly taciturn and conservative Yorkshire miners were ready for a change of pace. I made my way over to Barnsley, met Scargill in his office, was treated with disdain as a member of a prostituted profession but wrote nonetheless that something seismic was afoot in what had been a highly ossified union, and that there were treats in store for those who liked their politics militant. I claim this to be the first piece about the salience of Scargill, though Paul Routledge of the *Times* had, it turned out, done a decent report on the election results as they occurred. In a few months such claims were moot. Scargill led a mass picket of miners to the Saltley coke depot outside Birmingham, recruited the support of the local engineers' union and saw the thick blue line of the forces of law and order snap and the cops scamper for higher ground.

The Saltley événements and their analogues put an end, at some remove, to the businessman's government of Grocer Heath. By the end of the 1970s, I had seen the fruits of a Labour administration in the bare-faced Special Branch framing of two of my journalist colleagues (Crispin Aubrey and Duncan Campbell—two of the then celebrated ABC defendants) and had written several editorials about torture in Ulster when Roy Mason was Callaghan's minister for the province and a Yorkshire area-sponsored NUM Member of Parliament. Forgive me this free association; I'm getting to the point in a second. The Official Secrets Act persecution of the ABC defendants, which included warrant-free searches and seizures, the blackmailing of witnesses and the rigging of a High Court jury, exposed the complete dependence of the Labour home secretary, Merlyn Rees, on the "advice" of comical yet sinister reactionaries in the security underworld—forces that had demonstrated many times that they did not care about election results and did not care *for* election results that returned non-Tory governments. Roy Mason's slavish defense of the same forces, as they busied themselves in the Six Counties, was to lead to the defection of the civilian Irish nationalists from the Labour lobby in the crucial parliamentary vote of no confidence in 1979. Thus old British Labourism perished forever, not in the light (as Dangerfield wrote about the last stand of the old House of Lords), but in the creepy twilight of a rotten compromise.

Milne's narrative makes me relive my youth, because it demonstrates the fashion in which these events were imbricated and affiliated. I thought I had been watching events carefully, but nothing like as carefully, it turns out, as the general staff of the Conservative Party. The Tories used to be fond of saying that the idea of class struggle was old hat. Believe that, sir, and you'll be ready to credit any damned thing. Even before Thatcher carried the vote of no confidence in Callaghan, she had commissioned her friend Nicholas Ridley to design a campaign of revenge on the mineworkers, and to ensure that all the arsenals and all the tactical designs were in place in advance. Nigel Lawson, who was later to cover himself with glory as energy secretary in this bannered campaign, wrote in his memoirs that preparation for it was "just like rearming to face the threat of Hitler in the later 1930s." That's quite a jest, when you remember how active the Tory Party actually was in the cause of anti-fascism. And it lends poignance to Harold Macmillan's later lachrymose invocation of the splendor of the British mining communities, as they brass-banded off to war against the Kaiser and thus, presumably, earned the right of any survivor to a home fit for a hero. In 1914 Karl Liebknecht told the German labor movement that "the main enemy is at home." In our own time the British Tories came to the same conclusion by a different route. We may thank Lawson for making this connection in its most crass and insulting form.

The idea of the Great War as the template of the miners' strike was not restricted to elderly sentimentalists like Macmillan. It became a favored trope of the industrial correspondents, one of whom I remember telling me that such and such a pithead punch-up had been "the Sarajevo of the dispute." It occurred to Neil Kinnock as a convenience too, because it enabled him to seem to stand with the rank and file while denouncing the supposed generals. "Lions led by donkeys"— the remark of a French general about British cannon-fodder in Flanders—became the OK vernacular in which to discuss events. (The Donkeys, interestingly enough, was the title of a history of the Somme that formed the inspiration for Joan

Littlewood's *Oh, What a Lovely War*. Its author was Alan Clark. He at least did not pretend that Generals Haig and French, unlike Privates Scargill and Heathfield, were not responsible for a million dead.)

To all this invocation of high and evasive metaphor, Milne opposes one hard and fast, earthy injunction. It is, in effect, the same injunction that Deep Throat laid upon Woodward and Bernstein in that DC underground car park. "Follow the money." Nothing was more damaging, in the entire course of the strike, than the accusation that Scargill and his colleagues had solicited funny money from overseas, and put that funny money to funny purposes. In particular, the idea that Scargill and Heathfield had paid off their own mortgages with dubious subventions from Colonel Gaddafi—a suggestion that made a brilliant lunge at several layers of the collective subconscious—was perfectly designed to split the union. If you are on strike pay, and you wonder about your family, and what keeps you going is the tradition of equal sacrifice, and you read in the *Daily Mirror* (friend of the working man) that your leaders are high on the hog—well, then, your anger and anxiety is well programmed to find an alternative outlet. Perhaps in a sweetheart "democratic" union prepared in advance by some Bulldog Drummond like David Hart.

I read Milne's book with a faint blush of shame because, not having paid daily attention to the strike and not having much liked Scargill when I met him, I had not disbelieved everything I read about the union funds. Furthermore, some of the bylines on some of the stories had been known to me and not axiomatically distrusted. At one level, what he discloses could have been known by anybody. Scargill and

Heathfield did not have mortgages, ergo these mortgages had not been paid off in Tripoli. Why did no newspaper bother with that trivial fact-check? But, correctly taking this failure as symptomatic or synecdochic of a larger one, Milne inquires how the original allegation came to be made. In detail that is impossible to summarize, he pursues a banking trail that demonstrates, beyond any doubt at all, that a series of dummy deposits and phoney receipts was created. The intent of this paperchase was to suggest that an embattled union, forced to protect its assets from state sequestration, had resorted to the terrorist and communist financial demi-monde, and had awarded large kickbacks to its own leadership in the process.

In *The Manchurian Candidate*, if you recall, the poor sap who acts as front man for the McCarthy inquisition breaks down at one point and asks for clearer instructions. On one day, he has alleged that there are 83 communists in the State Department, and on another that there are 66. Can't he be given a simple figure, and stick to it? With a pitying glance, Angela Lansbury (Mrs. Thatcher to the life in those days, now that I think of it) tells him that he's missed the whole point. People are no longer asking: "*Are* there communists in the State Department?" They are asking: "How *many* are there?" So with the bewildering series of accusations against Scargill. Libyan money, Russian money, Czech money. Laundered through Ireland, through France, through Switzerland. Something was supposed to stick, and stick it did thanks to the assiduous repetitions of Captain Robert Maxwell and his "Labour paper." But the actual money, as Milne shows, cannot have and did not come from Libya. And the timing of its deployment and discovery was so exquisitely calibrated as to require the intervention of someone with knowledge gained by surveillance, and resources only available to governments or corporations. Someone, also, who was capable of taking friendly journalists and proprietors on one side and feeding them a corking scoop. Someone, finally, who was capable of putting an agent into the NUM and keeping him there for some time before ordering him to mutate from *agent* to *provocateur*.

If the Tories had not prepared for a showdown as assiduously as they claim to have done, and if the intelligence services were not so leaky and boastful, and if Robert Maxwell's empire of fraud and mendacity had not imploded when and how it did, there might be some benefit of the doubt involved here. But, as it happens, having carefully reconstructed the movements of Roger Windsor, the NUM's chief turncoat, and of Mohammed Altaf Abbasi, the demi-monde's chief bagman, Milne is able to state with complete forensic confidence that

It is self-evident that the Libyan money, still in dollars in Lloyds Bank on 3 December and deposited into a sterling account on 4 December, cannot have been the money Windsor produced from his safe on 29 October, some five weeks earlier. It cannot have been the money brought through customs by Altaf Abbasi —if indeed that ever happened. It cannot have been the money picked up by Windsor in Sheffield and Rotherham and stored in his larder for ten days in late November. And it cannot have been the money used to "repay" the repairs on the NUM officials' homes and Roger Windsor's bridging loan. Nor is there the slightest possibility that, having deposited £163,000 in a Lloyds Bank account on 4 December, Abbasi could have withdrawn the same money immediately and rushed it over to Sheffield for Windsor to pass on £50,000 to Scargill...The only rational explanation for what took place in the light of the new documentary evidence is that there must have been *two* sets of money.

Good intuitive and supportive evidence of this hypothesis is provided by the GCHQ employees who later contacted the *Guardian* to reveal that the British security services had tried to make a bogus and incriminating deposit in a Scargill-linked bank account several years after the strike was over. One of Mrs. Thatcher's few mistakes appears to have been her removal of legal trade-union rights from the honest toilers at GCHQ.

Things being what they are in the libel courts (which protected Maxwell to the end, but which never afforded Scargill the majesty of the law) Milne treads very carefully on the tracks of Roger Windsor, who emerged mole-like from the heart of the NUM to tell the most alarming stories about the Scargill entourage, and who became the pet of the *Daily Mirror*, and who seems to have shown something like an excess of zeal in getting himself photographed with his arms around Colonel Gaddafi while allegedly on union business. My best advice to readers who want to know more about this man, who rose without trace and who seems to have sunk without trace, is to consult the remarks made under parliamentary privilege by Tam Dalyell MP, which have so far survived all challenge and which are cited on pages 170–75 of this densely documented book.

A name with which Roger Windsor's has been linked, to use the coy formulation of Fleet Street, is that of Stella Rimington. Now resold to us all as the user-friendly face of a newly feminized secret police, Ms. Rimington's career at MI5 has in fact been rather more hatchet-visaged than her handlers pretend. The MI5 defector Cathy Massiter spoke of Rimington's earlier role in bending all the rules of surveillance in order to gratify her masters (and mistress) by going after CND. If Mr. Dalyell's inquiries are on the right track, she seems to have taken her interest in industrial relations along the same stellar career path. Of course, we do not know for absolutely certain. But that is not the fault of Milne or Dalyell. It is the responsibility of a Parliament that has begged to remain in ignorance, and that has voted unaudited sums for undisclosed security purposes, and that has permitted infringements on the privileges of its constituents and members that are far greater than any cod fax ever composed. A vast failure of nerve here on the part of the Labour leadership. Merlyn Rees and Peter Archer, former senior minister and law officer in Labour cabinets, now admit that they were kept in the dark about highly politicized cowboy activities run by both MI5 and MI6, and not infrequently directed at their own colleagues. The dodgy world of the Ulster "security forces," which combines the Orange card with the black-bag operation, has acted like a hothouse for corner-cutting dirty-tricks types, death-squad penis-enviers and all the other banana republic heavies who were later turned against working men and women on the mainland. Sir Kenneth Newman was perhaps unintentionally revealing when he spoke of the Six Counties as the "laboratory" of modern British police tactics.

So the disclosures made by Peter Wright, for whatever sordid motive, turn out to be a better guide to reality than the naive social democratic belief in the impartiality of the permanent government. Nothing is more depressing, in Milne's narrative, than the eagerness of Neil Kinnock and Norman Willis, even in opposition, to act as conduits for raw, untreated disinformation served up by the security elite with the help of their long-term asset Captain Maxwell. (And where was the Serious Fraud Office and all the other apparatus of financial scrutiny, so harshly and falsely deployed against the NUM, when Maxwell was riding high?) In the days when Labour's HQ was Transport House, and the TUC's was at Congress House, someone once remarked: "Transport House and Congress House! What simply *marvelous* names for brothels!" Many a true word is spoken in jest.

It seems a long time ago that the *Daily Mirror*, under the stewardship of Cecil King, was at the center of a loony 1968 conspiracy to install a junta under the benign leadership of Lord Mountbatten. But we only know about that episode through the grace and accident of certain people's memoirs. What we need is to know how we are governed, and by whom, in real time. If Milne's book receives a tithe of the attention it deserves, it will present the first serious test of the caliber of Tony Blair. In his well-received speech to the last Labour Party Conference, Mr. Blair went out of his way to promise the restoration of union rights at GCHQ, and received much praise for his attacks on official secrecy and the unaccountable bureaucratic state. Here, then, is his opportunity. Can he demand less than a Parliamentary Select Committee, along the lines of Senator Frank Church's hearings on the CIA, to investigate the abuse of power by the intelligence services? And can he state without looking a fool that he will, on his first day in Downing Street, receive the traditional off-the-record briefing from Stella Rimington? When the Tories first went to the trenches against their coal-mining fellow citizens in 1974, Edward Heath called an election on the slogan "Who runs Britain?" I thought then, and I think now, that this was and is a very good and pertinent question.

Lucky Kim
On Kim Philby
1995

W HILE I was still reading these books, and thinking about them, I chanced to have two annoying near KGB experiences. A creepy individual named Yuri Shvets published a book called *Washington Station: My Life as a KGB Spy in America*, which was fully as lurid and preposterous as its title (put out by the "respected firm" of Simon and Schuster) might suggest. Its central allegation was that an old personal enemy of mine had been a key "agent of influence" in Reagan-era Washington. I could believe anything of this man except that his controllers had awarded him the hilarious code-name of "Socrates." And every checkable allegation in the book turned out to be grotesquely false. So that was irritating, because it meant another portentous non-scare about a virtual non-person. Then, at a party in Georgetown, I found myself being introduced to Mr. Oleg Kalugin. Now apparently retired from his foul career as a secret policeman, Mr. Kalugin gave me a card with the name of his consulting firm (offices in Moscow and Washington) on it. The outfit was called Intercon, which seemed more appropriate than was perhaps intentional. Mr. Kalugin looked as if he had been dreamed up in an Ian Fleming nightmare. His idea of light conversation, since I decided to ask him about some of the books under re-view, was to hint that he could say a lot if he chose. "Your Kim Philby... ha, ha, ha, that's quite another story... Yuri Modin—well, he's a character..." and so on. I found myself get-ting irrationally pissed off. Here am I, a journalist and a free citizen of the Anglo-American world. But if I seek to know what was really done in the Cold War dark, I must attend on someone who was a criminal in that war. My "own side" has no intention of enlightening me, and the spook industry has built up such an oligopoly in journalism and publishing that no untainted rival—such as the old-fashioned idea of full dis-closure—has been permitted to challenge the self-interested ghouls who pay out their ration of "secrets" in a niggardly and mysterious fashion as a form of individual and collective wel-fare. What if, I decided, what if, just for once, one read this output as if history mattered and as if the war of ideas was a real thing?

For some people, the defining, molding episode of this moribund century is the Final Solution; for others it is the Gulag, the 1989 revolutions, the Spanish Civil War, the Somme, Hiroshima, the storming of the Winter Palace or the Easter Rising. All of these can still lay great claims on the minds and emotions even of people who do not remember them. They furnish our stocks of imagery and they define what we mean by moments of truth and choice. Revisiting these territories we find that, as Auden phrased it about Spain, "Our thoughts have bodies" and "The menacing shapes of our fever are pre-cise and alive." For me, anyway, the most absorbing moment is the Hitler-Stalin Pact. It was not merely a test of global in-stitutions and of ideologies and principles and individuals, but a sort of key to how power really thinks and how potentates truly behave. The declared interests or manifestos of great contending parties are never what they are proclaimed to be. (Salient current example: the obvious collusion of those "historic, atavistic foes" Serbia and Croatia in the dismemberment of Bosnia. Memorable example: Brezhnev's intimate consultation with Lyndon Johnson in the days before the invasion of Czechoslovakia.)

The Cold War was ostensibly about some quite important differences, arising from the postwar Stalinization of Eastern Europe and from the competition for nuclear superiority. But it also had remarkable elements of superpower collaboration and symbiosis. And, though this could never be admitted by the ideologues of the supposedly bipolar *Kulturkampf*, it did leak out to a wide public through the fictions of Len Deighton and John le Carré. Watching the shadowplay on the walls of the Cold War cave, and seeing the literal interpenetration of opposites as Karla penetrated "us," and "we" reciprocated, one could make the induction that the spy game was a thing in itself, and that those who took part in it, and those who paid them to do so, had more in common with one another than with the poor bloody infantry, which in Cold War terms meant the poor bloody civilians who lived under thermonuclear blackmail and paid through the nose for "protection."

Now that this stupid war is over, and a certain amount of daylight has been let in, we ought to be reading a grown-up account of what was done in our names, what was known, and in each case by whom. We ought not to be viewing history through the optic of penny dreadfuls, yellow journalism and adventure stories for boys. Instead, at least for the present, the opening of certain archives seems to have made the situation worse. Selective release of documents, very often by spies to other spies, or by spies to certain trusted journalists and freelancers, has turned any old snooper into a historian. One of the few people of any wit, seriousness or integrity to have done well out of this business is Phillip Knightley, and look what we find on page 190 of his book, produced with Genrikh Borovik.* Kim Philby is apparently talking:

> But if success does come, an agent has the obligation to take full advantage of it, even better, to take double advantage of it. To avail himself of all the opportunities that success brings, he has to examine them himself or at least intuitively guess what they are. I even wanted to entitle my book *Lucky Kim*, by analogy with Conrad's *Lucky Jim*. But then we decided that this title probably wasn't serious enough.

Well, no, I can quite see how it might fail a seriousness test. (One can almost hear the shade of Peter Cook, intoning regretfully how he "never had the reading for the spying.") *Lord Kim*, on the other hand, might just about have served, given the fact that H. St. John Philby got himself called everything from *sahib* to *tuan* all across the British Empire's eastern division, and given the obsession of all these authors with the English class system (Roland Perry gets so carried away that

---

* *The Philby Files* by Genrikh Borovik, edited by Phillip Knightley (Little, Brown, 1994). The piece also mentions *The Fifth Man* by Roland Perry (Sidgwick, 1994); *Treason in the Blood* by Anthony Cave Brown (Hale, 1995); *My Five Cambridge Friends* by Yuri Modin (Headline, 1994); *Looking for Mr. Nobody* by Jenny Rees (Weidenfeld, 1994).

he repeatedly refers to Lord Victor Rothschild in a book published by the ancient firm of Lord Frank Longford) and, finally, given the belief of Anthony Cave Brown that treason is a heritable trait, the *Bell Curve* theory of clubland skulduggery.

Yet this is the standard, both of writing and editing and research. When James Jesus Angleton, crazed and criminal head of the CIA, suffered himself to be asked a few questions by a panel of cringing congressmen, he took care to tell them that they had no right to inquire into his business, and were not in any case equipped to understand "the wilderness of mirrors" in which he operated. They were so impressed by the first assertion that, when it was revealed that the "spy master" (or was it "master spy"?—the two puerile terms are employed almost equivalently in this degraded literature) had actually been quoting from Eliot's "Gerontion," they were impressed almost out of their skins. This only added to the myth of austere, ascetic intellectual that was imposed by court writers on Angleton's actual persona of superstitious, credulous, addle-pated bully. The remark made above by Philby is supposed to have come from a taped transcript. All one can say is that the double error, in the context of fantasy talk about "double advantage," cannot have been made by him.

Hugh Trevor-Roper (God's little Dacre) once made the shrewd observation that the Cambridge clique probably amounted to very little in the sum of international violence and conspiracy, but that they could or might have done. They could or might have done, he went on to say, if during the period of the Hitler-Stalin Pact, they had conveyed Enigma or Ultra information to Moscow, and thus indirectly or accidentally to Berlin. Then they really would have altered the course of history. On the only occasion that I knowingly met a Cambridge spy, I broached the same question. Michael Straight, a distinguished East Coast American liberal and publisher (he had run the *New Republic* during the queasy years of McCarthy, and if exposed during that period could have helped discredit a cause larger than himself in much the same way as the wretched Richard Gott recently managed, on a smaller scale, to do), waited until 1982 to publish his book *After Long Silence*. It told the usual story: the high excitement of the 1930s; the precedence given in Cambridge circles to young men of background and pelf who possessed physical charm; the subordination of all ends and means to anti-Nazism. I had, in very truth, heard all this before. With the patriarchal Victor Navasky, editor of the *Nation*, as my witness, I drummed my faultlessly manicured fingertips with impatience on the snowy tablecloth in the fine Stanford White dining room of New York's prestigious Metropolitan Club (see how catching this rubbishy style can be). The fine silver gave off a discreet tinkle as I...no. I asked him flat out how those who hated Hitler enough to swallow all doubts about Stalin had swallowed the Hitler-Stalin Pact. Didn't he worry that he, who had only been recruited at that very period, might be (pardon a clapped-out expression) giving ammunition to the enemy? I shall not soon forget his response. With the telltale look of one who, at long last, had come in from the cold, he fixed me with a glance that told of a life spent in the shadows and...no. He told me that he had never, until that very moment, considered the possibility. He also promised, in answer to my subsequent question, to start considering it. He seemed not at all disconcerted, either by my questions or by his own answer. My tentative conclusion, since it was near incredible that he had *never* considered the matter, was that he was dissembling or was, possibly, in some sort of denial.

It's interesting to consult these latest volumes on the issue of the Nazi-Soviet Pact which, though everybody writes as if it didn't count as compared to its Munich predecessor, was actually a moral and intellectual earthquake in the life of all communists. Genrikh Borovik is the most interesting here, perhaps because he understands what the pact meant for Russia. He quotes from a Soviet intelligence source of the time, who even used the prevailing party-line euphemism in relating the fact that "the signing of the Soviet-German Non-Aggression Pact caused [Philby] to ask puzzled questions such as, 'Why was this necessary?,' 'What will happen to the single-front struggle against fascism now?' However, after several talks on this subject, [Philby] seemed to grasp the significance of the pact." Borovik also raises, for perhaps a sentence or two, the possibility that Philby's reports on the Maginot Line, sent to Moscow when Philby was still using a *Times* cover identity in France, might have proved more useful to Hitler than to Stalin. But you don't notice the subject at all unless you are looking for it, any more than you register the fact that, at about this time, the controllers of the Cambridge ring were being recalled to Moscow and put to death.

Roland Perry, an Australian who prefers to rely on the Yuri Modin school of history and who thinks he has proved that Victor Rothschild was the "fifth man," spends exactly one sentence saying that after the pact "the agents thought of abandoning their commitment until Gorsky made contact." Gorsky, the London control, was apparently able to convince

Maclean, Philby and Burgess, but not Blunt and Rothschild, that Stalin's realpolitik was "buying time." This could be accurate, I suppose, though it isn't consistent with Borovik, whose ex-KGB credentials are superficially as good as Modin's. And anyway, Perry writes like this:

> Gorsky hated being late for Anthony Blunt, who was always militarily punctual. The tall, lanky agent with the long face and gravity-drawn mouth often complained about meeting in public houses, but Gorsky knew he was more than partial to the Scotches he bought, which soothed the MI5 man's perpetual worry about being seen by "someone from Whitehall."

The fastidious Anthony Blunt, lured to a pub in Hammersmith by the promise of a free malt. At least it bulks out the narrative.

Anthony Cave Brown understands the Hitler-Stalin Pact in the following historical sense. He knows that the Soviet defector Walter Krivitsky had warned Washington of growing Moscow-Berlin rapprochement (though he does not connect this to the Munich sell-out) and he runs the whole development together by saying: "Time ran out. When Hitler and Stalin made the pact to which Krivitsky had alluded in Washington and the German army invaded Poland, Britain declared war on Germany."

That takes care of that, except for some briefly appended gobbets of boilerplate, lifted by Cave Brown from Philby's own very constrained memoir, *My Silent War* (as the "Lord Kim" effort was eventually titled). But then, Cave Brown is such a political primitive that he describes "Fabian socialism" as "Marxism without the blood," and admonishes St. John Philby in the following manner:

It was laid down in the 17th century in the *History of the Pleas of the Crown* that "because as the subject hath his protection from the King and his laws, so on the other side the subject is bound by his allegiance to be true and faithful to the King." This legal contention was binding on all Britons at all times during their lives. Whether Philby was entirely loyal was, and will remain, a major consideration in the life of conspiracy on which he now embarked.

Cave Brown employs this very shaky piece of authority to suggest that old St. John was being a traitor when he persuaded his friend, the no less presumptuous king of Saudi Arabia, that American corporations would give him a better deal than British ones for his oil. If influence-peddling in the Gulf is to be rated treasonous, the attorney general should lose no time in getting Mr. Cave Brown out of his Virginia retreat, and making him some kind of consultant.

Something I owe to the soil that grew,

says Rudyard Kipling's Kim,

> More to the life that fed
> But most to Allah, who gave me two
> Separate sides to my head.

Much speculative commentary—an entire edifice of it, in fact —has arisen from the simple fact of the double life. How on earth could these chaps have lived their careers of deception, kept their nerve, done the dirty, got away with it, fooled the finest minds of their generations etc. Part of the difficulty here, if it really is a difficulty, arises from the failure of this or any earlier crop of espionage "experts" to agree on the simplest facts. Modin, for example, claims that Burgess did not flee "with" Maclean. He was ordered to accompany Maclean to Moscow so as to avoid any personal or alcoholic breakdown on his (Maclean's) part, and was assured by the KGB that he could be back in London before anyone had noticed his absence. "Yeah, right," as I scrawled, American style, in my margin at this point. Modin also says that Philby cracked under British interrogation in Beirut in 1963 and confessed all before being allowed to escape. Borovik does not believe this, but he does succeed in showing that during the Stalin period there were those in the KGB who thought that the British agents were "double" and who even proposed liquidating them as infiltrators. This in turn helps license those—mainly drawn from the immense crackpot wing of British intelligence—who think that Kim always remained "one of us." Here, as a sort of meld of all this nonsense into one anecdote, is one of Cave Brown's riper efforts at narrative. The action occurs on the day of Philby's funeral in Moscow:

> In London, Philby's old comrade from the days of War Station XB, Nicholas Elliott, was in his club at St. James's at about this time, giving thought to a scheme to disrupt any attempt by the KGB leadership to iconise Philby posthumously, as indeed was their intention. The idea that formed in Elliott's mind was that the British Secret Service should comment [sic] to the Duke of Kent, the Grand Master of the Most Distinguished Order of St. Michael and St. George, that Philby be made a Companion of the Order. This was usually conferred upon British subjects as a reward for services abroad and often went to members of the foreign service. The Russians took such matters as honors and medals almost as seriously as did the British, and the award of a CMG to Philby posthumously might be expected to create a

thought in the KGB's mind—and perhaps in the minds of official England and Foggy Bottom—that Philby had been Whitehall's man after all. But the idea came to nothing, though it is not clear why. Elliott leaked the idea to the *Times*, and some notice was taken of it.

What a tremendous chance to send Boris the Bear into a frantic tizzy! What a stroke in the Great Game! Perhaps, though, it was wise to keep the CMG in reserve for another time, as a sort of super-weapon.

In other words, and as one trudges through these books, it is interesting to discover that as a young officer Monty was St. John Philby's best man. It is interesting to know that Philby junior, as a war correspondent in France in 1940, was buttonholed by the Duke of Windsor, who wanted some advice on how best to run away. But the whole business is becoming a case of more and more about less and less.

And the political and intellectual level gets lower and lower. Perry—who actually opens one of his chapters with the words "A shot rang out"—would not know the difference between Bukharin and Bakunin, and makes the case that Rothschild was a spy because he was a Jew. "He was never so committed to his country of birth and its established order. In fact, more than once when confronted with a conflict between race and country, he chose race." Well, why not come right out and say what's on your mind? However, Modin has been through the same set of coincidences as has Perry, though without making the stunning discovery that old Victor was a dedicated Zionist, and has concluded that the espionage "coups" attributed to Rothschild were actually the work of John Cairncross. Here we have what most of these *manqué* thriller writers would term an "irony" because though it seems that Cairncross was the most thorough and brilliant and successful of the spies, he wasn't a member of the upper class, wasn't gay, wasn't an alcoholic, wasn't a diplomat, didn't make a run for it and has indeed lived in France since 1952. He may not even have been an Apostle! He was a working-class lad from Scotland, a scholar and—guess what?—a believing communist. Where does this leave the celebrated hothouse that created "the climate of treason"?

Cairncross knew all about the climate of treason. He was working at the heart of the British government when an acquaintance of his, Sir John Colville, was told by Sir Arthur Rucker, then the prime minister's private secretary, that "communism is now the great danger, greater even than that of Nazi Germany." The date—which was October 1939—is what I would call a suggestive one. Not all that much later, having discovered that British intelligence was passing on watered-down information on Nazi war material to the Red Army, Cairncross got hold of the real stuff and sent them that. As a result, the Russians were enabled to re-equip in time to win the battle of the Kursk salient and to give the Wehrmacht a mauling from which it never recovered. So perhaps Trevor-Roper was wrong in suggesting that the period of the pact was the only one at which espionage might have made a difference.

I remember vividly, on the day when Mrs. Thatcher made her necessarily rather strangulated statement on the belated exposure of Sir Anthony Blunt, that she made an admission in the guise of an excuse. It had to be remembered, she said, that only in a great hurry and with some considerable improvisation did SIS begin to combat the Nazi menace in 1939–40. Was it then to be wondered at that a few wrong'uns escaped scrutiny and passed into the service? What this conceded was that nobody in the service or anywhere near it had been planning to do anything about the Nazis except give in to them. Every now and then this plain fact is glimpsed in one of these books. Philby is considered sound because he is ostensibly pro-Franco and an activist in the Anglo-German League. Burgess gains entrée by becoming private secretary to a leading pro-Nazi Tory MP. In order to win the confidence of "C" and the rest of them, the better to become a traitor to your country or your class, it was an advantage to pose as a traitor to civilization.

Only Jenny Rees, in her well-written and thoughtful memoir of her father, comes close to making intelligible literature out of all this self-referential palaver. Reading her account, we can at least scan the cultural and social and psychological (to say nothing of ideological) stresses that influenced one bright, active personality in the epoch of war and dictatorship. It seems—to begin at the end of the story—that Goronwy Rees was signed up by Burgess, on the authority of the celebrated Leonid Eitingon, to provide reports on the political atmosphere. His subsequent zigzags and recantations were never in perfect synch with his personal loyalties and friendships, and the strain can be read in his columns for Encounter, in his family life as related here, and in his academic career. Rees was not an important agent, and is of moment to the professional spy writers only for the role he eventually played in "unmasking" former associates, but at least one can learn something about society and about the conflict of ideas from

Ms. Rees's account. One may also learn how much of Goronwy Rees's life was wasted on this stuff.

As so much of ours has been. These endless quasi-disclosures and planted rigmaroles are what we get instead of something really useful like, for instance, a serious post–Cold War reform of the insulting rules governing the Public Record Office. Allen Dulles once edited, from clippings in the *Reader's Digest* and elsewhere, a book entitled *Great True Spy Stories* (all the title needed was the suffix *"for Boys,"* or perhaps *"for the Birds"*). Time at last to stop recycling the clippings, and to replace the history of conspiracy with the modern history, of unaccountable power and unelected arrogance, of which it forms a squalid part.

Diary

At the Oscars

1995

EVERY SPRING, American camera crews and sound teams and the boys and girls of the "pencil press" (as it is still quaintly known) load their equipment or stuff their notebooks in a pocket and set off for the unthrilling town of Punxsutawney, Pennsylvania. The occasion is Groundhog Day, when a local creature named Punxsutawney Phil is reputed to predict the coming season's weather. I think it's the angle of his shadow that is supposed to work the trick. A long time ago, this media ritual passed the point at which it could be called self-satirizing, and became instead a ludicrous and embarrassing chore. The reading and viewing and listening public would not notice if this non-event went uncovered, and the media would be glad to be shot of the tedium of "covering" it, but nobody quite knows how to stop the dance. Locked together and sobbing with boredom (as in *They Shoot Horses, Don't They?*), the numbed partners drag their way across the floor one more time. Russell Baker once wrote a brilliant column about these gruesome proceedings, which summarized for him the participation of the press in events that are staged only for the press's benefit.

There are several other pseudo-spectacles which evoke or produce the same ritualized, desperately inauthentic sensation.

The State of the Union speech. The New Hampshire primary. The White House Easter egg roll. The presentation of the presidential Thanksgiving turkey (which even comes complete with its own self-satirizing pun). I would add the Nobel Prizes though not, oddly enough, the Booker ones. Nothing that *has* to be done every year is, however, likely to be much good (think of Christmas). And now, the Oscars themselves are starting to bore people. When the original non-event goes stale, then the society of spectacle is in serious trouble.

Groundhog Day actually produced a very good sub-Dada movie starring Bill Murray, which took the piss out of the repetitious and the banal by capturing the star in a time warp where he was doomed to enact the same day over and over again until he could learn to act his way out of it. Other smart films have been made on dumb subjects, or about apparently dumb people. *Rain Man* was a masterly study of the idiot savant. *Wayne's World* and *Ace Ventura: Pet Detective* took the intrinsic humor of the condition of stupidity and, as they say in Hollywood, ran with it. So, at the very dawn of the Reagan era, did *Being There*. Even *Dumb and Dumber* managed to take lavatory comedy to a height so far unattained. But *Forrest Gump*, or perhaps better say the reception accorded to *Forrest Gump*, is a departure of a different kind. Here is stupidity being, not mocked or even exploited, but positively and wholesomely and simply and touchingly *celebrated*.

I believe in not getting too excited about supposed cultural signifiers such as Oscar night, but for once I found myself paying attention to the conversation. Perhaps because, for the first time, I was actually present. I also believe in not writing about either one's children or one's ailments, but it is germane to the plot to mention that I attended in the company of my cinéaste ten-year-old son (without whom I would not have gone to see *Dumb and Dumber*, true, but without whom I would not have gone to see *Groundhog Day* either). My generous employers at *Vanity Fair* threw a post-Oscars bash, which now replaces the one that used to be thrown at Spago by Swifty Lazar. In spite of trade rumors that Mike Ovitz of Creative Artists had not liked his ink in our special Hollywood number, and had been working the phones to keep people away, everybody came. Or almost everybody. Madonna, who was next to me on the dinner *placement*, cancelled at the last moment, as is her right. Perhaps she didn't feel she had been well seated. Never mind; I was able to introduce Alexander Hitchens to Arnold Schwarzenegger and Sylvester Stallone, both of whom were very nice to him, as was Jessica Lange and as were Uma Thurman and Oprah Winfrey. His only autograph refusal came from Jane Fonda.

I was impressed by how many people didn't go for *Gump*. Usually, success is everything and brings everything in its train, but the idea that the industry regarded this as its best effort was widely thought to be embarrassing. As the movie's director, Robert Zemeckis, gave his speech of acceptance (which he did, excruciatingly, by speaking "on behalf of Forrest Gumps everywhere"), the girl seated next to Madonna, in the words of my colleague Frank DiGiacomo, "turned to the pop star and displayed the universal hand symbol for masturbation." The Material Girl herself interrupted a speech on how FG "stood for several qualities" by chirping: "How about mediocrity?" So there is sales resistance even to the biggest gross.

Nor did the press play its customary role of acting as a cheering section for Movieland. "Welcome to Oscar night," grinned Johnny Carson as emcee a few years ago. "Two hours of sparkling entertainment spread out over a four-hour show." People laughed that time. This time, the critics were asking how come an industry whose whole point is *entertainment*, for Chrissake, can't keep the ball in the air for even an hour? Especially hard to take were the innumerable acceptance speeches. On the preceding Sunday, the *New York Times* Sunday magazine had run quite a witty page of advice to winners, printing all the dull and conceited and hypocritical things that winners have been prone to say and constructing an all-purpose "don't give" speech out of them. And yet, on the night, speaker after speaker came to the microphone to say that the award was really for teamwork, or really for all the little people, or really for their spouses and children. It's interesting and rather frightening when people ignore, or don't understand, jokes made at their expense. Julian Barnes once wrote a salutary essay on this, recalling the great Monty Python sketch about an obscure island completely inhabited by men sounding and looking like Alan Whicker. They paced to and fro, droning horribly and trailing microphones. It was, as Barnes pointed out, impossible for Whicker to have missed the item, or the point. Yet on his very next appearance there he was, pacing about and droning horribly and trailing a mike. What can you do?

At least this year there were not very many "cause" speeches. The liberal conscience of Hollywood was never as strong as the conservatives made out, and the only occasions on which really hard political positions were taken at the

Oscars were also occasions on which boos and hisses and gasps resulted. (The director of *Hearts and Minds* welcomed the "victory of the Vietnamese" in the 1970s, and in the 1980s, Vanessa Redgrave took the opportunity of a not-too-heavily-goyish captive audience to give her views on "Zionist thugs.") In recent years, Richard Gere's moist tribute to the dalai lama has been more the sort of thing. That, plus a lot of red ribbons in solidarity with AIDS victims. This year, the red ribbons were down a bit and the preferred cause was public broadcasting, which the Gingrich majority wants to defund. Mr. Gingrich and his ally and publisher Rupert Murdoch both have shares in commercial cable and television, so any removal of public subsidy from America's only non-commercial airwaves would benefit them directly, as well as confirming the hold of Beavis and Butt-Head on program scheduling. Thus, the general dumbing down of America was a topic both on and off the screen as the evening wore on, or off.

Somewhere over on the other side of town, the O. J. Simpson jury sat in sequestration. Judge Lance Ito had decreed, in yet another of his loopy rulings, that they should not even be allowed to watch the Oscars on TV. He feared, irrationally but not without reason, that there might be some O.J. gags during the proceedings and that these might be prejudicial. So, heightening the atmosphere of unreality in which they already dwell, the jurors were prevented from sharing a quintessential experience with their fellow Americans. As it turned out, not even the terrible David Letterman managed to squeeze off a burst about Mr. Simpson or anything related to the trial. The evening was, as some magazines have taken to claiming on their covers, "100 percent O.J.-free." In truth, the industry does not quite know what to make of the Simpson affair. Pity, if you will, he who pulls the job of making a motion picture or a mini-series out of the story. It has, from its very first moments, all been on screen already. In the very week of the Oscars, the pathetic film extra Kato Kaelin won and lost his fifteen minutes; parlaying a slight acquaintance with the superstar defendant into a Gump-like appearance on the witness stand, the offer of a book contract, more bit-part work than he can handle and the grand sum of $50,000 for spilling the beans to Rupert Murdoch's trash-TV flagship *A Current Affair*. If Andy Warhol were still alive, he would not be thought of as a satirist of the postmodern.

In the bad old days, there used to be something called the Hays Office in Hollywood. This office laid down certain dos and don'ts for movie-makers, most but not all of them to do with indecency but all tending to a respect for authority and family values. (Warhol's early movie *Kiss*, which showed couples kissing for a grueling three minutes apiece, was originally made as an explicit defiance of the Hays Office rule that limited lip contact to three seconds.) I think movie people secretly miss the Hays Office, because it provided a comforting formula and some reassuring ground rules and a safe context in which to operate. It was ideal for an industry which likes to repeat itself and which is generally terrified of risk.

In *Minima Moralia*, Theodor Adorno wrote that an aesthetically faultless movie could be made in perfect conformity with all the rules and requirements of the Hays Office, as long as there was no Hays Office. This Frankfurt *koan* has always struck me as especially pregnant. It is the attachment to formula itself; the sort of derivative, poll-driven, synthetic compromise so well depicted (not satirized) by Robert Altman in *The Player*, that is turning out turkey upon turkey. A few years ago, Pauline Kael wrote a celebrated article, based on a season spent in Hollywood, about why the movies were so rank these days. She anatomized the process now known as development, by which every drop of blood and every smidgen of originality was extracted from a script.

Now John H. Richardson, a writer for *Premiere* magazine, has updated the Kael concept. When Richardson writes that "the only big-canvas film-maker of stature we have today is Oliver Stone," he meant it to sting. His essay is full of good lines. (A Hollywood publicist tells him that when he goes out to push a new movie, he feels "like the emperor's new dry cleaner.") It also contains a fine John Huston joke:

> These two producers were lost in the desert. They're dying of thirst, crawling along when they come upon an oasis. What a beautiful sight. They're saved! They fall to their knees and one of them scoops up the delicious sweet water to his face when the other producer stops him. "Wait!" he shouts. "Let me piss in it first."

But the meat of the article is its revelation of the formula now taught in screenwriting programs. Richardson took one of these ever more influential courses and discovered that "a movie should introduce two buddies, build their relationship to a crisis, separate the buddies so that they can learn some lessons on their own, and then bring them back together." This is the model of movies as different as *Rain Man* and ET.

Lost in this process is the idea that any real work will be in the last instance the work of an individual. Writers and directors—the temperamental and creative X factor in any movie—are now seen as necessary and (at least individually) disposable evils. Did you know that it took thirty writers to produce *The Flintstones*? (Not even Alexander Hitchens had a good word for *that* mother.) As a consequence, the final cut of *The Flintstones* was even more Gumpish and moronic than the first version. And the first version was less good than the old and unpretentious 1950s cartoon had been.

This is indirectly reassuring, because such steep dives in standards cannot be the result of increasing cretinization among the populace. (Any more than the rises in IQ performance cited in *The Bell Curve* can be the outcome of changes in genetic makeup.) Calcified slogans about popular culture and more meaning worse don't do much work either. Market forces are giving people what the studios want, and the studios have enslaved themselves to an intellectual version of Gresham's law.

That this is so can be illustrated by the fate of two of this year's movies: one of them a surprise winner and the other not even nominated. *Blue Sky*, Tony Richardson's last film, sat in a can on the shelf for years before anyone got around to releasing it. And when it was finally released you had to avoid blinking if you wanted to avoid missing it. I caught it in a deserted semi-art-house in Washington with not so much as a ten-year-old for company. It is an intelligent and amusing and upsetting film about a services marriage in the early years of American nuclear testing. Tommy Lee Jones is good as usual (I can't imagine him as Al Gore's roommate in college, try as I may, but so he was) and Jessica Lange gives the performance of her lifetime. When people could get to this picture, they loved it and rewarded it. So there is an unslaked demand for quality out there.

Hoop Dreams, the documentary which created a huge fuss by its exclusion from the nominating process, sounds sentimental in most of its reviews and descriptions but is actually anything but. It is an arresting depiction of the use of basketball as upward mobility. And it tells a grainier and grittier story of life in the inner city, so-called, than many of the drive-by fictionalizations. Whenever it was mentioned in passing during the ceremony, it was clapped. But that was all.

I have never found out why this outfit calls itself the Academy and I have never met anybody who understands how the process of nomination works. But at lunch in Santa Monica the day after the gala, I did learn a useful piece of Hollywood etiquette. What do you say when you are introduced to somebody who has just made, or starred in, a film that you think should never have been made, let alone screened? Answer: you shake the hand and smile and say: "You must be very proud..."

Look Over Your Shoulder
The *Oklahoma Bombing*
1995

"YOU CAN READ about neo-Nazis all the time in the *New York Times*," said a sardonic acquaintance of mine the other day, "as long as they are in Germany." And indeed, the existence of an all-American underground composed of paranoid fascist mutants was until recently considered a fit topic only for those who are themselves labeled paranoid. When Costa-Gavras made a film on the subject about ten years ago (*Betrayed*, starring Debra Winger and Tom Berenger) he was laughed to scorn by the mainstream critics, who diagnosed a bad case of Euro-Marxist condescension toward the nightmare side of the American dream. There were no big funds available to law enforcement agencies to track down the violent right, as there would have been if the targets were Libyans or Cubans or (best of all) "drug kingpins." Every now and then, the American Jewish Committee or the Anti-Defamation League or Morris Dees's heroic Klanwatch outfit would issue a report, warning of the weed-like growth of ostensibly anti-tax militias who also sold *Mein Kampf* and inveighed against ZOG, their sinister acronym for what they term the "Zionist Occupation Government." I must confess that I used to ignore some of these reports myself. One pamphlet, put out by the Aryan Nations, had run a wanted list of mug-shots, exposing the real powers behind ZOG. My own name appeared next to that of Norman Podhoretz. Momentarily chilling as it was to feel "wanted" by these people (let alone to be gazetted with Podhoretz), the overwhelming impression was of crankiness cut with impotent, pitiable hatred.

No longer. The Oklahoma detonation has exposed the militarization of a wing of the American right, and could perhaps permanently alter the locus of the national debate. It has also made 19 April into a date of cultish significance. It was on 19 April 1992 that a supremacist guerrilla named Randy Weaver saw his wife and child shot dead during a shootout with federal agents in Idaho. On 19 April 1994, the Bureau of Alcohol, Tobacco, and Firearms—a leftover from the Untouch-ables of the Prohibition era, and a state militia that cries out for scrapping—broke every rule in the book and ignited the compound of wigged-out millennialists in Waco, Texas. On 19 April 1995, a real charmer named Richard Wayne Snell was led to execution in Arkansas. He had boasted of murdering a Jewish storekeeper and a black policeman. Leaflets had gone out across the South, warning of reprisal if he was executed by the Zoggists. As Snell was being readied for the lethal in-jection, he snarled: "Look over your shoulder. Justice is com-ing." And then hours later the center of bureaucratic Okla-homa, complete with subsidized daycare center, tax records, criminal case evidence and the rest of it, vehicle registration and all, slid into the street with a tremendous roar. In Mas-sachusetts, 19 April is a state holiday known as Patriots' Day. It commemorates the militiamen of the American Revolution who "fired the shot heard round the world."

There is a feeble insurgent pulse that beats at the heart of the bucolic fascist movement, and it is the same pulse that animated Daniel Shays, the Whiskey Rebellion and some of the early populist movements. A man can't brew his own booze no more, can't hunt when he wants, can't build an outhouse on his own land without filling forms into next week, can't educate his children with the Good Book in one hand and a strap in the other. A man needs a permit to get married, to set a trap for a wild animal, to own a gun which the Constitution says he has a right to. He has to pay taxes and answer questions about his income, just so the shiftless can get their welfare checks. It's a constant whine, like the endless bleating of white Rhodesian peasants reported by Doris Lessing and called by her "the conversation." The country is going to the dawgs/to hell on a sled/to hell in a handcart. The pointy-heads and the desk-job white-collar drones are responsible. At different pitches and with different timbres, this refrain has been part of the Joe McCarthy movement, the George Wallace campaign and every Republican surge from Nixon to Gingrich. (But let's not be too partisan about it; the rhetoric evolved from the days when the Ku Klux Klan and the Southern Democratic Party were each other's official and provisional wings.) As Richard Hofstadter, in The Paranoid Style in American Politics, and Theodor Adorno, in The Authoritarian Personality, have both taught us, this kind of American populism has always been tainted by its kinship with racism and superstition, and by its servility to the very power it ostensibly rails against. It leads to Huey Long and Ross Perot, not to Walden.

This makes it very hard to guess how many people, on learning of the Oklahoma explosion, made a little holiday in their hearts. The question was, in any case, overtaken at once by the appalling images of death and mutilation, and by the competition to be first in the spin-control stakes. But if the Internal Revenue Service computer had been blown up with no loss of life, or if the same had happened to the Untouchables or the Interior Department, there would have been an audible growl of satisfaction. The Nazi David Duke, it doesn't pay to forget, got a clear majority of the white vote in the gubernatorial race in Louisiana. And several of the new conservative intake of the Senate and House have made either electoral or political pacts with members of the militia movement.

Bill Clinton's approval rating has climbed several points since his own intervention in this argument, and since I live in a city where the approval rating is God I feel almost profane in saying that I think he made a big mistake. Two big mistakes, actually. In his first set of remarks, he associated the bombing with the incendiary rhetoric of his tormentors on the talk-radio circuit; the ones who won't let up on him and his wife and who insinuate that he murdered Vince Foster. Now, it is true that people like Rush Limbaugh and Gordon Liddy and Oliver North, the soldiers of fortune of the airwaves, have made observations that flirt with incitement. Limbaugh recently predicted a second and "violent" American revolution in approving tones, and Liddy actually recommended the shooting of federal agents if they came at you with guns. You would get the idea, listening to these jerks, that the United States was already (as Evelyn Waugh said about Britain under Labour in 1945) "an occupied country." But the gun-freaks and white supremo types have been organizing, and using deadly force, for longer than the right-wing bigmouths have had corporate sponsorship of the air. In June 1984, in fact, they murdered Alan Berg, an anti-fascist talk-show jockey in Colorado, who had taunted the Nazis on his own program. It was the investigation of that slaying, which uncovered a ramified movement of well-armed Aryan bullies all across the western states, that first alerted the FBI to a problem it has failed to keep in its sights—blind as they are in the right eye. (An excellent book on the phenomenon also resulted from the Berg case: *Armed and Dangerous* by James Coates.)

So, as well as being ahistorical in suggesting guilt by association, Clinton gave the conservative demagogues an excuse to change the subject. They began to talk in injured tones about American traditions of free speech and the First Amendment. And certainly, in his few known utterances, the gaunt and ghoulish-looking Mr. McVeigh has not spoken of hearing voices from the ether. He has droned obscurely about animal rights, the purity of hunting and the wide open spaces. Indeed he does resemble, as William Burroughs once wrote of his own visage, "one of them sheep-killing dogs." He and his kind hate the cities and the city-dwellers, especially those cities that have become sinks of immigration and race-mixing and alien religions.

Clinton's second mistaken emphasis was the equally predictable one of law and order. He proposed greatly increased powers of search and seizure, even though the FBI director, Louis Freeh, testified publicly that the bureau doesn't need them, and then he and his useless attorney general, Janet Reno, both rushed to say that the culprits, whoever they might be, would and should be executed. For some reason—

perhaps for a good one—Democrats always sound unconvincing when they make jaw-jutting remarks about "toughness on crime." Furthermore, they invariably come second in the auction of toughness that follows. Here again was a change of subject from which the right could only benefit.

Newt Gingrich is leading a charmed life at the moment. Two of his newly elected "Republican Revolution" colleagues, Helen Chenoweth of Idaho and Steve Stockman of Texas, have proud and open ties to the militia movement and have parroted its propaganda about the sinister New World Order. Two Republican senators, Larry Craig of Idaho and Lauch Faircloth of North Carolina, have also shown a willingness to express the same concerns as the ultra-right. Moreover, the largest single organized faction in the Republican Party today is the so-called Christian Coalition led by Pat Robertson. The key text of this movement, Robertson's own tract on the New World Order, can be demonstrated to be a line-by-line plagiarism from classic European antisemitism. In Robertson's worldview, it is the Warburg and Rothschild families, the Freemasons and the Illuminati all over again. Yet nobody ever calls Gingrich on it; ever asks him, on the record, if these characters and these ideas are really part of the "big tent" that is said to enclose Republicanism. A couple of cosmetic shifts have been made in the past few days. Senator Alfonse D'Amato of New York, a man best known for his free and easy business dealings and his unfunny racist imitations of Judge Lance Ito, incredibly broadcast live on a radio talk show, has backed out of an evening intended to honor Gordon Liddy. But in general, that convicted Watergate criminal (who once expressed a willingness to kill people in the great cause of saving Richard

Nixon's face) is still a darling of the "movement," as is the Iran-Contra criminal Oliver North. Pensioners of the state and servants of power that they are, the pair make a weird sort of advertisement for the rugged frontier values they so hoarsely proclaim.

So the moment is slipping by in which political lessons are likely to be learned from the Oklahoma atrocity. Those who used the first days to call for the bombing of any old Ay-rab country have survived the embarrassment intact. (Rush Limbaugh said we should bomb the Middle East, starting with Gaddafi, "even if we don't know exactly who did it.") There have been no calls for surgical strikes against the training camps in Idaho and Montana. Caliban doesn't like looking in the glass. Meanwhile, the attempt to give federal bureaucrats and their families a human face, as victims and survivors instead of anonymous pen-pushers, is insipid almost to the point of masochism. If the best the Democrats can do is to ask people to be grateful for all that the state does for them, then they will repeat exactly the condescending errors that cost them the Congress in 1994 and may lose them the White House next year.

So the language of therapy and recovery is kicking in, if anything so bland and superficial can be said to have any kick at all. The words "fascist" and "racist" are never employed—perhaps from some exaggerated anxiety about political correctness—so the terms "anti-fascist" and "anti-racist" are likewise muted. Instead, we have trauma-management seminars, and the rebarbative spectacle of the Clintons at the White House, pictured with a flock of tots, and speaking earnestly about how children shouldn't be afraid to go to school. I can picture a few wolfish smiles among the perpetrators at this response; not a bad return of respect and fear for the investment of one fertilizer bomb device. Tom Metzger of the White Aryan Resistance went on radio to say that in any case, this being a war and all, there would be casualties. And if the federal bureaucracy insisted on putting creches in their buildings, what did they expect? No mincing of words there. I once spent some quality time debating Mr. Metzger on television, in the days when people to the left of center could still get on screen. He wasted a lot of his airtime explaining why Jews weren't white, and boasting of how his group had kicked to death an Ethiopian visitor to Seattle.

An especially irritating trope, invariably offered at times like this, is the stress on the loss of American innocence. I have at different times heard that this "innocence" was lost in 1898, in 1917, in 1929, in 1945, in Vietnam, in Dealey Plaza and (Robert Redford's most recent offering) at the time of the quiz show scandals in the late 1950s. How desirable is innocence as a condition anyway? And how come it is so easy to regain, only to be "lost" once more? How one yearns for just one moment that is not clotted with euphemism and sentimentality; one moment when someone in public life would call for a fight-back, and give these ostensibly libertarian movements their right name.

For some grotesque reason, it's been Yeats week in the Oval Office. To close his solemn speech at the White House Correspondents' Dinner on 29 April, Clinton quoted Auden's valediction to the poet: "In the deserts of the heart/Let the healing fountains start." The mere word "healing," presumably discovered in a computer keyword search, had evidently been enough to recommend this otherwise completely in-apposite verse. Then I got a call. "Hi. George Stephanopoulos thought you would know where that line about 'the center cannot hold' comes from..." As a result, I had the vaguely surreal experience of calling the White House and, George being absent, of reciting the first verse of "The Second Coming" over the telephone. The secretary's computer clacked oddly as I spelled and explained "gyre," and picked up a bit more speed when we got to "things fall apart." The repetition of "loosed" after "blood-dimmed tide" gave some difficulty, and then with a sinking feeling I heard my own voice saying: "The ceremony of innocence is drowned." If they pick that bit for the next speech, I realized, it'll be partly my fault. So I gave especial stress to the lines about how the best lack all conviction, while the worst... "Will he know what this is about?" she inquired, as if deploying all-American politeness on a slightly questionable but nonetheless registered voter. "Yes, he will. It's a poem he asked for." "A *poem*? Did you write it?"

And what rough beast, its hour come round at last...

Letters

22 June 1995

Christopher Hitchens's bit of yellow dog journalism in which he attempts to link the Republican Party with American neo-Nazis is nothing but reverse McCarthyism. David Duke is a total outcast in the Republican Party in Louisiana. Some state law makes it easy for anyone to run on a particular party's line; sinister types have managed to do it as Democrats. As a delegate for George McGovern in the 1972 Democratic Convention, I can recall the vehement racism of the "Democrats" who supported George Wallace, a candidate who won more popular votes in the primaries in 1972 than any other Democratic candidate, including McGovern.

Hitchens's suggestion that Ross Perot is somehow a figure of the neo-fascist right is absurd. He supported the liberal Democrat Ann Richards against George Bush (the former president's son) in the election for governor of Texas. His lawyer, who is Jewish, is the husband of Ruth Bader Ginsburg, associate justice of the Supreme Court of the United States. Perot endowed a chair for Ginsburg's husband at a prominent Washington, DC, law school. As for Huey Long, readers of the LRB should consult any number of excellent biographies for a more balanced view. Huey Long was the only American politician who was serious about the redistribution of wealth, which earned him the fear and loathing of the white American establishment and considerable support among blacks in Louisiana.

With regard to the role of the FBI, Hitchens neglected to point out that in the raid at Ruby Ridge, Idaho, that led to the stand-off with Randy Weaver, the FBI sniper shot and killed Weaver's wife, Vicki, while she was holding her child and did so as a result of a change in FBI policy implemented by Larry A. Potts, currently second in command of the organization. The official explanation by the director of the FBI, Louis Freeh, is that Potts had failed to read the change in the rules, which had been proposed by agents in the field. But the *New York Times* has reported that it was Potts himself who authorized the change:

> Under the bureau's lethal force rules, agents may use their weapons only if they reasonably perceive an imminent danger of serious bodily harm. But the rules were rewritten during the Ruby Ridge siege to authorize the shooting of any men seen near Mr. Weaver's cabin with weapons in their hands. One agent interviewed by the bureau after the stand-off said the change had been interpreted to mean: "If you see 'em, shoot 'em."

The FBI commander on the scene, Eugene Glenn, who is now special agent in charge of the bureau's Salt Lake City office, has said that Mr. Freeh's review was a cover-up intended to protect Mr. Potts and find lower-level scapegoats, and as the *Times* further reported, "indeed there is evidence that Mr. Potts personally approved the change." Congressman Stockman has called for an investigation into the cover-up—which, in Hitchens's book, seems to make him a neo-Nazi. Potts was given a mild reprimand and then promoted by Freeh, who assigned him to head up the Waco raid. It was Potts who urged the attorney general, Janet Reno, to invade the compound and use lethal force. He was subsequently put in charge of the Oklahoma City investigation and then made Freeh's deputy.

As for Pat Robertson's *New International Order*, there is no mention in that pamphlet of any Jewish financiers. In criticizing NAFTA and GATT, the pamphlet says that the only beneficiaries of those free trade agreements would be the international financial community. Hitchens is referring to Hitler's attack on Jewish bankers and I call on him to give us the "line by line" plagiarism from Hitler that he alleges. By listing the Warburgs and the Rothschilds, names found nowhere in Robertson's pamphlet, Hitchens would lead a reader to believe that Robertson has named these families, which is extremely misleading. When Harold Wilson referred to the gnomes of Zurich, no one in the Labour Party called him a Nazi. Robertson was referring to Citibank and others of this ilk, the business interests that care nothing for employment figures in the United States. Citibank itself has just fired all the union member employees who used to clean the bank's buildings and replaced them with contractors who employ non-union workers at barely minimum wage standards with no benefits. If an international banking institution makes loans to American industrialists so they can relocate to Mexico to benefit from the near slave labor one can obtain there, should this be beyond criticism? The products produced in Mexico on these terms are then imported to the United States with no tariff and cause increased American unemployment. This is the stuff that feeds the fires of extremism, as Hitchens should be aware. The fact is that NAFTA is a disaster, as Ross Perot pointed out in his debate with Al Gore, in which Gore misstated the actual economic facts of Mexico's economic condition. I don't believe Gore is a liar: he's just ignorant. But the fact is that Perot was right. As for GATT, the United States was in no economic shape to enter into such an agreement, which the Japanese are now going to invoke against the Clinton 100 percent tariff on luxury cars from Japan.

A more serious analysis of the Republican Party and the American economic crisis is in order than the one Hitchens offers. As for the FBI itself, one wonders about its sincerity when it shies away from a serious investigation of right-wing extremists but manages to have the resources to spy on Act-Up, the gay activist anti-AIDS group. We should certainly focus on the neo-Nazi threat in America, but we should be vigilant about a government that can promote the likes of Larry Potts.

Richard Cummings
Bridgehampton, New York

---

3 August 1995
In his rather loopy defense of the new American populist and conservative fauna Richard Cummings defends Pat Robertson from the charge of antisemitism and announces that, contrary to my claim, the names Warburg and Rothschild are "names found nowhere in Robertson's pamphlet." Let me refer him to the index of *The New World Order* (1991), which is now being passed from hand to hand by the Reverend Robertson's audience. The entry for "Warburg, Paul" reads "61, 65, 123, 124, 125, 178" followed at once by "Warburgs, 126." The Rothschild entry is not so voluminous but is in many ways more intriguing: "Rothschild, 123; Rothschild family,

123, 128; Rothschild, Lord, 111" may seem colorless even if it leaves Mr. Cummings looking—and dare I trust, feeling—a bit of a fool. More pregnant is the entry for "Rothschild publication, 7." Anyone who turns up this page, or who is otherwise familiar with the work of the Rev., will find that "Rothschild publication" is his term of choice for the London *Economist*. I rest my case.

In an exhaustive essay in the *New York Review of Books*, Michael Lind has shown the direct literary and political descent of Pat Robertson from classic anti-Jewish paranoids such as Nesta Webster. Given the venomous provenance of this worldview, I suppose it's reassuring in a way that some of Robertson's readers and followers are too dull to notice what he's driving at.

Christopher Hitchens
Washington, DC

After-Time
On Gore Vidal
1995

I RECENTLY paid a solemn and respectful visit to Gore Vidal's grave. It is to be found in Rock Creek Cemetery in Washington. You take a few paces down the slope from the graveyard's centerpiece, which is the lachrymose and androgynous figure sculpted by Augustus Saint-Gaudens for Henry Adams's unhappy wife, Clover (whose name always puts me in mind of an overworked pit pony). And there in the grass is a stone slab, bearing the names and dates of birth of Vidal and his lifelong companion Howard Austen. The hyphens that come after the years (1925 and 1928 respectively) lie like little marble asps, waiting to keep their dates. Who knows what decided the cemetery authorities to advertise their prospective clients in this way? Elsewhere among the crosses and headstones one may find Upton Sinclair, Nobel laureate and defeated socialist candidate for the governorship of California, Alice Warfield Allen (mother of Wallis Simpson) and Alice Roosevelt Longworth, grande dame of Washington dynastic bitchery. (She had a motto emblazoned on her sofa cushion in Georgetown: "If you can't think of anything nice to say about anybody, come and sit by me.") A clutch of Supreme Court justices, political bosses and Civil

War generals completes the roll. And all this seems fitting for Vidal: radical candidate in a California Senate race, collector and generator of gossip from the exiled Windsors and the Georgetown ladies, and master in novel form of the Washington of Henry Adams, John Hay and Teddy Roosevelt.

Or is it so fitting? On second thoughts, is not Vidal a natural for the Protestant Cemetery in Rome, hard by Keats and Shelley and Gramsci and Labriola, and sheltered, in serene pagan and Mediterranean style, by the pyramid of Sestius? What is an exile cosmopolitan doing in this WASP rockery in the District of Columbia? Even before *Palimpsest*, it was possible for close readers of Vidal's fiction to make a shrewd guess.* The following passage in the confessedly autobiographical *Two Sisters*, published a quarter of a century ago, supplies one clue. The narrator is set off by a recollection of Henry James, who after fifty years remembered "a boy cousin being sketched in the nude at Newport before his life was 'cut short, in a cavalry clash, by one of the Confederate bullets of 1863.' "

> Death, summer, youth—this triad contrives to haunt me every day of my life for it was in summer that my generation left school for war, and several dozen that one knew (but strictly speaking, did not love, except perhaps for one) were killed, and so never lived to know what I have known—the Beatles, black power, the administration of Richard Nixon—all this has taken place in a trivial after-time and has nothing to do with anything that really mattered, with summer and someone hardly remembered, a youth so abruptly translated from vivid, well-loved (if briefly) flesh to a few scraps of bone and cartilage scattered among the

* *Palimpsest: A Memoir* by Gore Vidal (Deutsch, 1995).

volcanic rocks of Iwo Jima. So much was cruelly lost and one still mourns the past, particularly in darkened movie houses, weeping at bad films, or getting drunk alone while watching the *Late Show* on television as our summer's war is again refought and one sees sometimes what seems to be a familiar face in the battle scenes—is it Jimmie?

A couple of years ago, Vidal dropped another hint in an article looking back on the Pacific War. He said that he gave way to emotion on hearing, even now, the song that goes:

Missed the Saturday dance
Heard they crowded the floor
Couldn't face it without you
Don't get around much any more.

And then, going back almost to the beginning, there was the matter of those initials on the dedication page of *The City and the Pillar*. This homoerotic drama, Vidal's third novel, won him attention and execration in about equal measure. The dedicatee was one "J. T." Just a few feet away from that marble slab in Rock Creek, one can discover a small gray stone with the inscription "James Trimble III. 1925–1945. Iwo Jima." And here the quest is over. Vidal intends to be buried as near as he can be to his first and only love, who played the saxophone and shone on the playing fields and whose anthem for doomed youth is in the refrain of "Don't Get Around Much Any More": a combination of Whitman's *Leaves of Grass* and the more candid letters of Wilfred Owen. *Palimpsest* fills in the blanks. For half a century, Gore Vidal has been living selfishly and hedonistically, because all this time he has been living for two.

It is via the Jimmie Trimble romance that the madeleine of these memoirs is unwrapped, and it is with that incomplete or uncompleted love that it closes. Along the way, it is the thread of Ariadne in the narrative. Vidal has written often and well about himself and others. In fact, he has written better. The chief enchantment of this book has not to do with the celebrated dust-ups between himself and Mailer, himself and Capote, himself and Tennessee Williams, or himself and William Buckley. Rather, we learn, not without preceding markers, but in many ways for the first time, about Vidal's family and about the Kennedy branch of it. We come to understand how divided a self he is; not just as between love and death but as between literature and politics, America and the world, the ancient and the modern, the sacred and the profane. And we get the goods not just about his sex life, but about his sexual nature.

To get the beastliness out of the way first, then. In his rather sere and melancholy condition, Vidal tells some old stories rather less well than he recounted them the first time. Of a disastrous visit to Cambridge, provoked by an invitation from E. M. Forster that had been meant for Tennessee Williams:

> Forster's look of disappointment was disheartening. But, dutifully, he took me on a tour. We crossed the river to the chapel, which I coldly termed "pretty," thus disheartening him.

Now from an essay ("On Prettiness," written for the *New Statesman* in 1978):

> As we approached the celebrated chapel (magnificent, superb, a bit much) I said, "Pretty." Forster thought that I meant the chapel when, actually, I was referring to a youthful couple in the

middle distance. A ruthless moralist, Forster publicized my use of the dread word. Told in Fitzrovia and published in the streets of Dacca, the daughters of the Philistines rejoiced; the daughters of the uncircumcised triumphed.

Of these two versions, the second and earlier is the more spirited and (frightful dangler in the last sentence notwithstanding) the better written. But in *Palimpsest*, much of which is set down in a terse, almost shorthand style, we learn that Forster had been cruel as a cat to Christopher Isherwood the night before, that he had sucked up to Williams in a queenly manner and that, in the opinion of the Bird (Vidal's usual term for Tennessee's person of plumage and flutter), he was an old gentleman "with urine-stained flies." Thus the newer version is more instructive and nearer to the nitty, if not indeed the actual gritty. In a letter to Jack Kerouac in April 1952, William Burroughs demanded to know: "Is Gore Vidal queer or not?" Burroughs, who had once been at the same boys' boarding school as Vidal, can now slake his curiosity. Or he could have pressed Kerouac himself, as Vidal certainly did almost a year later:

> At what might be nicely called loose ends, we rubbed bellies for a while; later he would publish a poem dedicated to me; "Didn't know I was a great come-onner, did you? (come-on-er)." I was not particularly touched by this belated Valentine, considering that I finally flipped him over on his stomach. Jack raised his head from the pillow to look at me over his left shoulder.

Come, now, this is more like it. And it also supplies part of the answer to Burroughs's question. Vidal is not a pillow-biter or a mattress-muncher. Nor does he suck. I once heard him declaim: "I don't want penises near me. I have *no* plans for them." It should by now be unnecessary to draw the reader a picture. Is he queer? Or is he on to something in saying that there are no homosexual people, only homosexual acts? The memoir also details many encounters with women, usually of the theater, like Diana Lynn, but also of the bar and the café and, in the case of Anaïs Nin, of the world of heterosexual narcissism. None of these matches is rekindled in order to prove any defensive point. Since Jimmie's death, sex and love have been blissfully decoupled. What might have arrested the development of some has emancipated it in our author. Though, as he commissions researchers to inspect the minutest reminiscence of Jimmie's short life and hard death, and as he discovers breakdowns and traumas among the boys and girls and even schoolmasters who knew the golden lad in real time, one wonders. In a last letter home from the Pacific, Jimmie asked his mother to send him some Walt Whitman poems. And Vidal wants very much, still, to know who it was that recommended this front-line reading to the hoplite. Is that a proof of an unsentimental carapace?

At various other points in the story, also, he makes himself out to be slightly more emotion-proof than I would guess he really is. The depiction of family life is amusing, often sideholdingly so, but must have been extremely grueling at the time. To *fear* one's mother, a drink-sodden bag of malice and conspiracy, may have accelerated the growing-up process and been useful in the dispelling of illusion, but still . . . Here is an account of mama's supposed *mariage blanc* to the rich footler Hugh ("Hughdie") Auchincloss:

> I should note that the only advantage for a child in having an alcoholic parent is that you acquire, prematurely, quite a bit

of valuable data. Apparently, there was going to be Sex whether
Nina liked it or not. She did not like it. But then no woman
could have liked Hughdie's importunate fumblings. He ejaculat-
ed normally but without that precedent erection which women
require as, if nothing else, totemic symbol of a man's true love,
not to mention a homely source of hedonistic friction. Since
Hughdie wanted children, Nina was obliged, in some fashion
that she, on several occasions in her admittedly never-long-empty
cups, vividly described to me and I would promptly erase from
memory. I think she inserted—with a spoon?—what she called
"the bugs" in order to create my demi-siblings.

Here is Hamlet contemplating "the nasty sty" but without
an ounce of feeling for either mother or stepfather. (His un-
affected liking for his father, an innovator in the age of aero-
space and an ornament of FDR's government, is one of the
charms of the book.) But who would not have preferred to flee
the home of fetid sex, booze and old money and embrace the
clean limbs of Jimmie? The memoir is partly diaristic and at
intervals loops back to the writing desk at Ravello and to the
present day. As often as not, this is to update us on a recent
lunch with Jimmie's mother, with a letter from a long-lost
trench mate on Iwo Jima, or with further bulletins from research into Jimmie's girlfriends and boyfriends. The love supplies a refuge from the everyday now, as indeed it must have
done then.

From his grandfather, the sightless Senator Thomas Gore
of Oklahoma (common ancestor with the current vice president, whom Vidal refuses to meet because of his connection to
Martin Peretz's plaything, the *New Republic*), the boy became
steeped in American political lore and in the unending battle

between "We the People" and the robber barons and malefactors of great wealth. Engaged as a reader to the blind old man, he also became an omnivorous consumer of books and lover of libraries. Here again, there is a sentimental ambivalence which is registered rather than resolved. Vidal knows that much American populist talk, with its loud affectation about the common man, is bullshit. He even backchatted the old senator about it: " 'When I was young, cheese and crackers was one word to me,' he used to say, emphasizing his poverty. Bored with this repetition, I am said to have responded, at the age of six or so: 'Well, ice cream and cake are one word to me.' " Not only is this a precociously Wildean remark and just the sort of thing that one writes a memoir in order to record, but it was a perfectly apt rejoinder to a wearisome pose. Yet not much later, Vidal writes approvingly that "for Gore and the other populists, the imperialism of the two Roosevelts and Woodrow Wilson—Polk, too, earlier—was a terrible distraction from our destiny, which was the perfection of our own unusual if not, in the end, particularly 'exceptional' society." The let-down at the end of that sentence is one that I wish he would pursue. He expounds at length his view of war and foreign entanglement as a racket run by the Morgans and Rockefellers, and recounts with some relish his student campaigns for "America First" in the run-up to the Second World War. Yet when he writes about his years in Guatemala in the 1950s (setting for *Dark Green, Bright Red*), he admits to great shock at the discovery of what American intervention in the southern hemisphere had really been like. Now, William Jennings Bryan and Colonel Lindbergh had not been opposed to the Monroe Doctrine or to the American empire: they had been opposed to American engagement in Europe. Moreover, the sort of "America First" isolationists who managed to be for war in China and Nicaragua but not in defense of the Spanish Republic or Czechoslovakia were exactly the kind of people who would have had *The City and the Pillar* burned by the public hangman. Vidal, most cosmopolitan and internationalist of American novelists, is in bizarre company when he views Europe as the polluter of American native innocence.

It is more honest to say, as he does, that the whole Second World War was not worth Jimmie's life. This is oddly reminiscent of his friend Isherwood's view that one could not risk harming a lover (admittedly a lover who would have been serving in the Wehrmacht) for any grand strategic consideration. But *Williwaw* is actually a rather fine novel of the American wartime and, though one agrees with Vidal's retrospective opinion that it is written in somewhat carpentered prose, it remains a source of pride to him to this day, and was at the time a healthy source of rivalry between himself, Norman Mailer and James Jones. There is no reason for him not to try and have this both ways, like so much else. But that would mean noticing that he was trying to do so.

In a way that is not perhaps quite dissimilar, Vidal returns again and again to his contempt for the life of the American professional politician. He saw it up close when young. He saw it up close in the Kennedy era. He has the lugubrious example of young cousin Al always before him. Yet he knows he could have been a player, and he still likes to tell of the advice that he gave to Jerry Brown as late as the 1992 Democratic primaries. It could of course be a luxury to be in this position. How wonderful to have been able to compose this paragraph, for example, about that hideous Palace of Culture that still squats—appropriately next to the Watergate building—on the banks of the Potomac: "The Kennedy Center, a real-estate metaphor for the arts in America."

> As a member of the Advisory Council on the Arts (my advice had been, Don't build the center), I was at the groundbreaking. The Kennedys were all on display. Hughdie and Janet, too. President Johnson wore a white camelhair coat and a suit of rich green never before seen on a first magistrate, or perhaps anywhere else on earth. He shoveled the dirt with casual contempt, more Kennedy gravedigger than keeper of the flame.

Vidal ran, not on the Kennedy ticket but with the somewhat sluggish Kennedy tide, for Congress in a reactionary district of upstate New York in 1960. With some rather feline help from Eleanor Roosevelt—who never trusted JFK—he came marvelously close to winning. Pressed to try again, or even to try for the Senate, he declined. In 1964, the year of the donkey *par excellence*, his mediocre Democrat successor was lifted into the seat by the LBJ surge. Can Vidal really say with complete composure that he is delighted not to have been that man? Clues in the text, and in other texts, suggest not. He could have been the perfect inside/outside Washington congressman, who was needed by his own party managers more than he needed them. (Not for nothing was he a friend of Tom Driberg, whose own non-political needs also made him the perfect division-of-labor cruising companion.) Vidal has spoken elsewhere of never missing a sexual trick, and of not having to decline in years while brooding over the lost chance of this one and that one. I suspect that he still wishes he had given the rough trade of Congress a fair shake.

But in general, what a blessed life. Right places at right times. Sound bets made on the writing possibilities offered by Broadway and Hollywood, in both of which he shone while shining was still possible in those dark mills. Then, having succumbed to boredom but having proved that he could make his own way, off to Rome to write *Julian*. And a good companion, Howard Austen, of whom he says (twice) that the secret of their domestic felicity is—and has ever been—a strict "No Sex" rule. (On the gravestone in Rock Creek Cemetery, Howard is incised as "Howard Auster," the New York Jewish name that stopped him getting a job in advertising until Vidal proposed a one-letter amendment. How nice that such a deft piece of editing should have made such a difference, and how nice also that it is restored to the original when the lapidary question comes up. "They say I'm antisemitic," Vidal once intoned with sweet mockery in Howard's presence. "Every morning I breakfast with someone who looks more every day like —like *Golda Meir!*")

There are some excellent phrases, though Vidal prefers to think of himself as "making sentences." He says that he tortured his mother "with heartless kindness." Seeing Henry Kissinger in the Sistine Chapel at an American Academy soirée, and noticing his gaping at the Hell section of *The Last Judgment*, he observes: "Look, he's apartment-hunting." Campaigning in 1960, he comes up against the titanic subsidies paid to the farm interest and quips about "socialism for the rich and free enterprise for the poor," which I think pre-empts Milton Friedman as author of that essential line about the way we live now. There is also a pregnant observation borrowed by Vidal from his postwar visits to the monkish cell of George

Santayana. He judges the author of *Egotism in German Philos-ophy* to have been an opponent of fanaticism rather than an antisemite, and cites his critique of Fichte's and Hegel's propaganda (about German destiny) as "the heir of Judaism." In the continuing quarrel between Vidal and the Podhoretz school of New York neoconservative Zionism, I have heard Vidal defended as someone who doesn't dislike organized Jewry *an sich* but who a) blames the Zionists for keeping the militarist and interventionist home fires burning and b) blames Judaism for leading to monotheism and the militant Pauline theology of heterosexual and repressive family values. So here is a new take, which by no means invalidates the earlier ones (especially when you reflect on what family did to, and for, Vidal). Podhoretz, I always thought, made his fatal mistake when he accused Vidal not of being antisemitic but of being anti-American. The blood of the clan was thereby aroused. Vidal, chronicler of the Civil War and the birth of America, was just not going to take this from someone who once said that the battlefields of Gettysburg and Bull Run were as remote to him "as the Wars of the Roses." If you don't want tribalism, in other words, don't incite it. Rather in the way that he doesn't care about his bad reviews, while remember-ing every last one of them, Vidal maintains indifference to the charge of antisemitism and includes a learned piece of genealogy which strongly suggests that he is, by virtue of his ancient surname, not unconnected with *converso* or *marrano* lineage. Could be. The fact is that Vidal is and was one of the few "gentiles"—ghastly term—to have written for *Partisan Review*, *Commentary* and the *Nation* in their heroic periods (when he also made his most surprising friend—Saul Bellow), and would be better off protesting not at all about such a cheap and politicized slander.

The finest and most revealing passages in *Palimpsest*, those which best synthesize the public and the personal, are the ones which treat of the Kennedy court. It's a test of character whether one repudiates Camelot or not, and Vidal passes this test with all pennons flying. (He even admits, with a moue of distaste, to having helped deceive Richard Rovere as early as 1960 about Kennedy suffering, as he obviously did, from the disabling ravages of Addison's disease.) For this and other services to power and family and deceit, the triptych under review, he is properly contrite. His description of a vacation spent in the Kennedy compound at Hyannis, at the time of the bogus crisis over Berlin, is a real document of tawdriness and vulgarity and opportunism. Jack and Bobby argue about which of them first hilariously called James Baldwin "Martin Luther Queen." Portentous and shallow power-worship pervades the scene, and it becomes appallingly clear that JFK himself can only be interested or excited by risky and violent and gamey solutions to the boredom and impotence which he is already feeling. Young Bobby appears in the character of an envious thug, anxious to please and eager to show that he is no faggot (an impression which Rudolf Nureyev elsewhere slyly revises). Written from notes made at the time, this is a seriously revealing chapter. As for the hugely overrated Jackie (stepsister of Vidal's half-sister), she appears as a spoiled and mercenary minx:

> I have often wondered what would have become of Jackie had Nina stayed with Hughdie. Jackie would certainly have married money. That is to be taken for granted. But she would never have

got Jack. One shudders to think that there would never have been a Jacqueline Kennedy Onassis if Hughdie could have had a satisfactory erection.

The business of "making sentences," as Vidal likes to put it, is intimately connected to the *pronouncing* of sentences. Both faculties get their outing here. Vidal's sentence on himself is that he will only be whole when he is in some way reunited with Jimmie. His sentence on the culture is that it has mistaken showbiz for diversion, and has abandoned literature and the novel for the vacuously meretricious. He fears that he himself has been forgotten, dismissed even from TV and exiled from an academy that rewards only the arid practice of "theory." (He should make more of not having gone to university, an unusual distinction in the now totally "credentialed" America. For one thing, he has always followed the practice of I. A. Richards in reading literature without any canonical crib.) A faint self-pity disfigures the closing staves of the book, which are much preoccupied with the possibility of a last career in "the films": "I arrive back in Ravello. Three offers to act, but the agent is firm: 'The parts are too small.'" Experience might have taught him that there are no small parts, only small players. This palimpsest, however much scored out and scribbled over, and however much a keening for the golden gone to dust, is nonetheless a record of the transmutation, of the base into the gold, that is the raw stuff of literature—and our slight and sardonic hope.

A Hard Dog to Keep on the Porch
On Bill Clinton
1996

O XFORD 1968–69. In the evenings, after dinner in hall, groups would take shape informally in the quad. There was Richard Cobb's lot, making for the buttery and another round of worldly banter. There was this or that sodality, taking a cigarette break or killing time before revision. There was my own cohort, usually divided between the opposing tasks of selling the factional newspaper, or distributing the latest leaflet, or procuring another drink. And there were the Americans. I remember James Fenton noticing how they would cluster a little closer together and talk in a fashion slightly more intense. Mainly Rhodes or Fulbright scholars, they had come from every state of the union with what amounted to a free pass. The Yanks of Oxford were accustomed to going home and taking up a lot of available space in the American academy, in the American media and in American politics or diplomacy. Yet for this contingent, the whole experience had become deeply and abruptly fraught. They were far from home and they were deeply patriotic. You could tell that they had been told by their selection committees, before embarking on the Atlantic crossing, that they should comport themselves as ambassadors and emissaries. But those local lawyers and Rotarians and Chambers of Commerce had not prepared them to hurry up, finish their studies and take ship to Vietnam.

It's often been said since that these young men would not have been bothered by the war if it were not for their own impending draft notices, and that they were quite prepared to let the underclass be conscripted in their stead. This is quite simply a slander. The arguments and conversations of those years disclosed a group of very serious and principled people. They did not like to criticize their own country while overseas, but they could not bear to see it befouled by warmongers and racists. All of them could see the self-evident connection between the rise of the war party in Washington and the defeat of civil rights and the Great Society. Many of them came from families where military service was a proud axiom. All of them felt guilty and indebted for their luck. At 46 Leckford Road, in a scruffy house where many of them hung out, there were debates of a high quality. (There were also biscuits and brownies made out of marijuana, which meant that you didn't have to inhale if you didn't desire.) Frank Aller, the brilliant scholar of China who was one of the chief ornaments of that address, later took his despair and disillusion to the length of self-slaughter. Most were more sanguine. I don't especially remember Bill Clinton, perhaps because he was one of the more moderate and conciliatory types. But I remember several of his girlfriends and I remember being impressed at a house that boasted its own duplicator for the production of Vietnam Moratorium leaflets. And now I live in Washington and I see the old Rhodes class of those years going about its business: Robert Reich running the Labor Department and Strobe Talbott managing U.S.-Russian relations from Foggy Bottom and Ira Magaziner trying to recover from his moment as person-in-charge of Bill and Hillary's healthcare reform.

When I want to recall those Leckford Road days, I can turn up a letter that William Jefferson Clinton wrote, on 3 December 1969, to a certain Colonel Holmes of the University of Arkansas Reserve Officers Training Corps. Clinton wanted to clarify his attitude to the military draft:

> Let me try to explain. As you know, I worked for two years in a very minor position on the Senate Foreign Relations Committee. I did it for the experience and the salary but also for the opportunity, however small, of working every day against a war I opposed and despised with a depth of feeling I had reserved solely for racism in America before Vietnam... Because of my opposition to the draft and the war, I am in great sympathy with those who are not willing to fight, kill and maybe die for their country (i.e. the particular policy of a particular government) right or wrong.

(My friend Todd Gitlin, author of the best book on this period, points out the ranking of "fight, kill and maybe die" as the correct order in which antiwar people listed their objections.) But toward the close of this telling letter, Clinton explains to Holmes why it is that, after all, he does not propose to become a full-blown refusenik:

> The decision not to be a resister and related subsequent decisions were the most difficult of my life. I decided to accept the draft in spite of my beliefs for one reason: *to maintain my political viability within the system.* For years I have worked to prepare myself for a political life characterized by both practical political ability and concern for rapid social progress. [Italics mine.]

Since Clinton went on both to dodge the actual draft *and* to be something of an antiwar activist, this missive from an old head on young shoulders has been adduced as the early indication of a desire, if not a need, to have everything both ways. In the 1992 presidential elections the letter surfaced, not as the confirmation of an early stand on principle, but as proof of an ingrained tendency toward excuse-making and evasion. And it set people remembering. When *had* they first noticed Clinton's talent for being all things to all men? Even as Cecil Rhodes's legatees were taking the liner across to Southampton in October 1968, and viewing their own destiny with a high seriousness and purity, they found themselves sharing a ship with Bobby Baker. Mr. Baker, who was Lyndon Johnson's bagman and fixer within the Democratic Party and throughout the capital city, had been convicted in a sensational trial of tax fraud and conspiracy. His attorney, the no less legendary Edward Bennett Williams (known as "the man to see"), was in effect sending him off on a cruise while he played out the appeals procedure. Confronted with this gargoyle of the old gang, many of the Rhodes boys kept a fastidious distance. "But Clinton was there," in one account, "standing at Baker's side, soaking in tales of power and intrigue...It was while watching his performance with Bobby Baker that Strobe Talbott said he first understood Clinton's 'raw political talent.'"

New Hampshire, January 1992. Before a single vote has been cast, the prestige press has announced that the Democrats have their frontrunner. This is Bill Clinton, New Democrat and governor of Arkansas. In the two invisible primaries, which are the press primary and the fundraising or "money" primary, he has passed every test with aplomb. Tough on welfare and crime, "flexible" on defense and foreign policy, solid for Israel, reputedly "good" with black people, he is moreover young and once shook hands with John F. Kennedy. At the bar of the Sheraton Wayfarer in Manchester, the HQ of the traveling press corps, most correspondents report that their editors only want good news about the new consensus candidate. And, generally, that's what they have been getting and transmitting. A flap has, however, broken out. A classic blonde troublemaker named Gennifer Flowers has gone public. Damage control is in progress, but things look a touch wobbly.

Outside a stricken factory somewhere downstate, Clinton is confronted by a host of questions about his Little Rock love nest. He looks like a dog being washed. Since I don't care about Flowers, I attempt to change the subject—never an easy thing to do at a pack-job press conference. I want to know about the execution of Ricky Ray Rector. Rector was a black cop-killer in Arkansas, lobotomized by a gunshot wound. He no longer knew his own name, and met most of the standard conditions for clemency. But Clinton left New Hampshire specifically to return to Arkansas and have him put to death. He did so in order to demonstrate, or "signal," that he was not soft on crime. Rector's condition was such that, as he left his cell for the last time, he saved the dessert from his last meal "for later." Strapped to a trolley for a lethal injection, he actually assisted the executioners in their hour-long search for a viable vein in which to place the lethal catheter. (He thought they were doctors trying to cure him.)

This, coupled with Clinton's ostentatious membership of an all-white golf club, strikes me as a more pressing issue of morals and character than l'affaire Flowers. But Clinton, who at first looks as if he welcomes a change of subject, doesn't care for this one. He turns his back and marches away. Later on television, his flack says that everything else is a diversion from the governor's real program, which is "a tax cut for the middle class." Rector is never mentioned again in the entire course of the campaign. There is a brief subsequent flap, when a few questions are asked about land deals in Arkansas, and a bankrupt savings-and-loan concern, and the role played in both by a law firm associated with Hillary Clinton. There's also something about a shady airport in Arkansas, said to have been used for murky transactions with Central America. But since these questions come from the Nation magazine, and from Ralph Nader and Jerry Brown, they can be, and are, easily shrugged off as "marginal." Understandably, the Republicans display little relish for dragging up the savings-and-loan scandal, or for raising the question of campaign donations, or for investigating property speculation. And as for reopening the Iran-Contra scandal...forget it. A sort of Mutual Assured Destruction guarantees that neither party will breach protocol on these questions. Instead, the Bush campaign concentrates on the old "draft-dodging" issue, and enlists the help of John Major's mediocre Central Office in rummaging through old passport files. They fail to gauge the extent to which the New Democrat has left all that behind him. Now, what would have happened if Bush or Reagan had executed a retarded black man in order to win a primary? Consensus politics has an interior logic of its very own.

Washington, DC, January 1993. On the Mall, there is what they call the People's Inaugural. Before a huge, informal and mainly young crowd, Aretha Franklin sings "Respect" and Bob Dylan makes a surprise appearance to perform "Chimes of Freedom." Clinton and his young family appear to sing along with both. There is much heady talk about the end of the 1980s, that decade of greed and self-delusion and secret government. But if the atmosphere on the Mall is populist, the tone of the real inaugural is anything but. Pamela Harriman gives a welcome to Washington party in Georgetown, which features wall-to-wall lobbyists and powerbrokers of the most traditional stripe. Campaign contributors are received and rewarded in proportion to the timeliness, and the size, of their subscriptions. The first harvest of cabinet appointments shows Georgetown beating the Mall every time. Lloyd Bentsen, the prince of Capitol influence-peddlers, gets the Treasury. Alan Greenspan, the reactionary fan of Ayn Rand, who has roosted at the Federal Reserve these many years, is beseeched to "stay on." Winston Lord, an old Kissinger hand, gets the Asia desk at State. Les Aspin, a plaything of the military contractors, is awarded to the Pentagon. And so it goes. Within a very few months, according to Bob Woodward's book, The Agenda, Clinton is exploding with rage at the way that Washington is running him, rather than the other way about. He has been told that the bond market will not permit some marginal adjustment on which he had staked credibility. This means, he advises his team, that they are all "Eisenhower Republicans" now. Have a care, Mr. President. Eisenhower was quite an activist chief executive. He built the interstate highway system and warned about the growth of the military-industrial complex. It may be rash to invite such bold comparisons.

The jokes about Clinton are always the same joke. "When he comes to a fork in the road," writes Paul Greenberg of the *Arkansas Democrat-Gazette*, "he takes it." He wants to have his dozen Big Macs and eat them too. And so forth. (I myself have contributed a one-liner: "Why did Bill Clinton cross the road? Because he wanted to get to the middle.") In earnest sessions with interviewers, the most overtly therapeutic of which was given to *Good Housekeeping*, Clinton himself has mused aloud about his dysfunctional childhood and his hunger and thirst for approval. Is there a connection between the essence of Clinton and the essence of Clintonism? Does either of them possess an essence?

The answer is yes, if you make the simple assumption that Clinton's consistent aim has been a national shift to the center-right. This of course is the very assumption that the consensus press and the Republican opposition are incapable of making. It is also an assumption that the liberal mainstream—and its Clintonoid centerpiece—is reluctant to see spelled out too starkly. But if it is sound, it explains Clinton's past and present, and also clarifies his strategy for gaining a second term. As I write, the president has the GOP more or less punching air. Instead of worrying about being an Eisenhower or Rockefeller Republican, he has embraced the idea. He has even hired a Republican political strategist, Dick Morris, to guide his campaign. And Mr. Morris has been sharing poll data with Robert Dole, who was until recently Clinton's complicit partner in the management of the Hill. Only the other week, speaking in Delaware, Dole repeated his call: "One reason to elect me in November 1996 is to keep the promises President Clinton made to you in 1992." The gap between New Democrat and moderate Republican could not be narrower, and probably never has been. So all those jokes, about Bill being adamant for drift, are to some extent at the expense of those who make them. When it came to a choice —between 1960s idealism and Bobby Baker; between Ricky Ray Rector and the opinion polls; between the crowd on the Mall and the crowd in Georgetown—Clinton was never anything but swift and decisive.

The origins of his protean and malleable politics can be traced partly to his upbringing, and partly to the morphology of his home state. Arkansas is a bizarre polity which on a single night in 1968 cast its vote like this: Winthrop Rockefeller for governor, William Fulbright for senator and George Wallace for president. It has correctly been described as one of the richest little poor states in the union. Today's Little Rock has a skyline of modern corporatism, housing numerous local monopolies such as Tyson Foods, the Worthen Bank, the Stephens Corporation and Walmart. In the Quapaw district of town, the Flaming Arrow club is the meeting point for lobbyists and legislators. (Gennifer Flowers used to be a lounge singer at this joint, but more to the point is its role as the site of Governor Clinton's off-the-record "budget breakfast" meetings.) Go south into the Delta, however, and you are in what H. L. Mencken once termed "the hookworm and incest belt." Here, sharecropper poverty and indebtedness are endemic, and the racial pattern is almost cartoonish. Prison farms are policed by armed men on horseback. Arkansas is a "right-to-work" state, which means union-busting and low wages. It is also the only state of the union without a civil rights statute. Elected by the lower-income voters, Clinton soon became the favorite son of the high-rolling stakeholders. The contradiction is best expressed by the white lie he often tells about coming from "a little place called Hope." No politician could reasonably be expected to pass up such a line, but though Clinton was technically born in the dull hamlet of Hope, Arkansas, he properly hails from the town of Hot Springs. And if Hope is a place of tin-roof piety and stagnation, Hot Springs is a wide-boy's town full of hustlers and whores and easy money. I once went to a Labor Day rally there; Bill and Hillary both spoke. The future First Lady was breathless with enthusiasm. "When Bill first brought me here, I said to him: 'Just look at all these *small businesses.*' " Yes indeedy, ma'am. Ready cash preferred. Bill's mother, Virginia, was a doyenne of the beauty parlors, bars and racetracks of this open city. His father, William Jefferson Blythe, was a smaller-time player in the traveling salesman line. Before his death in a roadside drainage ditch, he put flesh on the bones of every Dogpatch cliché about the region. ("You know you're from Arkansas if you find that you attend family reunions in search of a date.") He formed sexual alliances with two sisters of the same family at the same time, while married to yet another woman, and fathered progeny with unusual casualness. His death left Virginia at the mercy of an alcoholic wife-beating successor.

They say that in the boyhood of Judas, Jesus was betrayed. The saying itself shows the treacherous ground on which psychohistory is based. But in the closing days of his campaign for the presidency, Clinton began to tell the story of how he stood up to the brutal stepfather. Which makes it the odder that he then went to the registry and asked to take this man's surname. If you read the Clinton family profile "in neutral," so to speak, you would imagine yourself studying a problem kid from a ghetto, where it is a wise child who knows his own father. Yet Clinton's great contribution to American domestic politics has been his stress on the deplorable lack of moral continence among the underclass. His mantra, as a leader of the conservative Democratic Leadership Council, was "to end welfare as we know it." In pursuit of this goal, he has advanced a spending bill which removes perhaps some millions of American children from the welfare rolls. Even Senator Daniel Patrick Moynihan, who first opened the argument about the cultural pathology of poverty when he was working for the Nixon administration, has professed himself appalled at the callousness and want of discrimination which characterize the new dispensation. Marian Wright Edelman, one of Washington's best-loved advocates of civil rights, chairs the Children's Defense Fund. Hillary Clinton used to be the honorary president of this organization, and drew on the experience for her sentimental book *It Takes a Village...And Other Lessons Children Teach Us.* (This book, inter alia, recommends abstinence from sex until those troubled teen years are behind us.) Now, Ms. Edelman complains that she cannot get her phone-calls to the White House returned. It is important, therefore, to bear in mind that the Clintons do not seek *everybody's* approval. Below a certain threshold of power and income, they can be quite choosy.

It seems to me that they acquired this principle of selectivity while operating in Arkansas. There are, currently, three Clintonoid scandals still in play from that period. The first, which goes under the generic title of Whitewater, has to do with real-estate speculation. The second, which is vulgarly called Troopergate, has to do with Clinton's sexual appetite as recalled by his former bodyguards. The third concerns Mena airport. Taking these in random order, we find that no member of the Clinton entourage doubts the essence of the trooper testimony. The governor was, in the words of a local saying, a hard dog to keep on the porch. This would scarcely be worth mentioning if the leaders of official American feminism had not rallied to his defense and rallied, furthermore, by pointing to the relative trashiness of some of the women who have complained. Excuse me, but it is surely uneducated and impressionable girls like Paula Jones—vulnerable to predatory superiors and working on short-term contracts—for whose protection the sexual harassment laws were specifically designed. As ever, it is the class element in this dismal narrative that bears watching.

On Whitewater, it has become quite the liberal fashion to say that no laws were broken and that the investigation has been allowed to draw out its length for an unconscionable period of time. It may be too early to say that no laws were broken, but it's not by any means too early to say that this defense has a Reagan-era ring to it. And so do some of the business deals involved. "If Reaganomics works at all," wrote Hillary Rodham in a 1981 letter to the ill-starred speculator Jim McDougal, "Whitewater could become the Western hemisphere's Mecca." The proven record of the Whitewater partnerships is one of revolving doors, influence-brokering and greasy palms; that all this is legal in American politics is itself the scandal. As for the protraction of the hearings, these could have been wound up in a matter of weeks if it were not for skillful lawyering by the White House, and the seemingly endless outbreaks of amnesia that overcame its normally needle-sharp witnesses. The fact that the case has become an adventure playground for right-wing paranoids is not conclusive in itself, as some fastidious commentators affect to believe. Several senior White House Arkansans have already had to make hasty departures from politics, some of them clutching Go to Jail cards, and I would not expect these to be the last. Moreover, people with spin skills like the Clintons do not act as if there is something to hide if there is actually nothing to hide. Mrs. Clinton in one private missive expressed alarm that an investigation might involve the disclosure of ten years' worth of campaign financing in Arkansas. That's probably the thing to keep your eye on. In Little Rock and its gamey Hot Springs counterpart, the Clintons learned the dirty rudiments of retail politics—and how to wholesale them. And it seems pretty obvious that they brought these talents, and these operators, to Washington. For an example of how the small time connects to the big time, one need look no further than a recently leaked memo, the disclosure of which moved the Oval Office to a paroxysm of fury and mole-hunting.

At the anti-terrorism summit in Cairo last March, Clinton had a private meeting with Boris Yeltsin. An undertaking was given to provide American support for Mr. Yeltsin's reelection, and to accept his repeatedly broken word that the filthy war in Chechnya was being brought to a close. This aspect of business concluded, Clinton raised another outstanding matter. Russia had been threatening to prohibit imports of frozen poultry. "This is a big issue," says Clinton according to the notes of the meeting, "especially since 40 percent of U.S. poultry is produced in Arkansas." When Tyson Foods first bankrolled a governor's depleted campaign chest, the company can barely have hoped for representation at this level: chickens for Chechens, as you might say. (The whole finger-lickin' subject died within a few days, since Don Tyson is also a major benefactor of Bob Dole's. Mr. Tyson's executive suite is an exact scale-model of the Oval Office, except that the door handles are sculpted in the shape of hens' eggs. Recall what I wrote earlier about Mutual Assured Destruction.)

The third and most suggestive delayed-reaction charge from Arkansas receives the least attention. It also gives the right-wing paranoids the most trouble, since it is in essence a tale of depredation by right-wing paranoids. Reduced to its rudiments, the allegation is this. During the scoundrel time of the Central American war, an off-the-record airport in the Ouachita Mountains of Arkansas was used to fly illegal weapons to the Nicaraguan Contras. The returning planes were stuffed with cocaine, partly to finance the gunrunning and partly to pay off (and also to implicate and silence) those who took part in it. The least you can say for this story is that there is a lot to be said for it. I have myself interviewed Trooper L. D. Brown of Governor Clinton's police *équipe*, who claims to have been on more than one of the flights. He was able to show me documents given to him in Clinton's own handwriting, and to substantiate a good deal of what he alleged in other ways. And it is a fact that Clinton allowed the Arkansas National Guard to be sent to Central America at a time when other Democratic governors, such as Michael Dukakis of Massachusetts, were refusing the poisoned chalice. Indeed, it was Clinton's flexibility in the matter of this criminal and covert war (not unlike his subsequent haste to change sides and be on the winning side in the Gulf conflict) that won him the good opinion of several "responsible" establishment institutions, of the sort which never give up in the search for a trustworthy Democrat.

There are micro as well as macro elements in the Mena scandal, since one of the narcotics dealers involved was a man named Dan Lasater, a bond-dealer of the sort often described as "colorful." Lasater, too, was a major Clinton fundraiser and (until his imprisonment) a supplier of controlled substances to the president's chaotic brother Roger. As in the case of his disordered family and courtship background, so with his amateur experience on the drug scene: once in Washington Bill Clinton proselytizes for family values and the war on drugs with the zeal of a convert. Not since Nixon has the so-called drug war been prosecuted so sternly. Clinton all but fired his own surgeon-general merely for recommending a debate on decriminalization, and has now delegated narcotics "interdiction" to a senior member of the military. Bills on drugs and terrorism have stripped protection from citizens and defendants in a way that would never have been countenanced if the Democrats and liberals were in opposition. In his first reelection campaign video, Clinton announced himself the candidate of law and order and capital punishment.

Make no mistake, it is this version of realism that animates the Clintons. Rather than be attacked from the right, they will invariably move to occupy the conservative ground. This has been as true of the little things, like prayer in public schools, as it has been of the larger issues, like the demolition of the welfare state. In foreign policy matters, and on questions relating to the Pentagon or the CIA, Clinton has done rather more than demonstrate an impeccable orthodoxy. He has actually given the defense chiefs a larger budget than they asked for, and has kept in being some lavish military Keynesian projects (like the B-1 bomber and the Seawolf submarine) which the strategists have declared obsolete. During his campaign against Bush, Clinton ran against him from the right on two important matters—namely, Cuba and Israel. On Cuba, the Bush administration opposed a congressional amendment which extended the American boycott to third countries and foreign companies trading with Havana. Clinton flew to Miami and—once again in return for a handsome campaign contribution—adopted the position of the more farouche exile leaders. Similarly, Bush and James Baker were anxious to see Yitzhak Shamir's regime of petrified intransigence give way to Rabin and Peres. They therefore declined to make an unconditional loan guarantee to Israel, and as a result found themselves in a rugged domestic squabble with the lobby in Washington. Clinton took the earliest possible opportunity of saying that he was for giving the loan guarantee without strings. Again, perhaps, the psychohistorian could posit, in Clinton's strenuous eagerness on matters hawkish, an element of over-compensation for his draft-dodging past. Certainly the organized gay vote, which came out decisively for Clinton in 1992 because of his pledge to end discrimination in the armed forces, was to find out speedily that, when confronted with anything like uniformed opposition, the supposed commander-in-chief would start to cry loudly before he had even been hurt.

But political hypotheses may be more trustworthy than psychological ones. At Georgetown University, Clinton's mentor was Professor Carroll Quigley, known to us old special relationship hands as the author of arcane but original works on the Anglo-American ruling class. (Some of his books now have a half-life in those wobbly Pat Robertson circles which affect a belief in international banking as the engine of history. He was also a great expert on the power and ramification of the Rhodes Scholarship system.) In the course of his 1992 nomination speech, Clinton cited Quigley as a great influence. Could he have been thinking of Quigley's immense *Tragedy and Hope*, a book which argued for the domination of parties by business interests? As Quigley phrased it, perhaps a little too bluntly for some tastes:

> The argument that the two parties should represent opposed ideals and policies...is a foolish idea. Instead, the two parties should be almost identical, so that the American people could throw the rascals out at any election without leading to any profound or extensive shifts in policy. The policies that are vital and necessary for America are no longer subjects of significant disagreement, but are disputable only in detail, procedure, priority or method.

Quigley was alluding principally to the durable consensus on grand strategy, military alliance and trade, but his argument applies with equal force to the home front. Here, the Clintons only ever made one challenge to the status quo. Inspired by the obvious popularity and also the electoral potential of the idea, they proposed a system of universal healthcare. Now it may be true (as I think) that nothing could have saved George Bush in 1992. But the change in the political tempo began with a remarkable Democratic triumph in Pennsylvania, orchestrated by James Carville and based like all good campaigns on the ceaseless iteration of a single note. There were forty million Americans without health insurance. No comparable society except South Africa lacked a health system. (Or, as Carville put it with a clever appeal to a different kind of populism: "If a criminal has the legal right to a lawyer, working Americans should have the legal right to a doctor.")

Of course, the cry of "socialized medicine" is one of the hoariest slogans of the American right, so it had to be expected that there would be a political confrontation. But for once, the all-important opinion polls were aligned solidly and consistently with reform. There was expertise to spare among specialists on the subject. One group in particular, based at the Harvard Medical School, proposed the equivalent of a Canadian "single payer" or National Health plan, combining a wide repertory of benefits with a range of choice between different physicians. The Congressional Budget Office furthermore certified such a plan as the most cost-effective, not least because it would end the fantastically wasteful duplication and competition spawned by America's insurance racket. At an early White House meeting between the Harvard group and Hillary Clinton, the case for a straightforward National Health Bill was put by Dr. David Himmelstein. As he recalls the exchange:

> It was evident Hillary was thinking a lot about politics. Can you realistically tell me, she asked, that there are any big powers that support "single payer" and that can take on the insurance industry's lobbying and advertising budget? I said: "About 70 percent of the people in the U.S. favor something like a single-payer

system. With presidential leadership, that can be an overwhelming force." She said: "David, tell me something interesting."

So at the very beginning of the argument, the only possible winning hand was thrown into the discard. The end of the argument—the utter humiliation of the Clinton administration on Capitol Hill and the relegation of healthcare to the bottom of the political heap—could not, even in pragmatic terms, have been worse than a stand on principle would have been. Except that to contrast pragmatism with principle in this old-fashioned manner might be a mistake. What if the collapse in the face of the insurance racket is the principle? In order to try and construct a more centrist consensus of their own, the Clintons coined the phrase "managed competition" to describe the highly bureaucratized free market in healthcare that they proposed. (Something like Milton Friedman's famous allusion to "socialism for the rich and free enterprise for the poor.") That term might well do duty for the whole menu of Clintonian rule, from the free-trade agreements with Mexico and Japan, to the care and feeding of the war economy, the distribution of favors for clients like Yeltsin and the quid pro quo relationship between tax exemptions and corporate campaign contributions.

There almost certainly is a relation between Clinton the man and Clintonism as politics, though it may not be as obvious as it seems. If one had to nominate a hinge moment, it would probably be the last days of the George McGovern campaign, in Texas, in 1972. Clinton was sent down to the Lone Star state, along with his friend Taylor Branch, at a moment when the Nixon forces seemed almost unstoppable.

(A subsequent post-Watergate myth has depicted the press as anti-Nixon during this period. In point of fact, the general refusal of the media to discuss Nixon's illegal use of state power was one of the most striking features of the election.) Taylor Branch, later the outstanding biographer of Martin Luther King, remembers the dying days of McGovernism very clearly. The Texas Democratic Party was riven with faction, and generally uninterested in the pro–civil rights and anti-war position taken by the young volunteers from up North. More time was spent in hand-holding, log-rolling and back-scratching than on the issues. But as Branch suddenly noticed, his friend Bill was very good indeed at the back-slapping and palm-greasing bit. As the vote drew near, senior Texas Democrats like Lloyd Bentsen and John Connally either deserted the McGovern campaign or joined the front organization calling itself Democrats for Nixon. It was from this sort of timber that Clinton and others were later to carpenter the Democratic Leadership Council. He evidently decided, for whatever mixture of private and public reasons, never to be on the losing side again.

In other words, Clinton's ambition became the same thing as his politics, and his approval rating from the powers that be became the same thing as his electability. From then on, the only test of courage was the ability—which had to be repeatedly demonstrated—to treat his own former principles and core supporters with distance and even contempt. He showed himself to be a swift learner. In many ways, then, his finest hour and his most maturing moment was his throaty speech at Nixon's graveside. Robert Dole cried. Governor Pete Wilson of California also cried. Clinton masked his tears but observed huskily that Nixon was a small-town self-made American who should be judged on his "whole record" and not just on one regrettable episode. (As I said to Mrs. Clinton on the one occasion I was able to mention this, I couldn't agree more. Breaking off from a discussion of how unkind the New Right was being to her, the First of all Ladies exclaimed: "Oh, you noticed that, did you?" I did not know where to look.)

In November 1981, David Stockman gave a long interview. He was then Ronald Reagan's director of the Office of Management and Budget, and had become the herald of the supply-side and trickle-down counter-revolution. Perhaps tempted by hubris, he bragged that the Reaganauts had put politics into a black box. By running up the deficit to a vertiginous level, and by promising deep cuts in taxation as well as a hugely swollen military-industrial budget, the new Republicans had ensured that no Democratic Congress, and no future Democratic presidency, could spend a dime more on anything without cutting at least a dime from somewhere else. Thus at last would come the long-delayed revenge on the New Deal and the civil rights movement. To get an impression of the sheer crookery of this, you have to recall that Stockman and Reagan predicted a zero deficit by 1984 and a $28 billion surplus by 1986. Thanks to a compliant media, the test of Democratic realism became that of a willingness to pretend that this was true. (The old Democratic saurians of the Hill, the Bentsens and Foleys and Rostenkowskis and Packwoods, all voted for the Reagan illusion before expiring in the Gingrich flood they had unknowingly beckoned on.) It was Clinton's unsentimental readiness to enter this auction of tax and spending cuts—while protecting the most "vulnerable," like the wealthy risk-taking donors and the recipients of company welfare—that demonstrated his readiness to govern. It also demonstrated his willingness to accept the limits of government, while hypocritically referring to these as some mysterious gridlock. When he needed a new director of communications after a spasm of local White House PR difficulty, he turned to the former Nixon-Reagan hack David Gergen— the very man who had sold the Stockman program to a credulous Washington elite. The resulting "managed insolvency," which might neutrally be termed the doctrine of limits, and is neutrally termed by the elite in that way, does not by definition extend to that elite itself. Meanwhile, the United States deficit has become a real peril to societies and economies other than its own.

And now I take another look out over my home town. The Democratic primary has just been held. Amid the pitted streets and gutted schools and rotting clinics, with a ratted-out city nominally run by a corrupt black demagogue, and actually run by a group of indifferent white congressmen, one can see the sordid end of the idea of participation. It was actually proposed that the primary be cancelled, in order to save money for a bankrupt neocolonial municipality. But that was thought too brutal and candid, so (even though the two party machines had long ago emitted their white smoke and announced *habemus candidatum*) the vote duly took place. Eleven thousand people turned out in the nation's capital; a total so shameful that it was barely reported. It is probably less than the statistical margin of error by which the opinion poll industry claims the status of a pseudo-science. Is this what the 1968 Rhodes generation intended when it set out with its easy talk of grassroots and empowerment? Perhaps not, but it is what it has wrought. Politics as a spectator sport, staged by fixers in a parallel universe and determined—in point of issues and candidates—before a single real elector has been invited to comment. Extreme public squalor and tribalism, coexisting with a triumph of special interests not seen since the Gilded Age. Everything more separate, more unequal and more rancorous. And everything accepted as somehow beyond the reach of political action.

Postmodern politics has dinned into us the concept of the lesser evil. One must, in other words, always be ready to accept Clinton (or Blair, or Mitterrand) lest worse befall. At one level, this is what is called a zero-sum game. If true, that is to say, it must be true all the time, and true in the same way as a theorem. How odd; that those who speak of a limitless offering of free will and free choice should be so insistent that one of the main items of decision involves no choice or alternative at all. The rise of Bill Clinton shows that there are indeed rewards for those who can learn to think this way. But those rewards are—shall we say—unevenly distributed, and they involve a certain amnesia about the choices that were avoided, or repressed, or not made at all. By stressing the idea of "no alternative," the non-ideological have redefined politics as a question of management, and eviscerated the idea that "the art of the possible" is indeed an art of possibility. But they may have outsmarted themselves, and their professional apparatus of consultants and pollsters and spin-meisters. The declining landscape of possibility—whether it is the prison-state for young African Americans, or the return of indentured labor in California, or the erosion of the First Amendment, or the collapse of environmental supervision, or the deregulated airline and food industries, or the free market in judges and legislators—now becomes their responsibility. The plea of a lesser evil will not displace it onto other shoulders. In their cleverness, the new class of the privileged have been slow to understand this. I hope to live long enough to see the day, not when they find it out, but when it is found out by the patient and the swindled—and the trusting.

The Trouble with HRH
On Princess Margaret
1997

AMID ALL the wretched declension of the British royal family, many people seem willing to suspend their general disapproval, disappointment, boredom, nausea—you name it—in the case of our Sovereign Lady the Queen. Unselfish, dutiful, serious, modest, faithful unto death, she rises above the showbiz values, disco ambitions and petty neuroses of her clan and brood. But does she truly deserve such a dispensation? Monarchs may be able to elude responsibility for many things, but surely the state of the monarchy is not among them. And the queen made at least two decisions of her own which contributed to the present zoo-like condition of her relatives. The first was her choice of consort: the hawkish and chilly authoritarian who made such a hell of his offspring's childhood. The second was her resolution, so pious and so carefully meditated, to sacrifice her only sister's happiness for the greater cause of family values and the high duty of setting an example. This is the House of Windsor, not the House of Atreus (let's keep our sense of proportion), but still, here if anywhere was its original sin. Does Brenda, even now, look wistfully back on a time when marriage to a divorced war hero was considered the height of scandal and required the officiousness of the aptly named Cantuar?

I wanted so much to be the first person to write about "the Royals" and not to employ Bagehot's rotund injunction about the danger of letting in "daylight upon magic." But the damn phrase is inescapable. The fascination of Princess Margaret, I suspect, is that she was the forerunner of the public, vulgar Windsor style: now such a drag but then such a sensation. If you were a commoner of average social mobility in London in the 1960s, 1970s and 1980s, there was a better than average chance that you would have *met* her in some club or at some party, or even on the pavement outside. Martin Amis remembers her showing up at the end of a dinner, on the arm of Nicholas Soames, and seating herself at the piano to sing "My Old Man's a Dustman" (to which, of course, the only answer was "No he ain't"). Two members of the *New Left Review* editorial board, known to me, were confronted by her at some do or another. It was the fashion in those days to address everybody as "man," and they concluded later that HRH hadn't objected to this informality because she thought they were saying "Ma'am." I myself cannoned into her, flesh-tinted and well into the gin (her, I mean), as I entered a cocktail party. She was unescorted, and seized on me as a new arrival. "Know anything about china?" she demanded. I truly did not know whether she meant porcelain or the Middle Kingdom, and was very grateful for whatever rescue eventuated. There she was, I mean to say, going around the place letting in daylight on magic like billy-oh. In those pre-Tampax, pre-Squidgy, pre-bulimic days there was an element of antic subversion involved, as well as some unhappiness and boredom and, one suspects, a teeny tincture of the vengeful.

Mr. Aronson is the author of a much more interesting royal book, about "Prince Eddie" and the Cleveland Street homosexual racket, but he has the soul of a courtier and writes about being given "audience" and even being "received."* This lends a certain ludicrous tone even to his gravest chapters. (At one point he describes the queen mother as "blessed with typically Celtic good looks: black hair, blue eyes and a skin like cream," when any modern student of the subject could have begun the sentence in the same way and gone on with: "gingery pube-like rug, yellowish eyes and a hide like a pizza.") But he is a writer of the pre-daylight era. He describes with near solemnity the situation at Glamis Castle on the night of Margaret's birth. In 1930 it was still a requirement that a minister of the crown, usually the home secretary, should be present for any royal birth. (This "ancient tradition" dated back to the reign of James II and the rumor about the warming-pan baby delivered covertly to his consort, Mary of Modena.) So J. R. Clynes, home secretary to Ramsay Mac-Donald, had to journey to Glamis Castle and wait for sixteen days for the waters to break. He passed the time profitably enough being shown around the local estates by Lady Airlie, a lady-in-waiting, who was pleased to find "under his homely exterior a deeply sensitive mind, touchingly appreciative of beauty." In the company of the ceremonial secretary of the Home Office, Clynes was able duly to vouch that the royal parturition was on the level, and that the loyal bonfires could

---

* *Princess Margaret: A Biography* by Theo Aronson (O'Mara, 1997).

be lit. Aronson concludes this story—a profile in capsule of the whole Ramsay MacDonald experience—with a mixture of lyricism and foreboding:

> Particularly gratifying to the local people was the fact that the baby had been born in Scotland. Because of this Scottish birth, Princess Margaret was often to be described, in the years ahead, as being typically "Stuart," in contrast to what was regarded, in the same journalistic shorthand, as Princess Elizabeth's stolid, more "Hanoverian" appearance. And indeed, for a while, the younger princess's looks did seem to reflect something of the elegance and romance of the ill-starred Stuart dynasty. Only in the face of Princess Margaret's increasingly Hanoverian appetites did such references begin to die.

Hanoverian appetites! I like the ring of it. But all the poor thing wanted to do (then at least) was to marry a dashing group captain who had been married before. The humiliation of Mr. Clynes was as nothing to the imperial time-wasting that went on as a result. Entire cabinet meetings and sessions of Parliament were devoted to the question. Under the Royal Marriages Act of 1772 (another piece of mystic and antique tradition, designed to prevent the ghastly offspring of George III from letting down the side) the sovereign's consent was required for a marriage of any member of the family who was younger than 25. After the quarter-century mark had been reached, things became simpler. All that was required was the consent of the British and Dominion Parliaments. But the year was 1953, and there was a coronation on the way, and Canon 107 of the Church of England's 1603 doctrines expressly forbade divorce, so it was thought better to inter the issue with the maximum of surreptitiousness and dishonesty. After

Churchill and all his private secretaries had discussed it exhaustively—the latter overruling the initial sympathies of the former—and after the cabinet had been brought in, and the archbishop of Canterbury, and after the attorney general had done a canvass of Commonwealth prime ministers, it was decided to post Townsend to Brussels and, here being the devilish cunning and mature statecraft of the thing, *not to tell Princess Margaret the secret.* She was shipped off on a royal progress through Rhodesia with the queen mother, and not given the tidings until she had been radiant at the Rhodes Centenary Exhibition in Bulawayo.

She threw such a fit at this point that, later in the annus horribilis of 1953, it was determined to amend the Regency Act. Privy Council meetings, drafting committees, huggermugger select committees, portentous exchanges in both Houses—the lot. The Regency Act—wafting us back to the tradition-laden year of 1937—provided that if the queen croaked or went barmy then Princess Margaret would be regent until Charles turned eighteen. As amended, it would now provide for Prince Philip to fill the slot. It was a clear demotion. The yellow press, in an early and faint-hearted version of mutinies against discretion still to come, asked John Bullishly why a foreign-born consort should assume precedence over a daughter of King George VI.

But this was as nothing to the squalor and piety which marked the Year of Grace 1955. In August, Margaret turned 25 and tried to pick up the threads with Townsend. More cabinet meetings, more crisis sessions at Lambeth and Buckingham Palaces, and at Balmoral. The Marquess of Salisbury threatened to resign if the match was allowed by the government.

Sir Anthony Eden boarded planes and flew hither and yon to talk in grave tones to the queen. The queen pointedly took all her dogs for a walk on one occasion, in order to avoid having to talk to her sister on such a distasteful subject. The shivering girl was told that if she persisted in her folly, a Bill of Renunciation would be placed before Parliament, and would require her exile from the realm as well as the loss of all titles and income. Finally, at a meeting with the archbishop of Canterbury himself, she crumbled and said she'd give up the man in her life. The prelate, Dr. Geoffrey Fisher, rather outdid himself for the occasion. "What a wonderful person," he exclaimed, "the Holy Spirit is!" Here we see, in early prefiguration, both the chill dysfunction and denial practiced by the Windsors, and the degeneration of the C. of E. into the cracker motto Jesus Movement.

Of course, if J. R. Clynes had been present at Glamis for the birth of a baby boy, Margaret would have become king in 1953. Such are the beauties of primogeniture. Having become a black ewe instead, she began to live a little and cultivate a few affectations. The cigarette-holder, the decanter, the reputation of being dreadfully hard on the staff and just a little brittle with the family "firm." (By the way, the Duke of York—so Aronson instructs us—was known in the 1920s as "the Foreman" for his supposed interest in industrial matters, so the rather trying business of the royal family comparing itself to a going concern is not as recent as some may think. In fact, it's almost a hallowed tradition.) She behaved with wonderful surliness at occasions of duty. Nancy Mitford related one such fiasco: a dinner in honor of the princess in Paris in 1959:

Dinner was at 8.30 and at 8.30 Princess Margaret's hairdresser arrived, so we waited for hours while he concocted a ghastly coiffure. She looked like a huge ball of fur on two well-developed legs. Shortest dress I ever saw—a Frenchman said it begins so low and ends so soon. In fact the whole appearance was excessively common.

Lady Jebb, the wife of the British ambassador, told her diary that the trouble with HRH was that she insisted on being treated as a princess without showing any willingness to shoulder the responsibilities of being one. Where has one heard that recently? The establishment says things like this with an air of complete assurance and rectitude, even while it insists on maintaining a mediocre extended family which breeds more people than are necessary for any conceivable "job." Most European royal houses lost their thrones in part for the simple reason that there were too many redundant princelings and princesses. The House of Windsor has not been exempted, but then it made Margaret surplus to requirements from the start.

Not long before the Townsend business, she had been sent on a tour of the Caribbean. Sir Hugh Foot, then governor of Jamaica, received instructions that she was not to share a dance with any "colored person." (Foot had been through this before. Confiding his support for elections in Jamaica to the visiting Princess Alice, he had been told that he was talking "balderdash.") From what one hears of, say, the queen mother's admiration for Ian Smith, there was a good deal of this sort of thing in royal circles. So it would be nice to think that there was another element of revenge in Princess Margaret's later decision to head for Mustique when things got tough. Or perhaps, like Margot Beste-Chetwynde with her darling Chokey, she just enjoyed creating a frisson. One used to hear the most extraordinary things about one of the barmen on the island ...Unfortunately, Aronson doesn't keep the promise of his early hint about "appetites," and he adds little to the dreary tale of Margaret's marriage to Snowdon and fling with Llewellyn (sounds like a grueling tour of Welsh hillsides). I had not known before that Wallis Simpson, on being brought the news of the princess's engagement to a commoner, said: "At least we're keeping up with the Armstrong-Joneses." And apparently it is true that the dashing Snowdon once yelled at her: "You look like a Jewish manicurist and I hate you." Quite a facer for a Hanoverian.

Her vile treatment by the dynasty prompts one's sympathy every now and then, but she generally succeeds in dissipating it by reserving all her own sympathy for herself. Her performances in America, for example, have been uniformly repellent. She referred to the Irish as "pigs" during a visit to Chicago and then tried to get out of it—first by saying that she'd said "Irish jigs" and then by taking refuge behind anti-terrorist security measures. At a Hollywood dinner, where she had insisted on having Barry Manilow as her guest of choice, she flew into a rage when then governor Jerry Brown called her "Your Highness" instead of "Your Royal Highness." (It's a long time, it seems to me, since monarchists were wont to boast of the credit that the royals brought upon us overseas.) Had she been the elder sister, or even brother, she would probably have been no less hellish in the top job. It will soon seem— surely it does already seem—quite astonishing that so much establishment time has been spent on the "containment" of an averagely volatile woman from a disadvantaged family. All that the daylight proves is that there was no bloody magic to begin with.

Brief Shining Moments
Kennedy and Nixon
1998

I N ARTHUR SCHLESINGER'S court history, *A Thousand Days: John F. Kennedy in the White House*, which might without unfairness be called the founding breviary of the cult of JFK, there appears the following vignette. Schlesinger had been asked to carpenter a white paper justifying Washington's destabilization of Cuba, in which the high-flown rhetoric of the New Frontier might form a sort of scab over the fouler business of empire. This task he readily performed, scampering back to the Oval Office for a chat with the divine one:

> As we finished, I said: "What do you think about this damned invasion?" He said wryly: "I think about it as little as possible." But it was clear, as we talked, that he had of course been thinking about it a good deal. In his judgment, the critical point—the weak part of the case for going ahead—lay in the theory that the landings would touch off a mass insurrection against the regime. How unpopular was Castro anyway? I mentioned a series written by Joseph Newman, who had just visited Cuba for the *New York Herald Tribune*, citing a piece which reported the strength of sentiment behind Castro. Kennedy said quickly: "That must have been the fourth piece—I missed it. Could you get it for me?" I sent it over that evening. In a short while he called back to ask

that I talk to Newman and obtain, as hypothetically as possible, his estimate about Cuban response to an invasion.

Allowing for Schlesinger's retrospective, self-serving grace notes (one has to love the placing of the word "wryly"), a conversation something like this one must have taken place in March 1961, just a few weeks after the bombastic, menacing "Ask not..." inaugural address, and very shortly before the invasion itself. And, even though Schlesinger was busily putting the arm on the press on Kennedy's behalf—persuading the *New Republic*, for example, to kill an accurate story about the training of Cuban mercenaries in Miami—he does want us to understand that he was always, privately, opposed to the folly of the Bay of Pigs. Let us suppose, then, that JFK had been hit by a bullet the day after he asked to read the Newman dispatches. Let us further suppose that Lyndon Johnson, finding the plans already in place, had authorized the invasion of Cuba. There would now be a herd of revisionist historians and propagandists, all assuring us that if he had lived, "Jack" would never have allowed the CIA and the joint chiefs to do anything so barbarous and stupid. Why, just the night before he fell to an assassin, he was "wryly" reconsidering...

I am not merely speculating here. During the last freshet of Kennedy-era retrospectives, there appeared a book, also by a man named Newman, entitled *JFK and Vietnam*. John Newman is a minor military historian who unearthed some papers showing that Kennedy had at one point had a contingency plan for withdrawal from Indochina. He became the house intellectual on the Oliver Stone movie *JFK*, and his work was much cried up by the Schlesinger school of apologetics. Kennedy might have started the Vietnam War, covertly committed men and resources to the war, argued forcefully for the symbolic importance of the war—but would have called it all off had he been reelected. So the war as we knew it, the actually existing war, so to speak, was all the fault of LBJ in spite of (go softly on this bit) his exclusively Kennedy-picked gang of warmongering advisers, not exempting the saintly Bobby.

There is no arguing with this kind of junk thinking. It all depends on an auto-da-fé among the intellectualoids. As he did so brilliantly with *Libra*, Don DeLillo has caught the tone of unwholesome adoration in his aptly titled *Underworld*, and put it into the caustic mouth of Lenny Bruce, found here delivering a monologue during the Cuban Missile Crisis: "Kennedy makes an appearance in public and you hear people say, I saw his hair! Or, I saw his teeth! The spectacle's so dazzling they can't take it all in. I saw his hair! They're venerating the sacred relics while the guy's still alive." Libertarians and anarchists tell us that the problem with humans is not the will to command, but the will to obey, and Bruce was rightly expressing contempt for the audience and not the demagogue. However, the charming Kennedy brothers conducted most of their business in secret and by deceit, so that much of the dirty work was done subfusc. It has taken nearly four decades to establish the following facts beyond doubt.

Their political careers were bought for them by a nasty old patriarch with a pronounced sympathy for fascism and a strong underworld connection.

They turned instinctively toward other crime families when there was any need for "wet jobs" or ballot-rigging at home or abroad.

They were willing to risk nuclear warfare even for relatively short-term domestic purposes.

For these reasons, whenever I see a grinning television anchor describe the Kennedy gang as "American royalty," I nod in silent assent. Nor can one object, except aesthetically, to the silly term "Camelot." Mrs. Kennedy did indeed tell William Manchester, for a fawning profile that he wrote just after the assassination, that her late husband—who loathed the classical music soirées that she arranged at the White House for artists like Pablo Casals—had thoroughly enjoyed the mediocre musical written by Lerner and Loewe where, "for one brief shining moment," King Arthur enjoyed absolute power over his knights. (And Sir Lancelot over their women.) You might think that an invocation of mythical yet absolute monarchy would put bow-tied American scholars and editors on their guard. But you would be dead wrong. "Camelot" is always cited without a breath of irony.

One day, I am going to drop everything and think exclusively about America and its celebrated loss of innocence. I have read that the country lost said innocence in the Civil War, in the Spanish-American War, in the First World War, during Prohibition, at Hiroshima and Nagasaki, at the McCarthy hearings, in Dallas, in Vietnam, over Watergate, and in the discovery that the TV contests in the Eisenhower era were fixed. This list is not exhaustive. Innocence, we were recently and quakingly informed, was lost again at the bombing of Oklahoma City. Clearly, a virginity so casually relinquished is fairly easily regained—only to be (damn!) mislaid once more. The same compound of the credulous and the ahistorical is to be noticed in the newest pile of

Kennedy-era books.* For the baby-boomers, the Kennedy-Nixon years represent the time when, for them at least, politics became vivid and real: when, to borrow Auden's lapidary words, the menacing shapes of our fever were precise and alive. And it's fair to say that nobody will be poring over, for example, the Reagan-Mondale debates a decade from now. Still less the Bush-Dukakis duel, and least of all the utter post-political vacuity that has descended since Bill Clinton became able (with the help of a fragment of archival footage) to proclaim himself the heir to a styrofoam Round Table and—one is forced to add—all the vulgar perks that went with it.

As with the flickering film shot by the accidental tourist Abraham Zapruder in Dallas on 22 November 1963, there exists a persistent and irrational desire to spool back and see what really happened and also—as if halting the film might somehow arrest or deflect the event—what might have happened. In the years between 1960 and 1968, there was a cultural and political revolution in the United States which altered everything for everybody. Kennedy, Nixon and Johnson form the enchanted or bewitched triad or triangle which still exerts power and fascination. Dr. Martin Luther King is the slain

---

* *The Dark Side of Camelot* by Seymour Hersh (Simon and Schuster, 1998); *"One Hell of a Gamble": Khrushchev, Castro and Kennedy, 1958–64* by Aleksandr Fursenko and Timothy Naftali (John Murray, 1997); *Taking Charge: The Johnson White House Tapes 1963–64* by Michael Beschloss (Simon and Schuster, 1998); *The Year the Dream Died* by Jules Witcover (Warner, 1997); *Abuse of Power: The New Nixon Tapes* edited by Stanley Kutler (Free Press, 1997); *Pillar of Fire: America in the King Years 1963–65* by Taylor Branch (Simon and Schuster, 1998).

hero and absent knight who—though they don't teach you this in school—fell victim to the swords of all three.

Now this is a fairly routine passage from Seymour Hersh's new book, ill-advisedly (and unironically) entitled *The Dark Side of Camelot*:

> Even aboard Air Force One, the president was forced to wear a stiff brace that stretched from his shoulders to his crotch—the aftermath of an errant poolside grab while he was on a campaign trip to the West Coast. Two months before the end, Hugh Sidey, *Time* magazine's White House correspondent, recalled in an interview for this book, a woman acquaintance of Sidey's "came to me and told me how Kennedy tried to put the make on her at the pool. She wrenched away and [the president] fell into the pool, hurting his back." The brace would keep the president upright for the bullets of Lee Harvey Oswald.

Makes you wonder about the lighter side of Camelot. Here, at any event, is a suggestive minor key connection between hubris and nemesis—or between Kennedy's frantically sordid private life and the events that punctuated and then terminated his sorry term in office. Nobody denies any of the facts. And Hugh Sidey—doyen of the old journalistic discretion, not to say journalistic whitewash—told me five years ago on a television panel that nobody dared print such things at the time. Yet, for proposing any correspondence between the crime family Kennedy and the serial fornicator Kennedy and the Kennedy of Cuba and Vietnam, Hersh has been pelted with dead dogs and old shoes from one end of Georgetown to another. It's true that he expended some effort on a false trail about Marilyn Monroe, where forged papers were dangled to improve slightly on what authentic papers had already demonstrated ("Follow the money" was the great and crass hack slogan to emerge from *All the President's Men*), but he did drop that line of inquiry just in time.

For the rest, Hersh's work makes harder and sharper and clearer what more scholarly books had already begun to assert. For example, in his splendid 1991 study, *The Crisis Years: Kennedy and Khrushchev 1960–63*, Michael Beschloss demonstrated that Kennedy had been privately relieved by the building of the Berlin Wall, had publicly almost refrained from commenting on it, and had waited until two years after it was safely built before using it as a sound stage for his *Ich bin* grandstanding. Hersh adds some more detail here, showing that Berlin was always subordinate to the sick Kennedy obsession with Cuba. Actually, almost everything became subordinate to that obsession. Again, we knew some of this already. In his book *The Kennedy Imprisonment*, Garry Wills showed elegantly that the Cuba crisis Mark II—the missile confrontation in October 1962—was intimately connected to the Cuba crisis Mark I: the Bay of Pigs and the incessant American-sponsored covert aggressions. Kennedy knew, in other words, that the Soviet allegations about his invasion and subversion plans had the merit of being true. But he could not afford to admit this publicly, and thus had no choice but to go to red alert when the "shocking" news of a Russian response became known. Even then, Robert McNamara and McGeorge Bundy opened the first meeting of his advisers by saying that the problem was principally one of American domestic politics. (That elusive, golden second term again.) It was Kennedy himself who secretly taped the meetings of this Executive Committee, or ExComm, so we can be fairly sure that he chose his own words with some care, and some eye for the record.

John J. McCloy, who implemented the decision to intern Japanese Americans after 1941, and who chaired the committee that decided on the Hiroshima and Nagasaki bombings, and who ran occupied Germany as a satrapy after the war, and who was later to serve as a trusty on the Warren Commission, and who was in every other respect the hardest of imperial and Cold War hardliners, told Theodore Sorensen after the Bay of Pigs that "even if the Soviet Union had missile bases in Cuba—which it hasn't—why would we have any more right to invade Cuba than Khrushchev has to invade Turkey?" This is the point to keep one's eye on, because it was based on the same pragmatic logic that Khrushchev himself was to employ. By applying pressure in Cuba, he secured the withdrawal of the roughly equivalent American Jupiter missiles in Turkey, but only at huge and unconscionable risk and only on the condition that no such deal or quid pro quo was ever mentioned in public. The Kennedys lied about this deal to Congress, to the American voters, and to the then hapless Vice President Johnson. "Face," you see. JFK placed a high value on face. Only the most servile masochist, it seems to me, can congratulate him on the coolness with which he defused a ghastly crisis almost entirely of his own making. But such was the relief that it can still be felt. So, hysterical gratitude is still offered to the lordling who, in the end, decided that the human species and his own face could probably both be saved. (At some remove, however, this needless war of nerves was to assist Brezhnev and his allies in toppling Khrushchev. An uncounted cost of the Cuban adventure is that it cost the pre-Gorbachev reformists a generation, which Eastern Europeans had to live through—and which the luckless Cubans still do.)

But it's very clear that Cuban democrats would not have been the winners if the Kennedy destabilization had succeeded. Reading back to the Bay of Pigs from the newly disclosed material on the missile crisis makes it clearer than ever that the White House and the CIA were relying on the most gruesome Cuban reactionaries, and on their allies in the Miami mob. There would have been, not a Cuban spring, but another Guatemala. Or another Guyana: even Arthur Schlesinger has grudgingly confirmed what Hersh fleshes out—the incitement of racial hatred and the use of sabotage and gangsterism to bring down the elected government of Cheddi Jagan. (There was a little help there from the London cousins, too, as a gesture toward the special relationship.)

Hersh helps clear up an old mystery, which involves Kennedy's famous reluctance to commit a second wave of air cover to the hired goons he had landed at the Bay of Pigs. This decision, which only guaranteed an outcome already certain, has been used for years by the right as evidence of a stab in the back. It also, and not only for paranoids, furnishes a motive for lethal Kennedy hatred among disaffected CIA and mafia types, insofar as the two species may be distinguished. The explanation turns out to be relatively simple, and consistent with the known facts. Kennedy was waiting to hear that Castro had been assassinated in Havana. When he didn't hear, he calmly betrayed the mercenary force as the laws of realpolitik required of him. He forgot to confide in Arthur Schlesinger, but Aleksandr Fursenko and Timothy Naftali, in their authoritative *"One Hell of a Gamble,"* also state plainly that "the Kennedy administration had expected Castro to die before he could rally support for destroying the invasion." The "expect" bit did not depend on the advice of astrologers, and the verb "to die" was being conjugated in the active, not the passive voice. The late Richard Bissell, who was Kennedy's personal Cuba hawk at the CIA, confirmed the plot on the record before his death. And the names and pseudonyms of known assassins and hitmen turn up in Bobby Kennedy's own office logs at the Kennedy Library. Garry Wills, who wrote with such contempt of Hersh's book in the *New York Review of Books*, might have had the grace to allow that these more recent findings amplify his own earlier ones.

Having made or bought the friendship of mobsters like Sam Giancana and Johnny Rosselli, the Kennedys seem to have acquired quite a taste for the quick fix of murder. How closely this was related to their simultaneous pursuit of sexual thrill and cheap glamour is good material for speculation. (That there was some connection is hard to doubt; Kennedy's best-documented affair was with Judith Campbell Exner, who was simultaneously entwined with the mafia chief Sam Giancana, who was himself involved in the attempts to murder Fidel Castro. Ben Bradlee has told us of his horrified astonishment at finding that Ms. Exner knew all of the secret telephone numbers for contacting the president out of hours. And of course Bradlee's status as a locker-room buddy of John Kennedy did nothing to dull the later rage of Nixonites when they found themselves invigilated by the *Washington Post*.) Anyway, orders were sent out from the Kennedy White House

Kennedy and Nixon

that Patrice Lumumba in the Congo, Rafael Trujillo in the Dominican Republic and Ngo Dinh Diem in South Vietnam were, with a bare minimum of deniability, to be taken off the chessboard. In some way, this was rationalized as a demonstration of manly toughness in a dangerous world. Both brothers were addicted to the accusation that anyone who had any scruples was inviting another Munich, and one remembers the enthusiasm of their terrible father for that pact —not because he was pro-Chamberlain so much as because he was pro-Hitler. (Franklin Roosevelt was right in saying that if Joe Kennedy ever got power, he would institute a fascist form of government.) One also remembers what most American liberals have organized themselves to forget, which is the prominence of both Kennedy boys in the inquisitorial campaign of Senator Joseph McCarthy.

I once had a Latin teacher who assured me that if I did what in fact I never did, and applied myself thoroughly to Julius Caesar's *De Bello Gallico* ("Concentrate, Hitchens"), I would discover that most of the great general's lauded victories were the anxious outcome of self-inflicted defeats. Since Caesar relied so heavily on the abortive expedient of partition, I am now sure without checking that this was so. Borrowing explicitly from the Joe McCarthy style, JFK in 1960 ran against Eisenhower and Nixon from the right—accusing them of selling out to Russia by allowing the development of a "missile gap," and impugning them for being soft on Castro. He knew that he was engaged in lies and defamations, and that in both instances the truth was the reverse of what he claimed. He also, as Hersh shows conclusively, used gangster muscle and money to swing two or three key states. Very well, say all the

189

clever spin-artists and sycophants, that's what it takes to get elected. But an unscrupulous campaign doesn't have to undergo much in the way of metamorphosis to evolve into an unscrupulous administration. When it became necessary to tell the truth in order to intimidate Khrushchev, Kennedy authorized his deputy secretary of defense, Roswell Gilpatric, to make a minatory speech asserting America's undoubted nuclear superiority, and its will (that bloody word again) to use it without compunction. (Kennedy reversed his demagogic election claims, also, when it suddenly suited him to say that his Cuba follies had been bequeathed by the Eisenhower-Nixon administration.) And in the meantime, keeping all his options open while he squandered the substance of democracy, he stalled on civil rights and flattered the Dixiecrats and prepared for another test of machismo in Indochina. This astonishing show, and the adoring press coverage that it reaped, was watched open-mouthed by Richard Nixon, whose bent presidency differs from other consequences of Kennedyism mainly in having been unintended. Everything that Nixon learned in 1968 and 1972, from the manipulation of foreign crises to the employment of underworld bagmen to the insinuation of treachery and weakness in high places, he had gleaned from his 1960 defeat.

Here one ought to pay a small debt of honor. Those of us who grew up despising Lyndon Baines Johnson don't have to take back very much. As senator and as president, he was a bully and a lout and an arm-twister, and at least as a senator he confused public and private monies on a heroic scale. But it is impossible to read Michael Beschloss's new book, *Taking Charge: The Johnson White House Tapes*, without experiencing a revisionist pang. For all his gung-ho coarseness—so much deplored by the allegedly more fastidious Kennedy claque—Johnson was revolted by what he termed the "god-damned Murder Incorporated" that his predecessors had been running from Miami. He had, as the missile crisis tapes now reveal, been remarkably sane during that episode of homicidal narcissism. He was also sure that the time was overdue to concede black Americans their natural rights as citizens, and used his coercive power on the Hill to this explicit end: the first time in history that such clout had ever been employed in that way. He threw away much of this gain by pursuing Kennedy's fantasy of standing tall in Indochina (where the military Neanderthals like Curtis LeMay, who had wanted pre-emptive nuclear war over Cuba, were allowed to test their strategic bombing theories on live subjects). He had to be ever watchful of the pro-Kennedy fanatics who refused any deviation from "Jack's" line and who seemed to think, as the partisans of Raul Castro now think, that the proper succession should anoint a brother and not a lowly vice president. But he had genuine, confused misgivings over the wisdom of the Vietnam commitment, and eventually resigned from public life over it. (It's almost touching to scrutinize the late-night conversations between LBJ and that old reactionary shellback senator Richard Russell, and to hear the two of them saying that this Vietnam War sure is a stupid proposition, and that it's high time to recognize "Red China"—except who wants to be called a commie sympathizer not just by Dick Nixon but by Bobby Kennedy?) Yet at least, on his way out, Johnson did leave behind a time bomb that could and should have destroyed Richard Nixon.

Whenever Nixon sought to justify an illegality or an atroc-ity, he did so by envious and bitter reference to the charm-ing Kennedy ability to commit such crimes and get away with them. Jules Witcover's new 1968 campaign journal, *The Year the Dream Died* (another unironic title), is the record of one mainstream reporter and his appalled and belated recogni-tion of the truth. It confirms earlier disclosures by Clark Clif-ford in his memoirs, and by Seymour Hersh in his biography of Kissinger and—indirectly but in detail—by Nixon's chief of staff, H. R. Haldeman, in his posthumous diaries. In plain words, Nixon's direct subordinates went to the South Viet-namese military junta, in the waning days of the Humphrey-Nixon election contest, and told them to sabotage the Paris peace talks and thus the main Humphrey peace plank. Do this, Saigon was told, and the incoming Republican admin-istration will smile on your cause. President Thieu, thus advised by Henry Kissinger and others, pulled out of the negotiations a few days before Americans went to the polls. Johnson's White House, by legally dubious methods of bug-ging, picked up this treasonous traffic. It did not dare make it public, because that would have been to admit to electronic eavesdropping, but it did tell the Nixon people that they had been rumbled. And Johnson warned Nixon several years later, from his Texas ranch, that he personally would release the crucial evidence if Nixon tried to justify his own crimes by reference to Democratic ones. Nixon and Kissinger mean-while kept the war going for four more years, at an excruci-ating cost in the lives of people better than themselves, before scuttling the enterprise on the exact terms offered by the pathetic Hubert Humphrey back in 1968.

It's fascinating, in reading the old and new Watergate tapes, to be able to discern and detect the outlines of this old skeleton. Whenever Nixon and his crew are scared of exposure, they threaten in their turn to go public with what they know about the Kennedys and the Democrats. Jerry Zeifman, chief counsel to the House Judiciary Committee, was visited many times during the Watergate inquiry and browbeaten with exactly this threat of reprisal. To Zeifman's disgust, this tactic was successful with several Democratic luminaries on the committee staff—among them the young Hillary Rodham —and as a result Nixon was able to leave power with the moral equivalent of a plea bargain. One consequence of that period of moral and political leniency, misrepresented by self-pitying Nixonites as a lynching, was that Nixon's estate kept hold of reels and reels of decisive Watergate tapes. Only thanks to Stanley Kutler of the University of Wisconsin, who sued for the release of the tapes and has now edited and annotated them with great panache, do we now have something like a clear record. On the tape for 23 June 1972—the day of the so-called "smoking gun" conversation between Nixon and Haldeman—not only do the two desperate men discuss using the CIA to cut off the FBI investigation of the burglary, but Nixon is heard clearly to say:

> When you get in these people, say, "Look, the problem is that this will open the whole, the whole Bay of Pigs thing, and the president just feels that"—without going into the details—don't, don't lie to them to the extent to say there is no involvement, but just say this is sort of a comedy of errors, bizarre, without getting into it—"The president's belief is that this is going to open the whole Bay of Pigs thing up again."

It was the politicization of one state police agency, in the effort to suborn and corrupt another one, that in the end meant Nixon had to go. We used to have to guess at what dread secret from Camelot he used in his extremity. At least now our guess can be an educated one.

In *Pillar of Fire*, the second volume of Taylor Branch's biography of Martin Luther King, we learn more about the extreme domestic cowardice that was the domestic counterpart to the Kennedys' overseas imperial bluster. After the bombing of a black church in Birmingham, Alabama, and the death of four small girls, JFK temporized like mad in the face of racism and intimidation. In a meeting with Birmingham's white leadership he denounced the Student Nonviolent Coordinating Committee (SNCC) and echoed the claim that they were "sons of bitches." He then sent a former West Point football coach as a non-binding mediator between the bombers and the bombed before declaring that, really, he could do no more.

King never really forgave him for this and other capitulations. He watched the president's funeral on television in a hotel room and, as the cameras showed Jackie sinking to her knees before the coffin, he was heard to remark: "Look at her. Sucking him off one last time." I say "heard to remark" because this very coarse—and very inapposite and inaccurate—crack was picked up by the FBI men who were maintaining their surveillance of an official enemy. They lost no time in retelling the tale where it would do most harm.

I had almost finished writing this on the Martin Luther King holiday, the day after which Bill Clinton's own vulgar and exploiting and finally trivial past almost caught up with him. It's in reading Branch's biography of King that one may still lay hold of a worthwhile strand in the narrative. While a succession of insecure and dishonest statesmen committed high crimes and misdemeanors at home and abroad, always justifying themselves by a fear of being thought weak, or by a terror of being undercut by a rival, or by simple fear of the contents of J. Edgar Hoover's private dossiers, King rescued the language from their clotted and conspiratorial style and made three ringing points. America had a bill coming due, to the descendants of its slaves, which it was morally obliged to redeem. There was unlikely to be domestic tranquility, or the timely redemption of that bill, if a grossly expensive war of aggression was being prosecuted with a campaign of lies. And nuclear warfare, or the threat of it, was unpardonable because it would be "suicide and genocide at the same time." For these views he went to jail in JFK's New Frontier, had his telephone tapped by Bobby Kennedy, and was blackmailed by the head of the FBI in a crude attempt to force him to commit suicide. What, then, is the linkage between the private life of politicians and their public examples? There was certainly more on the King tapes than verbal obscenity. There is a great deal of foul-mouth talk on the Watergate tapes, much of it scabrously antisemitic, but no sex. The Clinton tapes are of interest for serious purposes not because of the lipstick stains but because of the possible use of lipstick subsidy (that of Revlon, on whose board sits Vernon Jordan) to procure hush money and soft jobs for friendly witnesses past and present. To take the two polar opposites, then, there is no discernible connection between King's lecherous indiscretions and his public persona, whereas there is at least a suggestive crossover between Kennedy's mobbed-up sex life and his thuggish foreign policy. Recall that Ian Fleming was one of his favorite authors. Bill Clinton has shown himself promiscuous about things like campaign finance and also about things like women met in a hurry along the trail. The two things may bear only an allegorical relationship. A baffled *New York Times* reporter noted from the heartland in the last days of January: "Time and again, people invoked the widespread reports of former President John F. Kennedy's infidelities as evidence that sexual conduct had little to do with leadership capabilities." This, as authors as different as Hersh and Wills have shown apparently in vain, is to get the personal and the political as confused as it is possible for them to be.

Letters

19 March 1998

Christopher Hitchens writes in the latest recycling of his anti-Kennedy rants that it was William Manchester on whom Jacqueline Kennedy planted the Camelot metaphor. This is typical both of Hitchens's hopeless ignorance of American affairs and of his preference for rant over fact. The rest of us think that Mrs. Kennedy was planting the Camelot idea on Theodore H. White. As for those "bow-tied American scholars" by whom, Hitchens proclaims, " 'Camelot' is always cited without a breath of irony," I would suggest that, if Hitchens could stop ranting long enough to read anything, he might look at the derision cast on the Camelot idea on pages 406–7 of the bow-tied *Cycles of American History*, including the remark that Camelot was hardly "a place known for marital fidelity." Or perhaps Hitchens doesn't get irony.

Hitchens must be the only journalist more gullible than Seymour Hersh, whose dreadful book he cites respectfully, as if Hersh's fantasies had any more than an accidental connection with reality. Seymour Hersh, who on page 123 of *The Dark Side of Camelot* has Lyndon Johnson, himself not a man known for marital fidelity, using Kennedy's sexual vagaries to blackmail his way onto the Democratic ticket in 1960—and then on page 406 about to be dropped from the 1964 ticket, his blackmail power evidently expiring, to make way for Robert Kennedy (though, as any schoolchild should know, if Hersh and Hitchens don't, the American Constitution requires the president and vice president to be from different states, and both Kennedys were then from Massachusetts)? Seymour Hersh, whose notion that the mobster Sam Giancana was the political boss of Chicago is an insult to the memory of Mayor Richard Daley? Seymour Hersh, who on page 4 has Kennedy sending money to the mob and on page 140 has the mob sending money to Kennedy without any explanation as to why either needed money from the other? Seymour Hersh, who fell for the forged Marilyn Monroe documents even though they had zip codes years before zip codes were invented? Christopher Hitchens is alone (except for Hersh) as a true believer in *The Dark Side of Camelot*.

I won't go into all Hitchens's fumbles, but one persisting theme in his anti-Kennedy rants is the systematic exoneration of President Eisenhower and his administration. You would not gather it from his piece, but it was the Eisenhower administration, not the Kennedy administration, that recruited mobsters to assassinate Castro. It was the Eisenhower administration, not the Kennedy administration, that contemplated the assassination of Lumumba in the Congo (he was killed by the Tshombe crowd a few days after Kennedy assumed office). It was the Eisenhower administration that planned the Bay of Pigs, and it was Ike himself who, in their last meeting before the inauguration, urged Kennedy to go full speed ahead.

Hitchens goes on about "the sick Kennedy obsession with Cuba." If Cuba was Kennedy's obsession, the Soviet nuclear missiles provided him with the best possible pretext for invading the country and smashing Castro forever. But Robert Kennedy led the fight against a sneak attack, and John Kennedy, overruling the joint chiefs of staff, made the decision against a military response. A year after the missile crisis, Kennedy was even exploring through Ambassador William Attwood (U.S.) and Ambassador Carlos Lechuga (Cuba), as well as through Jean Daniel of *Le Nouvel Observateur*, the possibility of normalizing relations with Cuba. Some sick obsession!

Let us rather mourn a really sick obsession—Christopher Hitchens's obsession with John F. Kennedy.

Arthur Schlesinger Jr.
New York

Christopher Hitchens writes: In my article I gave an imaginary instance, drawn from the imaginative work of Arthur Schlesinger, of the means by which an apologist for JFK might have proved that, had "He" lived, the Bay of Pigs invasion would not have taken place. Some readers may have found this counterfactual exercise too strenuous, or too cynical. But here, prompt upon its hour, is a letter from Pierre Salinger in the *Nation* of 16 February:

> You will remember that I was President Kennedy's press secretary. Five days before he was assassinated, he had a meeting at the White House with a French journalist, Jean Daniel, now editor of France's most important news magazine, *Le Nouvel Observateur*. During the meeting, Kennedy found out that Daniel was on his way to Havana for an interview with Fidel Castro. Kennedy asked Daniel to tell Castro that he was now ready to negotiate normal relations with Cuba and drop the embargo. Daniel was in a meeting with Castro when the phone rang and Castro discovered that Kennedy had been assassinated.
>
> If Kennedy had lived, I am confident he would have negotiated that agreement and dropped the embargo, because he was

upset with the way the Soviet Union was playing a strong role in Cuba and Latin America. Cuba would be a different country now and Castro would not be in power anymore.

There have since been seven other presidents, three of them Democrats, who have failed to lift the embargo. In the case of the first post–Cold War Democrat, who ran against George Bush from the right on the issue of Cuba—just as Kennedy did against Eisenhower—the embargo has been extended to include legally dubious sanctions even on third countries trading with Havana.

Mr. Salinger's choice of the word "upset" to describe his hero's view of Cuba and the former Soviet Union is a collector's item for those of us who study the mania of the JFK cult, and the imperviousness of its remaining devotees.

So no wonder that Arthur Schlesinger Jr., in dreaming the same dream, limits himself to the feeble word "exploring." As he shows even in the supposedly saving citation from his own book, euphemism is a necessity for the Kennedy fan. I'm mainly struck by what he does not contest—the Judith Campbell Exner/mob connection; the subversion of Guyana; the bugging of Martin Luther King; the timing of a murder plot to coincide with the Bay of Pigs; the killings of Diem in Saigon and Trujillo in the Dominican Republic. On these and other matters he won't come out to play anymore.

Future historians will no doubt be grateful for the information that the Bay of Pigs invasion, actually executed by Kennedy, was "planned" by the Eisenhower administration. I emphasized that myself, adding for the sake of the record that Kennedy fought an election on the claim—which he knew to be a lie—that Eisenhower and Nixon had gone soft on Castro. If Kennedy had ordered a nuclear strike, Schlesinger's last fawning words would doubtless have been that it was Eisenhower who built the bombs and missiles in the first place.

The fact that Eisenhower and Nixon also flirted with the mafia and would probably have killed Lumumba does not in the least undermine the point of my article, which almost pedantically stressed the permanent element of "bipartisanship" in these matters. It's contemptible of Schlesinger to seek apology for the state crimes of his patrons with the excuse that "everyone does it," just as it's laughable of him, having made a career out of scraping acquaintance with the divine Kennedy boys, to accuse me of being the obsessed one.

Seymour Hersh can stick up for himself, but I did point out that he'd been briefly gulled by a false Monroe trail before he recovered his balance. As to whether Giancana or Daley was the *capo de tutti capi* in Chicago, I leave it to Schlesinger's expertise.

I abase myself for confusing Pierre Schlesinger and Arthur Salinger Jr., just as I'm sorry to have mixed up Theodore Manchester with William White. But the Kennedy hydra sometimes has that hypnotic effect, even as its many stumps are serially cauterized by the slow emergence of true record.

---

2 April 1998

After all these years, Arthur Schlesinger Jr. might be wise to refrain from discussions of the Bay of Pigs fiasco. In 1961 I attended the Harvard International Seminar, under the aegis of Henry Kissinger. One July evening, Schlesinger talked informally about the policies of the Kennedy administration. The French participant in the seminar asked politely: "Would you care to say something about the Bay of Pigs?" Tersely, Schlesinger replied: "No, because the United States was in no way involved." When we broke off for coffee, the Frenchman complained to Kissinger that, while of course lies sometimes had to be told for public purposes, there was no point in repeating such lies on an off-the-record occasion with people sitting on the lawn. Kissinger said: "I don't think you quite understand what it's like to live in a Great Power." It was, I felt, quite a good riposte, but not exactly a contribution to history.

Mervyn Jones
London SW1

---

16 April 1998
Neither Henry Kissinger nor I have any recollection of the remarks attributed to us by Mervyn Jones. Nor do they make any sense. They lack even surface plausibility. Why, three months after the Bay of Pigs, by which time everyone knew of the CIA role, would I deny that the United States was in any way involved? (I might add that I had strongly opposed the operation.) Why would Henry Kissinger, then a young Harvard don with no experience as a government official, talk as if he were a world-weary national security adviser? The next time Mervyn Jones goes around attributing statements allegedly made nearly forty years ago, he should try to make them credible.

Arthur Schlesinger Jr.
New York

21 May 1998

Arthur Schlesinger insists that neither he nor Henry Kissinger has "any recollection" of that evening at the Harvard International Seminar. How I wish I could have overheard the ponderous discussion during which these two men, both congested by a lifetime of apologetics, agreed on this now classic line of defense. "Statements allegedly made nearly forty years ago" cannot be expected to be remembered by such busy fellows, who are not too busy to recall with crystalline clarity that they would certainly have denied making them. So it goes. I sympathize with Schlesinger almost as much as with Mervyn Jones in this instance, because the task of keeping pace with his own protean story is indeed a daunting one. It defeats even Schlesinger. Your readers ought to get hold of Noam Chomsky's short but annihilating book *Rethinking Camelot* (1993) and read pages 105 to 125. By the time they have read the multiple and incompatible versions of Schlesinger's "stand" on Vietnam, and seen how it has fluctuated over the years, they will have learned to appreciate that the job of the court historian, so subject to abrupt changes in fashion, is a queasy-making one at best. Mastering old Arthur's shifty positions on Cuba is a simple matter by comparison, though Mervyn Jones should probably not have attempted it merely by relying on the evidence of his own ears and eyes. Who does he think he is—a witness? I have never seen any attempt by Schlesinger to reply to Chomsky's close reading of his hilariously sinuous record, but I am pleased to learn that your correspondence columns are still open.

Christopher Hitchens
Berkeley, California

Acts of Violence in Grosvenor Square

On 1968

1998

I WAS JUST BEGINNING to write about 1968 when I learned of the death in New Orleans of Ron Ridenhour, the GI who exposed the massacre at My Lai. He was only 52, which means that he was in his early twenties when, as a helicopter gunner in the area, he learned of the murder of nearly 660 Vietnamese civilians. This was not some panicky collateral damage fire-fight: the men of Charlie Company took a long time to dishonor and dismember the women, round up and dispatch the children and make the rest of the villagers lie down in ditches while they walked up and down shooting them. Not one of the allegedly "searing" films about the war—not *Apocalypse Now*, not *Full Metal Jacket* or *Platoon*—has dared to show anything remotely like the truth of this and many other similar episodes, more evocative of Poland or Ukraine in 1941. And the thing of it was, as Ron pointed out, that it was "an act of policy, not an individual aberration. Above My Lai that day were helicopters filled with the entire command staff of the brigade, division and task force."

A few weeks ago, at the Vietnam Veterans Memorial in Washington, DC, the state finally got round to recognizing the only physical hero of the story, a decent guy named Hugh

Thompson who saw what was going on, landed his helicopter between Lieutenant Calley's killing squads and the remnant of the inhabitants, called for back-up and drew his sidearm. His citation had taken thirty years to come through. It was intended as part of the famous healing process which never seems quite to achieve closure.

Ron wasn't interested in any stupid healing process. He wanted justice to be done, and it never was. A single especially befouled culprit, the above mentioned Calley, was eventually court-martialed and served a brief period of house arrest before being exonerated by Nixon. The superiors, both immediate and remote, got clean away. A canny young military lawyer near the scene, Colin Powell by name, founded a lifelong reputation for promise and initiative by arranging to have the papers mixed up at the office of the judge advocate general.

I once asked Ron Ridenhour what had led him to risk everything by compiling his own report on the extermination at My Lai and sending it to Congress. He told me that, poor white boy as he was (he left school at fourteen and was drafted without protest), he had been in basic training when, in the hut one night, a group of good ol' boys had decided to have some fun with the only black soldier in the detail. The scheme was to castrate him. Nobody was more astonished than Ron to hear his own voice coming across the darkened bunks. " 'If you want to get to him, you've got to come through me.' I'd've been dead if I hadn't been white and poor like them, but they gave up." Later, when his troopship called in at Hawaii en route for Saigon, he went ashore and bought a book about Vietnam by the late Bernard Fall. "Shit, this is what I'm getting into."

A revolutionary moment requires both extraordinary times and extraordinary people, and Ron Ridenhour, despite his laconic attitude, was one of the latter. He wouldn't have denied, however, that there was "something in the air" in those days. It was getting to the point where you couldn't shove black people around so easily, or invade any country that took your fancy. There were people who wouldn't take it, and even people in the press and in the academy who were prepared to make an issue of that. (Though this can be overestimated: it took more than a year for the My Lai story to get into print—in the Cleveland *Plain Dealer*.) Nonetheless, the climacteric that was 1968 had been building for some time. What fused it into critical mass, and provided its most indelible slogans and imagery, was undoubtedly the correspondence between the civil rights and antiwar movements, both of them American and both of them therefore, in a time when "global village" was a new cliché, universal in scope and appeal and reach.

Something has to be done to rescue that time from the obfuscations that have descended over it and to fend off the sneers and jeers that now attach so easily. Some people, of course, take a kind of pleasure in repudiating their own past. Some, whether they wish to or not, live long enough to become negations or caricatures. Or indeed partial confirmations: I am thinking of Lionel Jospin, now chief minister of France and in those days a member of an unusually dogmatic trotskiant group; a groupuscule, indeed, and perhaps an excellent school for the inflexible later canons of neoliberalism. Robert Lowell once said that he was glad not to have been a revolutionary when young, because it prevented him from

becoming a reactionary bore in his old age. I see the point:
the fact remains that in midlife and in 1968 he acted eloquently and well, as a citizen of the republic of Emerson and Whitman should when the state is intoxicated with injustice and
war. Retrospectives which emphasize flowers, beads, dope
and simplistic anarchism tend to leave him out, as they also
omit the Ron Ridenhours.

I didn't really lift a finger to stop the colonial bloodbath in
Vietnam which was, let it never be forgotten, prosecuted by
liberal Democrats and robotically supported by an Old Labour government. I *did* give some blood for the Vietcong, at
a Blackfriars monastery which had been swept into enthusiasm by the mood of the time. ("Brother, your blood group
is a rare AB. Do you think you might possibly make it two
pints?" "No.") I invited Eduardo Mondlane, the soon to be assassinated leader of the rebels in Mozambique, to my rooms,
and helped organize a public meeting where he hailed the
Vietnamese revolution for presaging the defeat of Salazar-
ism in both Africa and Portugal, which indeed it did. I undertook a little work in helping American draft resisters in Oxford, thereby earning my first but not last file held by creepy
people nobody had voted for. I went out with the brush and
the poster paint. And I took part in a good-sized punch-up
outside the American Embassy in London, thus disproving
(as a pamphlet of the time pointed out) Lady Bracknell's
piercing words in *The Importance of Being Earnest*: "Fortunately,
in England at any rate, education produces no effect what-
soever. If it did, it would prove a serious danger to the upper
classes, and probably lead to acts of violence in Grosvenor
Square."

The My Lai massacre had taken place the day before: we weren't to know that, but it did seem very important to us that, half a world away, the Vietnamese might get to hear about this riot and somehow, I don't know, take heart. Mike Rosen, who was arrested and roughed up along with one or two other people who might be embarrassed if I printed their names today, wrote a rather fine agitprop poem making this simple point. It was a beautiful spring day and as one looked up from the big, heaving, horse-battered, clod-throwing tussle around the Roosevelt memorial one could see the reflection of binoculars and spyglasses as various members of the ruling class, foregathered on the roofs of North Audley Street, strove to catch the mood of the nation's supposedly insurgent youth. The editor of the *Daily Telegraph* the next morning published some sort of "I was there" piece in which he got all the slogans wrong, perhaps from listening through an ear trumpet. One of the fun things that year was to monitor the hopeless efforts of a rattled establishment to keep up. At Oxford the authorities had a solemn discussion about covering the medieval cobbles with tarmac, lest there be *a nuit des barricades*, and in the PPE examination papers an anxious and "with-it" question asked for elucidation of the sage "Herbert Maracuse." That was good for a chuckle. But it wasn't all doddering and quavering: Home Secretary Callaghan, that red-faced beadle, knew his stern duty. All the Fleet Street rags, the day after Grosvenor Square, printed a leering pic of a girl demonstrator in the grip of several stout bobbies, her skirt round her waist while one especially beefy constable administered a spanking. (For all I know, this is one of the many triggers that may have set Paul Johnson off.)

Tariq Ali was the moving spirit of that rally, and this book —which includes the spanking picture—brings it all back with exquisite vividness.* It's hard to recall what a hate figure he was in those days. I had a friend, a mustachioed Parsee Marxist named Jairus Banaji, who was forever getting picked up and smacked around by the forces of law and order just for the sake of appearances, as you might say. But then, 1968 was also the year when, also to the gloat and awe and wonder of the Tory press, London dockers marched to Westminster in support of Enoch Powell. Seeing the Kenyan high commissioner entering the precincts of Parliament, they bellowed "Go back to Jamaica," and were much admired in the suburbs for their John Bull spirit. The Communist Party, which was strong on the docks in those times and had the famous Jack Dash as its hate figure, took the day off and later tried to organize a conciliatory East End meeting addressed by the concerned priesthood. But this is to get ahead of the story somewhat.

Like most such years, 1968 began a few months early. Premonitory rumbles, in my memory, include the American-inspired military coup in Greece on 21 April 1967, which seemed to challenge the endlessly reiterated notion of reliable ideological convergence between Western European political forces (and also allowed us a second look at the "defensive posture" of NATO). One would have to add the hunting

---

* *1968: Marching in the Streets* by Tariq Ali and Susan Watkins (Bloomsbury, 1998). This piece also mentions *The Beginning of the End: France, May 1968* by Tom Nairn and Angelo Quattrocchi (Verso, 1998) and *The Love Germ* by Jill Neville (Verso, 1998).

down, by CIA men and the agents of a brutal dictatorship, of Che Guevara in Bolivia in October 1967, in which the local Communist Party also played a complaisant part. And, in quite another key, I recall the death at about that time of Isaac Deutscher, who had done so much in the early years of the teach-in movement to remind the young that "the end of ideology" was itself an ideological construct, and that there still existed factors such as class and power. (When he spoke at the main event in Berkeley, the communists tried to keep his appearance until last and then cut off the microphone.)

There's a kaleidoscopic feel to the pages of the Ali-Watkins volume. Turn the pages in a hurry and you go from the Tet offensive in Vietnam to the strikes in Poland to the murder of Dr. King and the ghetto insurrection, getting no time to take breath for les événements in France and the shooting of Robert Kennedy. Then comes the invasion of Czechoslovakia, the drama in the streets at the Chicago Democratic Convention, the butchery at the Mexico Olympics and the brave (now seemingly almost quixotic) We Shall Overcome moments of the first citizens' movement in Ulster. Some of these produced imperishable vignettes: microcosmic glimpses that were better recollected in tranquility. I remember Terry Barrett, a Tilbury docker, giving a brilliant rasping reply to the racists from a May Day platform, and the workers at the Berliet plant outside Paris rearranging the letters of their company logo to read Liberté, and Mayor Daley being lip-read by the cameras as he shouted across the convention floor at the composed, dignified figure of Senator Abraham Ribicoff: "Fuck you, you Jew son of a bitch. Fuck you. Go home." I also remember Dr. Frantisek Kriegel, the only member of the Czechoslovak leadership who refused to sign the humiliating post-invasion document. He was a veteran of the International Brigades, the Chinese revolution and the wartime resistance, and is often left out of the record (including, though not for this reason, of the Ali-Watkins book) because he put the signers to shame and also because he was attempting to save the honor of socialism.

Not entirely with hindsight, one can now identify the significance of 1968 as being perhaps the critical year in that Death of Communism that is now such a commonplace. Some of my best friends in those days, as well as some of my worst enemies, were members of the Communist Party. It was very striking to be able to observe, in both cases, to what a huge extent a year of crisis and opportunity exposed them to awkwardness, put them on the defensive, found them stammering and unprepared. Their international fraternity of parties had become so contorted and congested by past lies and compromises and reversals that they yearned mainly for a quiet life. Thus: the spring developments in Prague could not be accepted in their entirety even by the reform supporters, because they contained a frontal challenge to the leading role of the party. But the prospect of a Warsaw Pact fraternal intervention would compromise at one stroke the careful edifice of peace campaigns and broad fronts through which the party had ingratiatingly tried, with some success, to keep in with the Labour left and the trade-union apparat. I used to read the *Morning Star* (which had changed its name from the *Daily Worker* to become, as one comrade put it, a version of the *Daily Employee*) attentively. The Vietnam Solidarity Campaign was denounced, because the Soviet Union ostensibly put its faith in the good offices of U Thant. Enoch Powell was to be challenged by a bureaucratic fiat: prosecution under the incitement clause of the Race Relations Act. The Jew-baiting of the Polish authorities in the anti-Zionist purge in Warsaw in March 1968 was to be discussed only in a whisper. Most revealing of all, the stony and mediocre nomenklatura of the French Communist Party (those "crapules staliniennes," as Daniel Cohn-Bendit invigoratingly termed them) exerted their entire negative weight in order to abort the anti-Gaullist upheaval in France.

We know now what we knew then: the Soviet Union had given the PCF a direct instruction to become "the party of order." In a recent edition of the Paris magazine *L'Événement du jeudi*, one can read the testimony of Yuri Dobrynin, former fixer at the Soviet Embassy in Paris, who recalls in round terms: "La ligne dictée par Moscou était précise: pas toucher à de Gaulle." Thus, when the general returned mid-rebellion from a fraternal visit to Ceausescu's Romania, and disappeared to Germany to consult with his military caste and agreed to release the Algerian war criminals Raoul Salan and Jacques Soustelle as part of the deal, he had a *porte-parole* from the Kremlin in his pocket. The Fifth Republic with its cynical and fluctuating anti-Americanism didn't have long to run in fact, but Georges Marchais and Jacques Duclos and the others weren't to know that, any more than they did when they became the party of order once more and supported the "normalization" of Czechoslovakia a few months later. Somewhere between those two moments, the remaining breath fled the body of monolithic communism, which continued to decompose steadily in ways that some soixante-huitards found relatively easy to follow. (I was to have arguments with truly believing communists only once more, among certain American pro-Sandinistas in the late 1980s, but by then it was like dealing with the squeaks emitted long ago from a dead planet. The real laugh came when dealing with the neo-conservatives, who needed the illusion of an unsleeping and keenly ideological foe.)

Angelo Quattrocchi and Tom Nairn's book *The Beginning of the End*, which I read when it first came out, is more interesting now than it was then. It's rather sporting of the current Nairn to allow it to be reprinted. At the time, it seemed to those of us in the old International Socialists—who dismissed it scornfully as "a long poem"—to be the sentimentalization of a romantic moment; an almost hedonistic celebration of youth culture and spontaneity. (At the expense, naturally, of the sterner and more demanding task of educating and equipping the working classes to see through the illusions of Stalinism and social democracy, which I must say I still jolly well wish they had done.) There is an interesting change in the text, however. I am certain, without checking, that the original paperback had on its title page one of those mini-feuilletons which Robert Escarpit used to contribute, box-sized, to the front page of *Le Monde*. On this exciting occasion, slightly borrowing from the imagery of the old specter and the old mole, he had imagined the think tank and dividend-drawing classes discussing the new and virulent infection; inquiring above all whether it might spread.

The book would obviously be more stale and depressing if this spirited but ephemeral contemporaneous thought had been left in. As it is, one winces to scan the Nairn-Quattrocchi afterword, the last two paragraphs of which read:

> Paradoxically, real inevitability has emerged only after the material century of its triumph, in the final product of its machines: the new society alive within it, invisible yesterday, visible everywhere today, the young negation of its nature.
>
> The anarchism of 1871 looked backward to a pre-capitalist past, doomed to defeat; the anarchism of 1968 looks forward to the future society almost within our grasp, certain of success.

Well no, actually, I don't think so. Although it is true that a certain esprit de soixante-huit survived the year of its birth, and had its final—and not least honorable—moments during the May days in Lisbon after the fall of fascism in 1974, there is no red thread of Ariadne, to paraphrase Clara Zetkin on Rosa Luxemburg, to be followed between the Sorbonne commune and the digital and cybernetic age. We are left to contemplate mainly the ironies of history—Deutscher's preferred trope—and the subtle, ironic, even surreptitious influences of language. *The Love Germ*, Jill Neville's rough little diamond of a novel, is a case in point. (It's as bitter to think of her early death as it is of Ron Ridenhour's.) As the mistress of the above Angelo Quattrocchi in the Latin Quarter in 1968, this tough and beautiful and brave woman was well placed to record the festival of the oppressed, with all its accompaniment of erotic and imaginative charge. She was also in a good/bad position to observe the way that male militants treated the girls' auxiliary, and thus to prefigure the imminent revival of feminism, which essentially began that year for those reasons. By an amazing chance, she chose the metaphor of sexually transmitted disease as the bonding element in a narrative of interpenetration. Her book reads more strongly now than that of her ex-lover, precisely because it subliminally knows that there may be a price to be paid for hedonism and narcissism. Jill did not for an instant echo those sadistic authorities of the restored moral order, who said (and say) that AIDS was God's verdict. But she knew that there was more to politics, and to love, than doing your own thing.

So, in a very different way, did W. H. Auden, who, a few days after the Soviet invasion of Czechoslovakia, wrote a short poem entitled "August 1968":

> The Ogre does what ogres can
> Deeds quite impossible for Man,
> But one prize is beyond his reach,
> The Ogre cannot master Speech:
> About a subjugated plain,
> Among its desperate and slain,
> The Ogre stalks with hands on hips,
> While drivel gushes from his lips.

The term Velvet Revolution, used to describe the humbling of secular power in Prague in 1989, may sound as vague and feel-good as the mantra of any "human be-in" from the Bay Area ragtags of the Summer of Love. But it conceals, within its irritating geniality and inclusiveness, the signal and salient fact that satirists and poets and subversive wordsmiths had simply, bloodlessly worn down the monster of what Ernst Fischer called *Panzercommunismus*. Auden was more audaciously prescient than he'd realized. The dank, gruesome regime of the *langue de bois*, of peace-loving forces and progressive elements and internal affairs, gave way before wit and music and understatement—just as if Allen Ginsberg had fulfilled his dream of levitating the Pentagon. To the extent that 1968 metamorphosed into 1989, then, it carried its point. But no date will ever mark history's high tide.

In a work-camp of enthusiasts which I attended in Cuba that summer, where the ideological level was not as low as some of you may think, there was a sort of dress rehearsal when the Warsaw Pact went grinding into Czechoslovakia. All the conventional arguments, about Great Power tyranny and the "socialist camp," or about self-determination v. "giving ammunition to the enemy," were gone over as a matter of course. Somewhere in there, but waiting for an idiom in which to be unambivalently uttered, was an expression, or affirmation, of human and civil rights as a good thing in themselves. Easy enough, you say, and of course I'm with you all the way, but neither side in the Cold War had proved, or ever proved, capable of stating such a principle in practice. Double standards can waste an awful lot of time. Anyway, I found the exact phrase for it when I met Adam Michnik, one of the Polish sixty-eighters, a few years later. "After all, like socialism, the words freedom and democracy have been discredited by governments and parties. But we do not abandon them for this reason. The real struggle, for us, is for citizens to cease being the property of the state."

Good man, I thought at the time, having then no idea that Michnik would easily outlive Stalinism and go on to be the leading Polish critic of clerical fascism, brute nationalism and all the other mental rubbish of post-1989. Now let's see if we can't stop citizens being anybody's property, or anyone's disposable resource, or nuclear statistic. In order for that to occur, as William Morris put it in A Dream of John Ball, people will have to cogitate how it comes that they so often fight for something and lose, or think they have won, only to get another thing, and leave to others the task of fighting for the same thing under another name.

Diary
The "Almanach de Gotha"
1998

I N HIS MEMOIRS, Claud Cockburn wrote about the occasional charm of things being just the way they're supposed to be. Thus, the first time he went on the Orient Express he met a tempestuous woman who was later arrested for espionage; the first time he interviewed a politician he was told a breathtaking lie in the first five minutes; the first time he entered an Irish castle a fine large pig ran squealing across the main hall. Sometime in the 1970s, I was taken to one of those nightclubs in Berkeley Square, and there ran into Jonathan Guinness and his party. Introductions were effected; I didn't catch all the names and said to the small dark man who still had hold of my hand: "Sorry, did you say you were Paul from Romania?" He released the mitt and drew himself up somewhat. "Paul of Romania." I burbled something about it being dreadfully noisy in here, he unbent a little and produced from his inside pocket an enticing brochure about real estate in the Seychelles.

Well, I mean to say, a sprig of Balkan royalty nightclubbing with a sideline in real estate...I sent a postcard to Claud the next day. And now I look up my friend in the new reborn and revived edition of the *Almanach de Gotha*. Romania has less than two pages devoted to its royal house, which is rather modest considering that His Majesty King Michael I of Romania serves as chairman of the Comité de Patronage of the Société des Amis de l'*Almanach de Gotha* 1998. From these pages I learn that Michael, or Mihai, was born to King Carol in 1921 and "reigned, firstly," from 1927 to 1930, or in other words between the ages of six and nine. He was then made crown prince and grand voivode of Alba Julia, before becoming sovereign again between 1940 and 1947. He now lives in Switzerland. He has several daughters, among them Princess Maria, whose address is listed as that of her husband, the financial analyst Casimir Mystkowski of New Rochelle, NY. But there are no sons or brothers or crown princes in the lineage. Could it be that my chance acquaintance was that even finer specimen of Cockburnian central casting—an impostor? Romania and mythomania are close kin, as Dorothy Parker knew when she wrote:

> Oh, life is a glorious cycle of song
> A medley of extemporanea;
> And love is a thing that can never go wrong;
> And I am Marie of Romania.

One of the prime purposes of the old *Almanach* was precisely to clear up the question of who was who, and in what order of precedence. The issue more than once became critical. On 20 October 1807 the Emperor Napoleon, feeling even more upwardly mobile than was customary, wrote a stiff note to his foreign minister, de Champagny.

> This year's *Almanach de Gotha* is badly done. I protest. There should be more of the French nobility I have created and less of the German Princes who are no longer sovereign. Furthermore,

the Imperial Family of Bonaparte should appear before all other royal dynasties, and let it be clear that we and *not* the Bourbons are the House of France. Summon the Minister of the Interior of Gotha at once so that I personally may order these changes.

The next year, the *Almanach* serenely carried two versions, one entitled "Edition for France—at his Imperial Majesty's Request" and the second "*The Gotha*—Correct in All Detail." This stratagem was more than a temporary solution, as Lord Lambton emphasizes in his history of the Mountbatten family. "The newly mediatized families were allowed into the second section of the *Almanach de Gotha*, while the unmediatized withered in the third. The Bonapartes, despite their overthrow, were placed in the second section of this royal bible. How could they not be? Napoleon had married a member of the Hapsburg family."

A note may be necessary here on "mediatization," which applies to the second-order families of the Holy Roman Empire and of its successor states. "An 'immediate' fief was held by feudal tenure directly from the emperor, with no intervening superior lord. When such a fief was placed under the authority of a feudal superior other than the emperor and that superior was himself a tenant within the empire, this fief was thereby 'mediatized.' " The distinction was felt most keenly in Germany, which in its form between the 1871 empire and the Weimar Republic was an association of sovereign states, grand duchies, duchies and principalities. At the May 1913 wedding of Princess Victoria of Prussia to Prince Ernst August of Hanover, it mattered like anything that a specially composed waltz was reserved for guests listed in *Gotha* Part One, holding the rank of royal highness or higher. Feverish courtiers flapped through the book as the orchestra struck up. You laugh, perhaps. Possibly you scoff. But this Saxe-Coburg-Gotha racket is the origin of our own dear house of Battenberg-Windsor, which had a momentous "King and Country" row with its German cousins the following year. And don't I recall a tiny fuss only a little while ago, about the removal of the title HRH from one delinquent Windsor by marriage? "The wires of democracy cannot take too high a social voltage," Leon Trotsky wrote in *The German Puzzle* in 1932, as Weimar was collapsing. "Such are, however, the voltages of our time. The worthy *Almanach de Gotha* once had trouble in defining Russia's political system, which combined popular representation and an autocratic tsar." One of those new-old dilemmas, affecting any modern nation with an ancien régime. Nancy Mitford was premature in saying: "An aristocracy in a republic is like a chicken whose head has been cut off: it may run about in a lively way, but in fact it is dead." We shall see.

The Duchy of Saxe-Coburg-Gotha was overrun by the Red Army in 1944 and the *Almanach* went into what is technically known as abeyance. Its reappearance, in a rather tackily bound edition with microscopic computer-generated print, is one of the unintended consequences of a reunified Germany. An accompanying press release gurgles excitedly of the relevance and up-to-dateness of it all, and speaks of an *Almanach* website as well as the fact that almost half the member states of the EU have a reigning royal house. But this sales talk obscures the true pleasure of the text, which lies in its evocation of the world of Saki and Rudolf Rassendyll and Fouché d'Otrante and Fratting und Pullitz and (my darling among the entries) Sayn-Wittgenstein-Sayn, not by any means to be confused with Sayn-Wittgenstein-Berleburg. Saki was especially good on this world, in both taking it seriously and not seriously. The dialogue between Reginald and the duchess in *Reginald at the Theatre*, for instance:

> There are certain fixed rules that one observes for one's own comfort. For instance, never be flippantly rude to any inoffensive, gray-bearded stranger that you may meet in pine-forests or hotel smoking-rooms on the Continent. It always turns out to be the king of Sweden.

And later:

> "Which reminds me of the man I read about in some sacred book who was given a choice of what he most desired. And because he didn't ask for titles and honors and dignities, but only for immense wealth, these other things came to him also."
>
> "I am sure you didn't read about him in any sacred book."
>
> "Yes, I fancy you will find him in *Debrett*."

King Juan Carlos of Spain is the other co-sponsor of the Comité de Patronage. He is generally accounted the best of the Bourbons. In the same Prado where hang the Goya portraits of his dubious ancestors, you may go and view the *Caprichos*. Number 39 of this sequence has a smirking jackass, pointing proudly with his hoof at two pages of a family album. There, in silhouette, Goya has etched in a line of jackass forebears. "Hasta su abuelo" says the title—"as far back as his grandfather." (Goya invariably renders donkeys and asses, not as beasts of burden, but as burdens themselves. In other *Caprichos* peasants are shown carrying them.) This catches the innate absurdity of all genealogical fetishism, but it doesn't quite answer the question of why everybody is fascinated by it, and why people other than "the quality" cling to their ancestors and their family albums. The cult of the blood royal, with its supposed connection to antiquity and service to continuity, is actually little better than an attempt to breed, not a hereditary master race, but a hereditary master class. As the *Almanach*'s own propaganda gloatingly states: "Under some royal and princely and dynastic laws still in existence, members who marry a spouse from outside a *Gotha* Part One family lose all dynastic rights and titles. In some German families this still means forfeiture of estates and property." How quaint! But, just as those states and nations that opt for racial purity have always brought calamity on themselves and others, so the families and houses that self-select for breeding have declined in a welter of cretinism and porphyria, to say nothing of disputed codicils.

Nonetheless, the interest in forebears and provenance is human and natural and often harmless—or absurd, as in the thousand generations of Kinnocks that we once had to hear about. My own Great-Uncle Harry, who was sunk at Jutland yet managed to save not only himself but also the ship's Maltese mess steward, was painted as a lad in a "Young England" portrait competition, and I have the oil to this day because in boyhood I was held to have a likeness to the old mariner. I won't say I wasn't touched when a visitor mistook it recently for a painting of my firstborn son. So it's the minute fanaticism and superiority of the *Almanach* that offends: the chilling and narrowing of the kinship tie into something denatured and artificial.

Mind you, at the demotic and plebeian end of the heredity biz, things can get pretty grotesque also. One of the few complete sets of the Almanach de Gotha, a collection of volumes from 1763 until 1944, is held by the Church of Jesus Christ of Latter-day Saints, vulgarly known as the Mormons of Utah. The purveyors of today's Almanach are vague as to what the Mormons want it for, but I know why. Perhaps oversensitive at having been founded by an unskilled huckster named Joseph Smith, the Mormons have been acquiring some background on the sly. They have established an International Genealogical Index, listing at least 147 million names. The aim—a classical piece of micro-megalomania where the monstrous scale of the effort dwarfs the essential pettiness of the enterprise—is to subject all these dead people to a retrospective Mormon baptism. Every day in Mormon temples, a proxy or surrogate living devotee is immersed while as many names as possible are recited. Every ancestor of every Mormon is inducted as a matter of course, but the proselytization has gone far beyond that, in an effort to Mormonize everyone who has ever been recorded. In Corinthians, St. Paul speaks sternly but vaguely, saying: "Else what shall they do, which are baptized for the dead? If the dead rise not at all, why then are they baptized for the dead?" Stupid question.

Adherents of other dogmas are not delighted by this tactic, which recalls that general of Chiang Kai-shek's who had his troops baptized en masse with fire hoses. There was a promising row two years ago, when American Jews discovered that the Mormons had "baptized" a list of 350,000 victims of the Nazis. Since these people, however misguided in failing to recognize the divinity of Jesus, had not lived as Mormons and certainly not been foully slain as Mormons, the zeal of Salt Lake City seemed exccssive, even offensive. The

Utah leadership now says it won't do this any more. But, over Catholic objections, it has baptized Ignatius Loyola, Joan of Arc and Francis of Assisi. (I must say I think that's quite funny.) In one temple in Provo, Utah, it has also laid claim to Jane Austen and Emily Dickinson. Most wondrous of all, though, it has obviously now baptized Franz Joseph Maximilian Maria Antonius Ignatius Lamoral, 9th Prince von Thurn und Taxis. As Elias Canetti has it in "The King-Proclaimer," the first part of his *Earwitness*:

> It is touching to see her with forgotten kings, she never forgets them, she retains even the worst has-beens among them, writes to them, sends them suitable small gifts, obtains work for them, and when the honor is long past, she is the only person still to remember it. Among the beggars with whom she pays her respects on grand occasions, one can find a former king or two.

Moderation or Death
On Isaiah Berlin
1998

I N *The Color of Truth*, the American scholar Kai Bird presents his study of McGeorge ("Mac") and William Bundy.
These were the two dynastic technocrats who organized
and justified the hideous war in Vietnam. Cold War liberals
themselves, with the kept conservative journalist Joseph Alsop
they formed a Three of Hearts in the less fastidious quarters
of Washington, DC. Another player made up an occasional
fourth man. Isaiah Berlin was happy, at least when Charles
(Chip) Bohlen was unavailable, to furnish an urbane ditto to
their ruthlessness. Almost as if to show that academics and
intellectuals may be tough guys, too—the most lethal temp-
tation to which the contemplative can fall victim—Berlin's
correspondence with this little cabal breathes with that abject
eagerness that was so much a part of the one-time Anglo-
American "special relationship." To Alsop he wrote, on 20 April
1966, an account of a dinner with McGeorge Bundy:

> I have never admired anyone so much, so intensely, for so long
> as I did him during those four hours . . . his character emerged
> in such exquisite form that I am now his devoted and dedicated
> slave. I like him very much indeed, and I think he likes me, now,
> which was not always the case.

Looking back on the fantastic bloodletting in Indonesia in 1965—an event which Alsop and the Bundys later decided was confirmation of their own sapience in Indochina—Mac Bundy returned the compliment, writing to Alsop in 1967 that he wished he had Berlin's stout resolution:

> I think more and more the truth of Vietnam is in the nearby countries...I don't have the wonderful self-confidence of Isaiah—"I'm a terrific domino man"—but I share the feeling that's where we have done best.

There were fainthearts, of course, as there always are when great enterprises of the will are afoot. As an ever increasing number even of establishment types began to sicken of the war, Alsop reflected bitterly that he might no longer be able to claim the standing of stern prophet and moral tutor to the military-industrial (and military-intellectual) complex. Berlin responded in the same tones of seasoned statesmanship:

> I can see the thin red line, formed by you and Mac and me, and Chip Bohlen—four old blimps, the last defenders of a dry, and disagreeably pessimistic, tough and hopelessly outmoded position—one will perish at least with one's eyes open.

"Take my arm, old toad. Help me down Cemetery Road." Except that it was actually many thousands of conscripted Americans, and uncountable numbers of Vietnamese, and not the intellectuals at the elbow of power, who were marched down that road before their time. Almost everything is wrong with the tone and address of the above extracts: the combined ingratiation and self-pity no less than the assumed and bogus late Roman stoicism. A "terrific domino man" indeed! What price "negative liberty" now? And what of the skeptical humanist who warned incessantly about the sacrifice of living people to abstract ends, or totemic dogmas?

As against all that, the pleadings of Alsop to Mac Bundy did succeed in getting the latter to release a huge tranche of Ford Foundation money to endow Wolfson College, Oxford, the foundation of which was Berlin's noblest enterprise. So perhaps he was on to something when he expatiated about ethical trade-offs between contrasting or alternative positions: the one transaction that he really did believe was historically inevitable. (The "color of truth," you will not be astonished to learn, was gray in the opinion of the Bundys.)

Now, I know that Michael Ignatieff was aware of the existence of the above correspondence at least a year ago. And I also urged Bird to send it to him. But the Vietnam drama takes up less than a page of his biography, and mentions Berlin's real positions not at all.* We are given, instead, a familiar impressionist sketch of an honest and troubled man—the word "detachment" makes its appearance—unable to ally himself with the extremists of either camp. There is scarcely a hint of his actual influence in post-Camelot Washington, or of the way in which it was actually employed. We hear that he "joked" in Oxford about being "an old mastodon of liberalism... a last feeble echo of J. S. Mill to be treated gently as a harmless, respectable old relic," which is certainly stylistically congruent with the more embarrassing letters to Alsop and the Bundys. (Please keep in mind, also, Berlin's choice of forebear in that last instance.) Typical is Ignatieff's sentence:

* *Isaiah Berlin: A Life* by Michael Ignatieff (Chatto, 1998).

"Berlin congratulated himself on remaining on good terms with friends who could barely stand to be in the same room." Ah yes, by all means: to be remote from both sides is a tremendous reinforcement of one's own rectitude and a tribute in its way to one's own lonely and yet somehow—yes—brave and upright objectivity. "Congratulated himself," however: isn't that slightly to give the game away? This congratulation was not, after all, being bestowed for the first time. Look up Berlin's essay on Turgenev in *Russian Thinkers*, and you will find yourself enlisted on the side of

> the small, hesitant, self-critical, not always very brave, band of men who occupy a position somewhere to the left of center, and are morally repelled both by the hard faces to their right and the hysteria and mindless violence and demagoguery on their left... This is the notoriously unsatisfactory, at times agonizing, position of the modern heirs of the liberal tradition.

Whether being rueful about Mill in some sheltered quadrangle, or vicariously biting Turgenev's bullet in the pages of any number of respectable quarterlies or, indeed, while seconding the efforts of unscrupulous powerbrokers in Washington, Berlin could not discard the affectation of the embattled, the lonely and even the agonized. Of liberalism and its quandaries and dilemmas it deserves to be asked, in this century in particular, and no less than of other ideologies: agonizing for whom?

Woe is me and lackaday. There is a sense in which, if you chafe at the present complacently "liberal" consensus, the reputation of Isaiah Berlin stands like a lion in your path. But the task of confronting said lion is not at all easy or simple: by no means as much as the preceding paragraphs may have made it appear. True, he was simultaneously pompous and dishonest in the face of a long moral crisis where his views and his connections could have made a difference. True, this is the kind of story that never, ever, gets told about Berlin by his legion of memorialists and admirers. I admit that I turned first to Ignatieff's scanty passage on Vietnam and, having some private knowledge, became incensed and thought for a while that his whole sodding book was going to bleed on in the same, so to speak, vein. But then I flipped back to the beginning and settled in. It swiftly broke in upon me that the lion was still there, in all his mingled splendors, part mangy, part magnificent. Isaiah Berlin may have been designed, by origin and by temperament and by life experience, to become one of those witty and accomplished *valets du pouvoir* who adorn, and even raise the tone of, the better class of court. But there was something in him that recognized this as an ignoble and insufficient aspiration, and impelled him to resist it where he dared.

The anecdotal is inescapable here, and I see no reason to be deprived of my portion. I first met Berlin in 1967, around the time of his Bundy/Alsop pact, when I was a fairly tremulous secretary of the Oxford University Labour Club. He'd agreed to talk on Marx, and to be given dinner at the Union beforehand, and he was the very picture of patient, non-condescending charm. Uncomplainingly eating the terrible food we offered him, he awarded imaginary Marx marks to the old Russophobe, making the assumption that he would have been a PPE student. ("A beta-alpha for economics—no, I rather think a beta—but an alpha, definitely an alpha for politics.") He gave his personal reasons for opposing Marxism

("I saw the revolution in St. Petersburg, and it quite cured me for life. Cured me for life") and I remember thinking that I'd never before met anyone who had a real-time memory of 1917. Ignatieff slightly harshly says that Berlin was "no wit, and no epigrams have attached themselves to his name," but when he said, "Kerensky, yes, Kerensky—I think we have to say one of the great *wets* of history," our laughter was unforced. The subsequent talk to the club was a bit medium-pace and up-and-down the wicket, because you can only really maintain that Marx was a determinist or inevitabilist if you do a lot of eliding between sufficient and necessary conditions. But I was thrilled to think that he'd made himself vulnerable to such unlicked cubs. A term or two later, at a cocktail party given by my tutor, he remembered our dinner, remembered my name without making a patronizing show of it, and stayed to tell a good story about Christopher Hill and John Sparrow, and of how he'd been the unwitting agent of a quarrel between them, while ignoring an ambitious and possessive American professor who kept yelling "Eye-zay-ah! Eye-zay-ah!" from across the room. ("Yes," he murmured at the conclusion of the story. "After that I'm afraid Christopher rather gave me up. Gave me up for the party.")

Many years later, reviewing *Personal Impressions* for the *New Statesman*, I mentioned the old story of Berlin acting as an academic gatekeeper, and barring the appointment of Isaac Deutscher to a chair at Sussex University. This denial had the sad effect of forcing Deutscher—who had once given Berlin a highly scornful review in the *Observer*—to churn out Kremlinology for a living, as a result of which he never finished his triad or troika of Stalin, Trotsky and Lenin biographies. In the next post came a letter from Berlin, stating with some anguish that while he didn't much approve of Deutscher, his opinion had not been the deciding one. I telephoned Tamara Deutscher and others, asking if they had definite proof that Berlin had administered the bare bodkin, and was told, well, no, not definite proof. So I published a retraction. Then came a postcard from Berlin, thanking me handsomely, saying that the allegation had always worried and upset him, and asking if he wasn't correct in thinking that he had once succeeded more in attracting me to Marxism than in repelling me from it. I was—I admit it—impressed. And now I read, in Ignatieff's book, that it was an annihilatingly hostile letter from Berlin to the vice-chancellor of Sussex University which "put paid to Deutscher's chances." The fox is crafty, we know, and the hedgehog is a spiky customer, and Ignatieff proposes that the foxy Berlin always harbored the wish to metamorphose into a hedgehog. All I know is that I was once told—even assured of—one small thing.

Close reading is necessary with a customer like this. The First World War was, like the abattoir in Vietnam, quite describable as a liberals' war. Any medium-run view of history will show that it did more damage to Western civilization than any form of ideology, not least in clearing the very path, through the ruins and cadavers, along which totalitarians could later instate and militarize themselves. (In that sense, and by his insistence that a gutted and humiliated Russia should stay in the war and meet its obligations to imperialism, Kerensky can be described as a little more bloody than merely "wet.") As a small Jewish boy, an only child with a defective left arm, tenderly raised in Riga and removed to St.

Petersburg because of the exigencies of combat and of disruptions in the timber trade, Isaiah Berlin saw a terrified tsarist cop being dragged away by a mob. The sight—it recurs in numerous interviews and reminiscences, including those recorded here—powerfully colored his view of disorder and insurrection; the more so, perhaps, because his infant imagination furnished the subsequent scene of lynching or drowning that he did not in fact witness. In only one interview ("Recollections of a Historian of Ideas," uncited by Ignatieff) did he remember to say that these cops were fond of firing on civilians.

One could argue that if he had been exposed to another contemporary scene of cruelty—the mass slaughter of peasant conscripts at Tannenberg, for example, or the Cossacks dealing with a demonstration, or perhaps the Black Hundreds falling to work in a shtetl—the formative effect would have or might have been different. Yet I think it's clear, from his own recurrence to the story, and from other evidence, that it was the disturbance to the natural order that made the young Isaiah tremble and flinch. Other members of his family, including a much loved uncle and aunt, were quite active supporters of the SR (Socialist Revolutionary) movement. Neither then nor in retrospect did he register any allegiance of that sort. Ignatieff is surely right to say that the episode with the arrested policeman "continued to work within Berlin, strengthening his horror of physical violence and his suspicion of political experiment." But it would have been more precise to say: only for certain sorts of physical violence and political experiment. Policemen are supposed to control crowds, not crowds policemen. Vietnam, for example, was not just an instance of horrific premeditated violence. It was a laboratory experiment run by technician-intellectuals and academic consultants, who furnished us with terms like "interdict," "relocate," "body count" and "strategic hamlet." To cope with the ensuing calamity, the Bundys and McNamaras later evolved the view that, while the war might have been a blunder, the error could, for reasons of state and for reasons of face, not be admitted. In this, too, they were seconded by Berlin. No doubt his reassuring "blimp" line came in handy here, as well. It's astonishing how often the men of power need, and appreciate, and also get, a hit of solid senior-common-room emollience.

The lifelong strength that Berlin drew from his 1917 baptism was, however, often applied in less obvious ways. I was fascinated to learn, from Ignatieff, that his Latvian family had a direct kinship with the Schneerson clan who ran, and still run, the fanatical sect known as Lubavitch or Chabad. (This family tree also includes Yehudi Menuhin, who might in other circumstances have become a mere fiddler on the roof.) So the charismatic loony rebbe from Brooklyn Heights, the late Menachem Schneerson—he who opposed blood transfusions because they compromised unique Jewish DNA—was Berlin's cousin. Any mention of these Hasidic fanatics, according to Ignatieff, would cause Berlin's face "to tighten into a rare and uncharacteristic expression of dislike." That's good, and good to know. (Leon Wieseltier, in his gushing goodbye to Berlin in the New Republic, could not have been more wrong than in depicting him as a medieval Jewish sage.) There are probably two additional and reinforcing reasons for Berlin's disdain. One is that the Russian rabbinate had historically supported the antisemitic tsar against Bonaparte, viewing the French as bearers of secularism and enlightenment. The other is that he saw, in the attachment of many Jewish intellectuals to Marxism, a sort of displaced messianic impulse. This certainly aided his persistent misreading of Marx and of what he thought of as Marx's teleology. But it also, by way of an internal mutation, made him distrust the zealotry of Zionism whether this was offered in political nationalist or black-coated Orthodox form, let alone in the nasty synthesis of the two that now defines the Israeli right.

Synthesis was Berlin's especial gift, while an educated wariness of any "tyranny of concept" larger than the human was his essential admonition, indeed constitutes his chief bequest. Yet, in his work and in his life, syntheses were often eclectic agglomerations and his allegiances—transferred not so much to England as to the Anglo-American supranational "understanding"—frequently bore the stamp of realpolitik and, well, calculation. He did, however, understand this part of himself and I was surprised at how often Ignatieff made a puzzle where none exists:

> He liked to say that his success—professorships, a knighthood, the Order of Merit—depended upon a systematic over-estimation of his abilities. "Long may this continue," he always said. Self-denigration came naturally, but it was also a pre-emptive strike against criticism. "I am an intellectual taxi; people flag me down and give me destinations and off I go" was all he would ever offer, when pressed to say what his intellectual agenda had been.

Ignatieff, himself a Russo-Canadian exile or émigré, never seems quite able to make up his mind about whether this was a joke, and (if it was) whether it was one of those jokes that are revealing and confessional. His confusion is expressed in the choice of the term "self-denigration." To deprecate self is one thing, while to denigrate self is masochistic. Without self-deprecation much English literary and academic conversation would become difficult to carry on. "Pre-emptive" comes closer to the mark: you say this sort of thing about yourself before anyone else can. But that's public, and a recognized act. In 1978, Berlin wrote a private letter to the psychiatrist Anthony Storr, wondering why he, a beloved only child, should still be visited with the feeling that his many attainments were "of very little or of no value." This takes us some way beyond the pose of false modesty, but nowhere near as far as self-hatred.

I propose that Berlin was somewhat haunted, all of his life, by the need to please and conciliate others; a need which in some people is base but which also happened to engage his most attractive and ebullient talents. I further propose that he sometimes felt or saw the need to be courageous, but usually —oh dear—at just the same moment that he remembered an urgent appointment elsewhere. That this was imbricated with both his Jewish and his Russian identities seems probable. He may also have felt that luck played too large a part in his success—a rare but human concession to superstition.

The difficulty with Berlin's views on political matters is that they are vulnerable to the charge not so much of contradiction as of tautology. (And perhaps of want of originality: Berlin's favorite, Benjamin Constant, proposed a distinction between the "liberty of the ancients" and the "liberty of the moderns"; T. H. Green spoke of liberty in the positive and negative, and the same antithesis is strongly present in

Hayek's *Road to Serfdom*—the title page of which quoted Lord Acton saying that "few discoveries are more irritating than those which expose the pedigree of ideas.") The greatest hardship experienced by a person trying to apprehend Berlin's presentation of "two concepts" of liberty is in remembering which is supposed to be which. I know of no serviceable mnemonic here. When Berlin delivered his original lectures on the subject, at Bryn Mawr College in Pennsylvania in 1952, he divided ideas about liberty between the liberal and the romantic. Positive and negative were the successor distinctions. To be let alone—the most desirable consummation in his own terms—is the negative. To be uplifted by others, or modernized or forcibly emancipated, is, somewhat counter-intuitively, the positive. Yet it is readily agreed, even asserted, that laissez-faire can lead to the most awful invasions and depredations of the private sphere, while an interventionist project like the New Deal can be a welcome aid to individual freedom. In a long interview, originally published in Italy, which appeared in full in the excellent *Salmagundi*, Berlin says that he likes the positive examples of Lloyd George and Franklin Roosevelt, not least because they insulated their respective societies from socialism *tout court*. One assumes that, with his sense of history, he means the Lloyd George who was the patron of Field Marshal Douglas Haig, and the guarded admirer of Hitler, just as much as he means the Lloyd George who was the father of Welsh Disestablishment. And one must suppose that he comprehends FDR the originator of the war economy, and FDR the prime mover of American acquisition of European empires, in the avuncular figure who proposed the Tennessee Valley Authority. At any rate, keen endorsement of either statesman is a distinctly bizarre way of registering any kind of objection to social engineering. Thus, there are contradictions in his view, but they languish from being untreated by their author. At least Lloyd George and Roosevelt, when they ordered up slaughters and conquests, or when they used authoritarian tactics, did not do so in obedience to any fancy theory. Once again, I think we may see the ghostly figure of that mobbed policeman—much more unsettling than a policed mob.

As it happens, Rosa Luxemburg in her great disagreement with Lenin said roundly that there was a real peril of practice hardening into theory, and vice versa. And, if you care, I agree with her. Dogma in power does have a unique chilling ingredient not exhibited by power, however ghastly, wielded for its own traditional sake. But the two concepts don't bridge the gap between the divine right of kings, overthrown by the Enlightenment, and the age of ideology. It's especially unhelpful, in this regard, that Berlin should have assumed that all Marxists were mechanists and determinists, and that there could be no quarrel in principle among them. (I don't recall him being so harsh on the fatuous and also tautological slogan about the "inevitability of gradualness" with which the Fabians advanced their own version of a managed and graded society. But then, the Fabians were quintessentially English, and their quiet authoritarianism was not threatening to power so much as envious of, and ancillary to, its customary exercise in these islands.)

In 1971, in an episode not explored by Ignatieff, Anthony Arblaster published a review of *Four Essays on Liberty* in the journal *Political Studies*. "Vision and Revision: A Note on the

Text of Isaiah Berlin's *Four Essays on Liberty*" was in some ways a minor key achievement; it took the form of a meticulous study of the alterations made between the different editions of Berlin's best-known work. But it resulted in a major chord huff, with Berlin making no effort to be urbane about his annoyance. It is easy to see what gave rise to his irritation. Arblaster instanced the following textual emendation:

> From Zeno to Spinoza, from the Gnostics to Leibniz, from Thomas Hobbes to Lenin and Freud, the battle-cry has been essentially the same; the object of knowledge and the methods of discovery have often been violently opposed, but that reality is knowable, and that knowledge and only knowledge liberates, and absolute knowledge liberates absolutely—that is common to many doctrines which are so large and valuable a part of Western civilization.

The earlier printed version had begun the list "From Plato to Lucretius," had stuck with the Gnostics and Leibniz, but had had Thomas Aquinas instead of Thomas Hobbes, almost, as Arblaster woundingly put it, "as if it had to be Thomas somebody." He went on, detailing other reworkings of the same passage: "Reality was 'wholly knowable,' not just 'knowable,' and this alteration, while typical of the general toning down, almost destroys the point of the sentence, for what is distinctive, let alone sinister, about the belief that reality is knowable?" Rather than taking Berlin up on the slothful prose that had led him to use clichés like "battle-cry," and to recycle the most worn and familiar Actonian trope, Arblaster inquired, mildly for him: "Where in the works of Hobbes is there anything which suggests that he believed that knowledge and only knowledge liberates, and absolute knowledge liberates absolutely?" It was Whitman, I think—I really must check this when I get the time—who said:

Do I contradict myself?
Very well then I contradict myself,
(I am large, I contain multitudes.)

Berlin, it seems, had a huge capacity for internal multitudes and for torrents of reference but, whoever he lit on or deployed, they turned out happily to confirm, in the first place, one another, and in the second place, whatever he was going to say anyway. Have you ever read an article on Berlin which did not mention his extraordinary facility with cross-fertilized "thinkers"—the conjuring names usually beginning with H rather than T? A biographer might have examined his subject more closely on the question: did an English society, and indeed academy, deeply wedded to compromise and to consensus, overvalue a polyglot chap who could mention a lot of Continental theorists and still come out with sound and no-nonsense views? I can't call to mind anybody in the native empiricist tradition who ever challenged Berlin on his high-wire juggling, or on his role as official greeter, waving the new arrivals through a normally rather suspicious customs. Ernest Gellner, however, always said he was a fraud. Berlin returned the lack of cordiality, perhaps feeling that it was uncomfortable having too many Central European polymaths about the place. (His distaste for George Steiner took something of the same form.) Incidentally, Perry Anderson's general matrix of the "white" intellectual emigration, which suggested that the radical exiles went to America while the conservative ones—with Gellner exempted—settled in England, understates the manner in which Berlin's Washington period was the making of him.

Berlin's promiscuous capaciousness also shows itself in his rather shifty attitude to Mill. In "John Stuart Mill and the Ends of Life," one of his essays on liberty, he could not lay enough stress on Mill's opposition to "some kind of hegemony of right-minded intellectuals." Again, it's not as if Mill's defenders continually and stupidly insist on this one point. Nor, on the other hand, is it the case that there is no evidence for his intellectual elitism. Berlin merely fails to cite any of it. And Mill possessed, in common with Marx and in bold contrast to Berlin, a consciousness of class. He clearly thought that the ends, of female suffrage, freedom for the Jamaicans, and other such utopian objectives, might require somewhat more discipline than could be summoned by mere appeals to reason or goodwill. It's quite possible to imagine him regarding the positive/negative duet as a distinction somewhat lacking in a difference. In the *Salmagundi* interview Berlin was asked his opinion about Mill:

I took Mill almost for granted.

But you wrote about him and gave a rather existentialist reading of him.

Well, I didn't think he was the utilitarian he thought he was. I didn't enjoy Mill. Save for the essay *On Liberty*. I didn't read Bentham properly. I read—who were the important names?—Carlyle, Emerson; who else was there in England?

T. H. Green?

I was not deeply impressed by him, nor by Hobhouse, admirable as they are. You see, it's the enemy who interests me; brilliant opponents who so to speak put their swords, their rapiers into one and find the weak spot.

Do you think that description applies to Marx?

Yes, up to a point it does. The point is that his particular criticism of the liberals he wrote about did not seem to me to be particularly effective. His positive ideas were of great importance but the idea that liberty is a bourgeois concept and all that sort of thing, or that it was a capitalist concept—no. But I did read Lassalle and I was impressed by his concept of profit and marginal utility. I want to retract what I said about J. S. Mill. I admire him immensely. He is a major, great, positive British thinker.

Whew! Not a moment too soon. Hobhouse and Green admirable in their way, even Marx quite impressive apart from some things he never said, and Mill not merely plucked from the burning, but hurriedly garlanded with the multiple encomia of being major, British and positive. Or should it be negative? The question is not merely sarcastic. Berlin supplied many admonitions that were strictly in the negative, most of them warning liberals against the hazard and fallacy of monism. But who can remember anything he suggested about what liberalism, or liberals, might actually accomplish? Rawls, Dworkin and Galbraith have all laid out avenues of potential meliorism. Berlin's design omits these spacious features.

The Oxford debating tradition does possess one great strength, drawn indirectly from the *Symposium*. You are supposed to be able to give an honest account of an opposing or different worldview, and even as an exercise to be able to present it as if you believed it yourself. It is a striking fact about Isaiah Berlin that, in his first and most serious and only full-length book, he is unable to meet this condition, even in the exegetical sense. The essay "Isaiah's Marx, and Mine," written by his pupil, and successor in the Chichele professorship, Gerry Cohen, is full of love and admiration for the man. But it cannot acquit Berlin of the charge of elementary misrepresentation, or at best misunderstanding. The fact that all the mistakes and omissions (alienation did not feature in the first edition, and is sketchily discussed in the second) are hostile is unlikely to be accidental. Berlin himself told *Salmagundi*:

> In 1933 Mr. [H. A. L.] Fisher, the warden of New College, asked me to write a book on Karl Marx for the Home University Library. I said: "What is the audience for the book?" He said: "Squash professionals." I had never read a line of Marx . . .

One sees the famous charm at work. But not even a line, by 1933, even after St. Petersburg? Anyway, it shows. And it's of interest that Berlin repeatedly describes his subject, admiringly for once, as a synthesizer. "A thinker of genius. I don't deny that. But it was the synthesis that was important. He never acknowledged a single debt."

Coming from the fabled synthesizer who acknowledged all debts and none, and could change his indebtedness from Hobbes to Aquinas at the drop of a hat, this is of interest also. Without checking, I can think of Marx's open indebtedness to Hegel, to Adam Smith, to the Blue Books of the Victorian factory inspectorate, to Balzac and to Charles Darwin. In other words, Berlin was being vulgar when it must decently be presumed that he knew better. Of his other subjects, not even Joseph de Maistre receives such offhand treatment.

Oddest of all, Berlin presents Marx and other "utopians" as apostles or prophets of ultimate harmony, while offering his agreeable and consensual self as the realistic man who recognizes the inevitability of conflict and contradiction. It is only the radicals who allegedly believe in the following prospectus:

> A society lives in a state of pure harmony, in which all its members live in peace, love one another, are free from physical danger, from want of any kind, from insecurity, from degrading work, from envy, from frustration, experience no injustice or violence, live in perpetual, even light, in a temperate climate, in the midst of infinitely fruitful, generous nature.

It is not possible to cite any authority for this florid caricature. Nobody, except the Christian church (by law established in his adored and adopted England), has ever proposed such an idiotic stasis as desirable, let alone attainable. But Berlin's facility for citation again chooses this moment to desert him. In the presentation of himself as the guardian of complexity and of unintended consequence, and of the inescapable clash of interests and desires, there may even be some element of displacement or transference. It was the despised Hegel who told us that tragedy consisted of a conflict of rights. It was Berlin, whenever faced with a conflict of rights, who sought to emulsify it. In other words, his emphasis on complexity had a strong element of... simplification.

I said earlier that Berlin was lucky. He did not actually consider himself fortunate, when posted as a diplomat to wartime Moscow on Guy Burgess's initiative, to find himself stranded and unwanted in New York instead. But, when told to make the best of his American contacts, he found himself in the perfect milieu. Ignatieff's passages on this period are excellent. Berlin's networking skills and, it's not unfair to say, his ability to be all things to all men, were ideally suited to address an American pluralism which exhibited multiple ambiguities about the war, and about the British. Once transferred to Washington, he could rotate—we would now say spin—between tough but stupid isolationists, between the old guard at the British Embassy and the new Churchillian bosses in London, between the Anglophile hostesses of Georgetown and the anti-Nazi émigrés from Central Europe. In what must have been at the time a dizzying subplot, he also involved himself intimately in the quarrel between Chaim Weizmann and David Ben-Gurion over the project of a Jewish National Home, and in the attempts by both to play off the British against the Americans. And, though he showed himself able to take risks in leaking classified material that favored the Zionist cause, he also found himself acutely sensitive to any suspicion, even on his own part, of a dual loyalty. (In a memo to Churchill on some Berlin cables from Washington that were thought to be too clever by more than half, Anthony Eden minuted his view that there was too much of the "Oriental" about this subordinate.) The resolution of this internal conflict took the form of backing Weizmann's moderation against Ben-Gurion's pugnacity, and also of repressing or postponing too much thought about the Final Solution. There was a small battle to be won in Palestine, and a larger one to be won in Europe, and the first had to wait, morally and tactically, on the latter. There was much to be brilliantly sublimated meanwhile.

This talent for compromise, and also for diplomatic and drawing-room maneuver, was to equip Berlin superbly for his later career in academic and intellectual politics. His slogan might well have been "surtout, pas de zèle," but muttered rather zealously. He had an instinct for multiplicity, and a liking for intrigue, but a need for conciliation. No wonder he was to write so contemptuously of those who saw a problem-free society, while so freely depicting himself as a proponent of hard choices. A foot in both camps of the Atlantic alliance, furthermore, was the ideal postwar "positioning" for a cosmopolitan, who had been a fluent and persuasive Greek at the initial moment of the new Rome. In the Cold War years, indeed, Berlin often found himself quite close to the throne. There are several accounts of an evening of electrifying embarrassment, when he was questioned about Russia in a close but philistine way by the young President Kennedy. Ignatieff puts the most lenient construction on these engagements with power. Describing an exchange between Berlin and the old mandarin George Kennan, he writes that "it was a fixed principle of his that so-called elites—intellectual or otherwise—had no business presuming that they knew better than the man or woman in the street." A recently unearthed interview between Berlin and Arthur Schlesinger shows that he omitted to clarify this fixed principle to the intellectuals of Camelot. When asked by Philip Toynbee and others to take a position on nuclear disarmament, as Ignatieff describes it,

> Berlin replied—with rather uncharacteristic bravado—that liberal principles were of little meaning unless one was prepared to risk one's very survival in their defense: "Unless there is some point at which you are prepared to fight against whatever odds, and whatever the threat may be, not merely to yourself, but to anybody, all principles become flexible, all codes melt, and all ends in themselves for which we live disappear."

This is bluster, not bravado. With its loud talk of survival, also, it is casuistry of a low order. The whole case against nuclear weapons is that they threaten to melt everything and make everything disappear, and thus that their use in geopolitical contests is or would be unpardonable. There was always another essential element to the critique: namely, that nuclearism creates an unaccountable and secret priesthood or elite which doesn't just think it knows better than the man and woman in the street, but is prepared to annihilate all of them, including all non-combatants in all other countries and indeed all people who have been born or might be born. The positive-negative poles, as you might say, are highly charged here. Rather feebly, Ignatieff attributes this vaporous reply to Berlin's hatred of the Soviet system. A non sequitur. Apart from anything else, it was Andrei Sakharov who educated millions of people to see the obviousness of the points I've just made.

(Incidentally, and on a point that often gives rise to gossip, Ignatieff asserts that Berlin was as shocked as anybody by the surreptitious CIA funding of *Encounter*, to which he often contributed, and further asserts that "he certainly had no official or unofficial relationship with either British intelligence or the CIA." He doesn't give an authority for this flat (and unprovoked) denial, but if we presume that its source was Berlin himself, the following inductive exercise might be permitted. It is improbable in the highest degree that Berlin was never even approached by either Smiley's people or the Cousins. So, if he turned them down, would that not have made a fine anecdote for his biographer? The *Encounter* disavowal, if taken literally, would mean that Berlin was abnormally incurious, or duller than we have been led to suppose, or had wasted his time in Washington. If you look up Peter Wright's *Spycatcher*, though, you will find a record of some affable chinwags with Berlin, tending to confirm Auden and MacNeice's award, in *Letters from Iceland*, of a "dish of milk" to the feline Isaiah. And some other living cloak-and-gown experts can tell a tale or two. Ignatieff's own respectful credulity on this minor point is a microcosm of the shortcomings of his approach.)

In every instance given by Ignatieff, or known to me, from the Cold War through Algeria to Suez to Vietnam, Berlin strove to find a high liberal justification either for the status quo or for the immediate needs of the conservative authorities. (I'm reserving the Israel-Palestine question for the moment.) There is a definite correlation between these positions and his scholarly praise for what he disarmingly termed the "banal": his general view that the main enemy was activism. At a State Department reception I once met a gloomy Argentine banker, a certain Señor della Porta, who discoursed about his country's greatest failure. With a good climate and much natural wealth, Argentina had failed to evolve a liberal and stable party of the middle class. "One day, however," he said, "we will indeed succeed in having such a party and such a leadership. And our slogan will be"—here he brightened up a bit—" 'Moderation or Death!' "

A lapidary phrase from Immanuel Kant—"Out of the crooked timber of humanity no straight thing was ever made" —served Berlin almost as a mantra. It appeared once in *Russian Thinkers*, twice in *Against the Current*, three times in *Four Essays on Liberty* and even more frequently in a 1990 volume entitled *The Crooked Timber of Humanity*. It features three times in Ignatieff's biography, in circumstances that are severally illuminating.

In November 1933, writing to Elizabeth Bowen, he advanced in capsule form his two chief propositions or preoccupations. I quote Ignatieff's summary:

> The philosopher Malebranche had observed that since the moral ends which human beings commonly pursued were in conflict with each other, the very idea of creating a perfect society was incoherent. This seminal idea had also cropped up elsewhere. Hadn't Kant said, he wrote to Bowen, that "out of the crooked timber of humanity no straight thing was ever made"? These were the chance encounters with ideas—not the fevered discussions with Ayer and Austin—that generated his later thought.

In 1950, Arthur Koestler gave an interview to the *Jewish Chronicle* in which he said that every diaspora Jew had a choice, but that it was only one choice, and a hard one at that. One could either assimilate fully into the non-Jewish world, and abandon Jewishness altogether. Or one could emigrate to Israel and there lead a fully Jewish life. In between, there was no room. Berlin wrote a reply to this, entitled "Jewish Slavery and Emancipation." He described Koestler's counterposing of the issue as coercive. Surely, if there was a point to Israel, it was that it increased freedom of decision for Jews. "There are too many individuals in the world who do not choose to see life in the form of radical choices between one course and another and whom we do not condemn for this reason. 'Out of the crooked timber of humanity,' said a great philosopher, 'no straight thing was ever made.'"

In 1969, he came upon a piece of moral idiocy from Herbert Marcuse—or at any rate a piece of moral idiocy from

Marcuse quoted in *Encounter*—and went into a towering rage, writing that people like Marcuse and indeed Hannah Arendt were products of

> the terrible twisted Mitteleuropa in which nothing is straight, simple, truthful, all human relations and all political attitudes are twisted into ghastly shapes by these awful casualties who, because they are crippled, recognize nothing pure and firm in the world!

It may be relevant that Berlin detested the assimilated German Jews, like Hannah Arendt, while pressing his hardest for assimilation in England. It may also be relevant that he always refused to reprint "Jewish Slavery and Emancipation," partly because his All Souls colleague Keith Joseph had been upset by an anti-assimilationist joke it contained. (Steinmetz the hunchback and Kahn the "accepted" *converso* are walking past the synagogue on Fifth Avenue. Kahn says, "I used to attend services there," and Steinmetz retorts: "And I used to be a hunchback." Every Jew, Berlin said, has his or her own hump: some deny it, some flaunt it and some—"timid and respectful cripples"—wear voluminous cloaks.)

In 1933, the date of the first known reference, Berlin was only 24, but he had obviously found and seized on his essential dictum. It is of course a thoughtful and provocative one, and full of implication. By the November of that particular year, however, it must have occurred to many people that politics and policy could indeed succeed in making humans *more* crooked, not to say more twisted. And, this being true, is it worth considering whether the converse might ever apply?

In the second extract, Berlin is making a perfectly intelligible attack on the Procrustean faction and the either/or tendency, as he would have been bound to do on general principles but as he felt additionally moved to do when faced with Jewish absolutism. The Kantian allusion is near superfluous, however. Koestler is not trying to make people grow straight at all. He is telling them that they must warp in one pronounced and final manner, from their current pattern of growth, or in another manner that is no less strenuous.

In the third case Berlin is suddenly willing to grant that there is purity and firmness to be attained, though not by people who are twisted and misshapen partly by environment. The specific location of this in Mitteleuropa is odd.

I shall not be able to improve on Perry Anderson's review of *The Crooked Timber of Humanity*, which appeared in the LRB in 1990, except perhaps to broaden his point with help from these later gleanings. Briefly, in his "Idea for a Universal History with a Cosmopolitan Purpose"—one sees how the very title might have magnetized Berlin's omnivorous attention— Kant stated that humanity was indeed capable of overcoming its tribal and backward heritage, and of realizing a latent common interest. However, the need for leadership in this great task is a problem in itself, because the innate brutishness that "we" need to overcome is also manifestly present in each one of us, and therefore poses a practically insuperable contradiction. "Das höchste Oberhaupt soll aber gerecht für sich selbst und doch ein Mensch sein"—"The highest magistrate should be just in himself and yet be a man." (I note, at the risk of attracting a raised eyebrow from Anderson, that the concept of an individual, no less than a class, needing to be "für sich" rather than "an sich," seems in this rendering to invert Marx's later usage.) There is but one way to assuage this need for a double positive that must still be derived from a double negative. As Kant phrases it, in Anderson's translation:

> Only in such an enclosure as civil unification offers can our inclinations achieve their best effects; as trees in a wood which seek to deprive each other of air and sunlight are forced to strive upward and so achieve a beautiful straight growth; while those that spread their branches at will in isolated freedom grow stunted, tilted and crooked.

There may be a slightly dank and collectivist timbre to the above, and the German forests may not have been greenhouses either of generous solidarity or of robust free thought, but that irony would seem to count at Berlin's expense. Kant is explicitly saying the opposite to what he supposes. At different points, indeed, in the *Four Essays on Liberty* Berlin returned the compliment by describing Kant both as an advocate of "severe individualism" and of "pure totalitarian doctrine." Then again, having found the rationalism of the Enlightenment to be forbidding and authoritarian, he invested his hopes in a Romantic movement that could hardly claim to be immune from visionary and unsettling temptations. But the wonder, even in a career as intellectually eclectic as Berlin's, is that he should have cut so many crutches (and so many cudgels) from such a frail—not to say, distorted—trunk as this.

Anderson amusingly, and I trust intentionally, describes the repetitive woodcutter and carpenter image that Berlin took from Kant as "a saw." It is an old saw of the English Tories, and their empiricist and pragmatist allies, that "you

can't change human nature." Rightly or wrongly, it was confirmation of this stout and hearty assertion that they took
from the anti-prophet Isaiah. The ur-Tory, Samuel Johnson,
phrased it most prettily in the lines he added to Goldsmith's
poem, *The Traveller*:

> How small, of all that human hearts endure,
> That part which laws or kings can cause or cure.
> Still to ourselves in every place consigned,
> Our own felicity we make or find.

(Of course, if the human timber can only grow crooked, then
there's no need for the exertion of the conservative interest to
maintain the situation.)

A word that rises naturally to the mind, in considering
the foregoing, is insecurity. Despite his great and confident
presence on the podium—which we know always put him
into an anticipatory state of nerves until the end of his days
—and despite his legendary performances in the salon and
at table, Berlin was uncertain of his welcome, unsure of himself and, possibly, uneasy about the uncritical admiration he
received from some acolytes. Ignatieff makes it abundantly
plain that Jewishness lay at the bottom of this unease. Using
much new material this time, he also demonstrates that Berlin suffered much private anxiety over Zionism. Though he
felt that his adopted England was uniquely tolerant of the
Jewish presence, he never allowed himself quite to relax. And,
though he thought that a Jewish national home in Palestine
was a necessary and even a good thing, he was acutely aware
that it was as much a project of the positive—the interventionist—as of the negative, or the right to be let alone.

Two instances illustrate this to perfection, and both involve his friend and ally Lewis Namier. In the *Salmagundi* interview, Berlin said of the problem of assimilation:

> Sir Lewis Namier explained this extremely clearly. He said that Eastern European Judaism was a frozen mass until the rays of the Western Enlightenment began to beat on it. Then some of it remained frozen, some evaporated—that meant assimilation and drifting—and some melted into powerful streams: one was socialism and the other Zionism. That's exactly right.

Score one for the poor old Enlightenment, at least: it emancipated Jews not just from legally imposed disabilities but from the control of their own stasis-oriented clerical authorities. (It wasn't the antisemites or Christians, after all, who persecuted Spinoza.) Then there is the single story which Berlin was most fond of relating. In the 1930s, a number of supposedly suave Germans were sent over to England to work on elite opinion. There was one academic setting in which they were always sure of a hearing. In the Ignatieff version of this much repeated anecdote:

> He remembered one particularly clumsy member of the German aristocracy who, in the common room of All Souls, happened to say that he thought German territorial demands in Europe were as reasonable as British imperial claims overseas. This remark, delivered into the stillness of the common room, was suddenly interrupted by a guttural growl from a man whom Isaiah had never seen before, seated in one of the window recesses. "Wir Juden und die andere Farbigen denken anders," ("We Jews and the other colored peoples think otherwise") the stranger growled, and stalked out. This was Isaiah's first encounter with the Polish-born historian and devoted Zionist, Lewis Namier.

One sees at once the utility as well as the beauty of such a piece of raconteurship. It puts the British, the Jews and the "colored peoples" all on one side, in a pleasingly multi-national manner. It leaves the fish-faced outsider gasping for air. It is an instance of a good return of serve, delivered across a celebrated common room. And it shows how even Galicians can become, if you like, Englishmen. It's the echt Berlin tale; arousing the same warm emotions as *Chariots of Fire* while illustrating grand matters.

This is of course the same Namier who not only became *plus anglais que les anglais*—no shame in that, one naturally hopes—but who wrote that "the future of the white race lies with empires, that is, those nations which hold vast expanses of land outside Europe." If he ever advocated Zionism as a movement for the emancipation of colored peoples, I think I would have read of it.

An ambivalence on this score is palpable in Berlin's own attitudes to Palestine, and to the British Empire of which it was for a long time a province. Benjamin Disraeli, proposed by Berlin in a famous essay as the Jew who overcame outsider-dom by identifying with the British upper class (a far more agreeable choice than Marx's rancorous allegiances in the opposite direction), was a stern racial nationalist as well as a mustard-keen promoter of imperialism. And Arthur Balfour, author of a famous declaration on the subject of Palestine, had been the British politician most opposed to Jewish immigration from Eastern Europe. (Berlin never alludes to this as far as I know, but he must have been aware of it.) Furthermore, whether or not the establishment of a Jewish state in Palestine was to be mainly dependent on British imperial goodwill, what were its founding principles to be? To his credit, Berlin never lied about Palestine being "a land without a people." But, if Jews were to demand, in that same land, not the equal rights that they demanded in America or Europe, but special and transcendent proprietorial rights, how could this claim be founded? It could only be founded on a) the claims of revealed and prophetic religion or b) the claims of an unbreakable tie of blood, and of that blood to that soil. Yet what could be less agreeable, to Berlin, than language or argument that originated from those ancient and superstitious sources?

An immediate answer to this conundrum of atavism was supplied, for Berlin and for many others, by the homicidal atavism of Christian and conservative Europe, which became infected with the madness of fascism and thus made Palestine a question of safety for Jews. Yet Berlin, again to his credit, did not allow this consideration to silence all of his misgivings. Visiting Mandate Palestine in 1932, he found the perfect English assimilationist metaphor to describe the conflict of rights. The place was an English public school, with the British high commissioner as headmaster, and two "houses." Most of the masters preferred the Arab house, whose boys were "gay, affectionate, high-spirited and tough, occasionally liable to break out and have a rag and break the skulls of a few Jews or an Englishman perhaps," while the Jewish house was full of clever rich boys, "allowed too much pocket money by their parents, rude, conceited, ugly, ostentatious, suspected of swapping stamps unfairly with the other boys, always saying they know better, liable to work too hard and not to play games with the rest." Golly. In one way, this illustrates a talent for stereotype. In another, it shows his gift for imagining the workings of other, opposed minds. Leaving Palestine by sea,

> He met a handsome, poetic young man named Abraham Stern, traveling to Italy to take up a scholarship in classics at the University of Florence, offered by Mussolini's government. When they got talking, Isaiah asked him what Stern thought of the recent British move to create a legislative council in Palestine. We shall fight that, Stern said. Why? Because it would give the Arabs representation in proportion to their demographic superiority. But, Isaiah countered, the council was merely advisory. It does not matter, Stern replied. We shall fight and fight, and if blood has to be shed...

Stern, and his distinctly less aesthetic deputy, Yitzhak Shamir, went on to offer military and political collaboration to Hitler in the battle to expel the British and to make a manly, even skull-breaking nation out of the Jews. And Berlin, normally so eager to please, was later to refuse to shake Menachem Begin's hand when he met him in the lift of the King David Hotel. For as long as seemed feasible, he took the part of those Jews who favored a binational state. It could be argued that he adopted this "moderate" line to try and defuse any quarrel between his new English home and a putative Jewish national one, but—though such a conflict was indeed an agony to him, especially during the war years in Washington—it would be paltry to reduce his dilemma to this proportion. He clearly saw it in the light of an issue of conscience, and of a serious challenge to his own philosophy, personal and political.

I was, however, quite surprised to read Ignatieff's disclosures under this heading. In public, Berlin always seemed to take the same damage control positions on the issue as he adopted on so many others. For example, in *Personal Impressions* he says of Chaim Weizmann that he "committed none of those enormities for which men of action, and later their biographers, claim justification on the ground of what is called raison d'état." Well, that's true only if you compare Weizmann to the usual suspects of this and other centuries. By the standard of mild and tolerant Jewish idealists, though, he justified a fair bit of ethnic cleansing on precisely that ground. (In 1944, he complained to FDR that "we could not rest our case on the consent of the Arabs." That consent was specified in the Balfour Declaration.) I know that Berlin once complained earnestly to the editor of the TLS about a fairly neutral review of a collection on Palestine edited by Edward Said and myself. I remember the huge row he forced, at the offices of *Index on Censorship* of all places, concerning an essay by Noam Chomsky which happened to mention in passing that Israel, under Weizmann's presidency, was only admitted to the UN on condition that Palestinian refugees would either be compensated or permitted to reclaim their homes. And there were many comparable instances. He even once told Susan Sontag that he had caught himself thinking of Israel as the old fellow-travelers thought of the Soviet Union. (In the context, or any context, a more than startling admission.) He kept his admonitions, and his reservations, extremely private until the very last possible moment when, on the verge of death, he dictated a statement critical of Netanyahu and in favor of a utilitarian two-state partition. The letter, I was recently told by its Israeli recipient, Avishai Margalit, contained, as he drily put it, "nothing to write home about." Coming well after the Oslo Agreement, and stressing Muslim holy places in Jerusalem rather than the actual Arab inhabitants of many denominations, it was little more than a coda to the loveless Arafat-Netanyahu embrace. But Margalit told me also that, before releasing it to the press, he decided to solicit Berlin's express permission. The request arrived as the old man was being taken to hospital in his last crisis. So his signal to go ahead and publish was his very last act on earth. Gerry Cohen tells me that at about the same time, Berlin was trying to evolve a petition calling on the British government to institute a major New Deal program of public works, in order to eradicate unemployment. Neither appeal was very muscular or particularly bold. However, the making or signing of public appeals had never been his practice. (A friend speculates that he avoided signing letters to the *Times* because his name began with B.) So at the very end, Berlin seemed to believe that he had an unredeemed debt to the friends on the left whom he had so often disappointed.

There's another instance of that same impulse, in a story told on tape to Ignatieff. Berlin claims that in 1968, while lecturing at Columbia during the campus rebellion,

> He gave a lecture so close to the police lines that his friends told him to wet a handkerchief to place over his mouth and eyes in case tear-gas canisters were fired in his vicinity. His Marxist graduate students Bert Ollmann and Marshall Berman attended the lecture, ready to defend him against hecklers and if necessary against physical attack. It was not an auspicious time to be a liberal philosopher.

Well, I know Bertell Ollmann and Marshall Berman, both of them members of that strange and interesting subset, Berlin's

Marxisant diaspora, and I've asked them about this episode. They both love "Isaiah," and they would both gladly have done that for him, and more. But they say they can't recall the event, and Ignatieff has certainly not checked it with them, and my own view is that—vertiginous though the times undoubtedly were—they are unlikely to have forgotten it. Had Berlin been menaced with martyrdom in the manner that he fondly invents, and Ignatieff fondly sets down, it would not, really, have been for his liberalism. (I don't know how to break it to the comrades about the Bundys.) One begins to see how myths are made.

Margalit was giving a lecture when I met him, at a New York conference on Post-Zionism organized for the centennial of Theodor Herzl's romantic Viennese project. He spoke with great brio about the startling proposition that European Jews—the *luftmensch*—could only be made healthy and whole by becoming farmers and peasants in the Levant. This, he said, both detached the Jews from their historic occupations and made it inevitable (because the land to be tilled had to come from somewhere, or rather from somebody) that there would be a confrontation with dispossessed Arabs. "If this is not the original sin," he remarked, "it is certainly the immaculate misconception." I close my eyes and think of Berlin's character and upbringing and preferences. To take educated and musical Latvian Jews and put hoes in their hands? Never mind the dire fate of the indigenous Palestinians, as Berlin's friend J. L. Talmon always painstakingly emphasized that he didn't. Does this not mean that the shtetl and the ghetto, and sooner or later the magical rabbi, will be back? And isn't there a class question involved?

Many people's attitude to Zionism is conditioned by their exposure to antisemitism and here, too, Berlin registered certain insecurities and uncertainties. He maintained two positions about Britain: first that it was the most "tolerant" country in which to be a Jew and, second, that you never knew when you might not get an old-fashioned reminder of your outsider status. In 1950, he was refused membership by the St. James's Club, even though put up by Oliver Lyttelton, and had to settle for Brooks's. The St. James's committee was blunt enough to leave Berlin in no doubt as to the reasons for his rejection. The following year, he became involved in a difficult correspondence with T. S. Eliot, to whose prose work he alluded in the same article on "Jewish Slavery and Emancipation" that had served as a rejoinder to Koestler. Eliot protested in a letter that, for him at least, "the Jewish problem is not a racial problem at all, but a religious problem." In that case, returned Berlin, why did his notorious lecture series, *After Strange Gods*, delivered at the University of Virginia in the year after Hitler's accession to power, insist that "reasons of race and religion make any large number of free-thinking Jews undesirable"? Other considerations apart, how did this observe a distinction between race and religion?

Eliot's reply mumbled some words of contrition for the odious sentence, asserted that Judaism had been made redundant by the marvelous advent of the foretold Christ, and warned that assimilated secularization would be death to both Christians and Jews. To this sectarian arrogance Berlin did not respond, at least not in public. (He wrote to Eliot in 1952, effusively complimenting him on "your most effective and fascinating letters about the Jews.") I said earlier that Berlin

suppressed republication of "Jewish Slavery and Emancipation," which in English at any rate he did. But in the essay's one
Israeli republication, he removed all the offending references
to Eliot. "Much later in life," Ignatieff observes rather briefly,
"he felt that his politeness had shaded into obsequiousness." I
admire the choice of "shaded."

Anglomane that he was, Berlin may have unconsciously
felt that Eliot was a native squire. He certainly did not suffer
from Jewish self-loathing. (That is, if one exempts the strictly
physical dislike which, Ignatieff reveals, he felt for his soft
and, as he thought, sexless and effeminate appearance.) It is
more that he wished to be English than that he yearned to be
other than what he was. In the essay contrasting Disraeli and
Marx, where every allowance is granted to Disraeli and nary a
one to the old incendiary, and where incidentally Berlin refers
unaffectedly to "the colonization of Palestine," there appear
the following lines, in praise of the "Jew d'esprit" who stole
the Suez Canal and proclaimed the empress of India:

> He wanted recognition by those on the inside, as one of them, at
> least as an equal if not as a superior. Hence the psychological
> need to establish an identity for himself, for which he would
> secure recognition, an identity that would enable him to develop
> his gifts freely, to their utmost extent. And in due course he did
> create a personality for himself, at least in his own imagination.
> He saw before him a society of aristocrats, free, arrogant and
> powerful, which, however sharply he may have seen through it,
> he nevertheless viewed with bemused eyes as a rich and marve-
> lous world.

The only inept word there is "bemused," which applies neither
to the brilliant and amoral Tory statesman nor to the man

who wrote of him with such vicarious, almost voluptuous admiration.

A crucial element of good form, in the case of those fortunate enough to have become securely recognized, is the ability to be light-hearted and lenient about some controversies over Jewishness, while reserving the right to be heavy-handed, even juridical, in others. (In case I'm being too elliptical, I mean to say how to avoid being thought of as chippy, while knowing when to call in your chips.) Berlin made himself master of the nuances of this code. I know of a pointed example. In 1960, Professor Norman Birnbaum, then at Oxford and a friend of Berlin's, wrote an article for *Commentary* about the English scene. In it—I possess the original typescript—he proposed to make the following observation for his readers in New York:

> It is a philosophical feat of no small order to celebrate, simultaneously, the essential Britishness of British politics and to derive from it prescriptions applicable to all of mankind's ideological ills. Not surprisingly, this feat has been accomplished by a very cosmopolitan group of philosophers long resident in the British Isles. The writings of Professor Isaiah Berlin, Michael Polanyi and Karl Popper are adduced wherever British self-congratulation seeks intellectually reputable credentials. Foreign voices have also been heard. Professor Jacob Talmon's writings have been praised by the *Times* itself, and Professor Raymond Aron has been honored as if he were a jazz-age Montesquieu, looking admiringly across the Channel from Paris.

One pauses to note that *Commentary* was once a critical magazine. Anyway, Birnbaum sent the essay up to Headington

House, in draft form, in a friendly manner, as one does. I also possess the excitedly annotated original reply:

> If you publish your piece as it stands I shall certainly find my-self compelled to write to *Commentary* to point out the following things . . . You speak of us all as "cosmopolitans" who have lived for various periods in England. The latter words are perfectly true. You do not add the adjective "rootless"; but since all the persons mentioned by you are Jews, the expression too strongly reminds one of the fact that this is how it is used by the pro-fessional antisemites in the Soviet Union—and indeed every-where else. This I shall certainly have to point out to *Commentary*, which is the very journal for such points. It would be better if instead of saying "cosmopolitans" you openly said "Jews of foreign origin." Other Jews, "ideologues" of equally foreign origin from Marx onwards: Namier, Laski, Deutscher, Shonfeld [*sic*], Hobsbawm—I need not go over the list—oppose "us" and dom-inate the discussion and influence gentiles. It may be a sound point, but it is certainly antisemitic; and as *Commentary* enjoys lacerating itself, it will surely not decline to print my letter.

Where to begin? With the idea of a point being simultaneous-ly "sound" and "antisemitic"? With the objection to the word "cosmopolitan" from the fan of Disraeli? Or with the bracket-ing of Namier and Deutscher? (Those lists of names, again.) The article, which must have made Norman Birnbaum wish that he had expended more fire on Michael Oakeshott, later appeared in a version only slightly toned down. Mark the sequel.

In the 1970s, when Hugh Trevor-Roper put up his fright-ful Christ Church friend Zulfikar Ali Bhutto for an honorary degree, there was a row. Richard Gombrich and Steven Lukes led a petition to deny Oxford's imprimatur to the man who had—among his many other crimes—displayed lethal chauvinism over Bangladesh. After the vote in the Sheldonian, which went heavily against Bhutto, I saw Trevor-Roper stalking away and asked him, in my journalist capacity, for a comment. "We've been ambushed," he yelled, "by the left. The left and the Jews." I invited him to repeat this, which he did, and which he did many times later on when the initial fury had abated. There was then another row. Lukes and others circulated a petition critical of the Egregious Regius, and of his . . . want of circumspection. It was Berlin who spent many patient hours trying to persuade them that this did not constitute prejudice. There are times to wheel out the big moral gun, and there are times to be discreet. And there are those who can decide which time is which. And that's power, of a kind.

In the long *Salmagundi* interview by which I help keep count, there appears the following exchange:

Do you think that liberalism is, in this sense, essentially European, then? Or Western?

It was certainly invented in Europe.

Historically, of course. But, I mean now—is it an essentially Western principle?

Yes. I suspect that there may not be much liberalism in Korea. I doubt if there is much liberalism even in Latin America. I think liberalism is essentially the belief of people who have lived on the same soil for a long time in comparative peace with each other. An English invention. The English have not been invaded for a very very long time. That's why they can afford to praise these virtues. I see that if you were exposed to constant pogroms you might be a little more suspicious of the possibility of liberalism.

Here is the rich man's John Rawls. Liberalism is for those who don't need it; free to those who can afford it and very expensive—if even conceivable—to those who cannot. But the clash of ideas here is more chaotic than confused. Should one deduce that liberalism can't be derived from the experience of pogroms? In that case, why did Berlin argue that liberalism was the answer to the experiences of this uniquely grim—as he thought—century? Meanwhile, if liberalism is geographically and even ethnically limited, where is its universality? (And what became of Namier's "Jews and other colored peoples"?) Should one be an English invader in order to be a carrier of liberal ideals? Finally, what's the point of a tumultuous and volatile and above all "cosmopolitan" society, like that of America, if high liberalism can only be established with common blood and on common soil?

Again, one gets the queasy impression that Berlin's opinions were a farrago: an unsorted box raided for lucky dips. Incidentally, "people who have lived on the same soil for a long time in comparative peace with one another" must be close kin to "the same people living in the same place"—Eliot's sine qua non for a stable and organic (and static) society in *After Strange Gods*.

I've kept for last Isaiah Berlin's most luminous moment: his encounter with Anna Akhmatova in St. Petersburg, as it was called when Berlin first saw it and as it is again called today. When he made his visit in November 1945, as a first secretary at the British Embassy, it was called Leningrad and had, under that name, resisted and thrown back the Nazis. During the unspeakable siege, Stalin and Zhdanov, in that mad way they had, took personal steps to rescue Anna Akhmatova and evacuate her to Tashkent, where she shared quarters with Nadezhda Mandelstam. But they did this insincerely and pedantically (and in Stalin's own case perhaps superstitiously), regarding her as part asset and part witch. Many people were not sure that she had survived. Berlin himself only discovered her whereabouts by accident, while visiting a rugged and bohemian bookstore. Wherever he traveled, Berlin carried a certain idea of Oxford. He had not yet read any of Akhmatova's poems, but he knew that they had been kept in print by his friend Maurice Bowra. (Score one, then, for the Wadham man so often described as having squandered his gifts.)

When he set off to call at N.44 Fontanka, therefore, Berlin stepped out of his usual cocoon. He was taking a risk, leaving everything to chance, acting on human instinct. The resulting meetings are much better rendered by Ignatieff than by György Dalos.[*] Not only was Berlin, in a later phrase of an Akhmatova poem, "the guest from the future," he was also a revenant from the past and a catalyst for the fusion of the Russian intellectual diaspora with those, like Akhmatova, who had decided to stay on, no matter what. He brought her some Kafka. They disagreed vividly about Turgenev and Dostoevsky, with Berlin naturally preferring the more vulpine Turgenev. In a freezing flat with nothing to eat but cold spuds, the emotional thermostat was set very high. Dalos doesn't mind pruriently canvassing the possibility of a

---

[*] *The Guest from the Future: Anna Akhmatova and Isaiah Berlin* by György Dalos, translated by Antony Wood (John Murray, 1998).

tryst, but it's very clear that this was one of those few occasions where that really would have spoiled everything. Ignatieff, who gives us the impression that Berlin was a virgin until middle age, is emphatic and on good authority. Berlin, he writes,

> remained on one side of the room, she on the other. Far from being a Don Juan, he was a sexual neophyte alone in the apartment of a fabled seductress, who had enjoyed deep romantic entanglements with half a dozen supremely talented men... Besides, he was also aware of more quotidian needs. He had already been there six hours and he wanted to go to the lavatory. But it would have broken the mood to do so, and in any case, the communal toilet was down the dark hallway.

At last, a Boswellian moment. Berlin's subsequent report to the Foreign Office, instead of processing political intelligence in the conventional way, was a learned and spirited brief on the artists and writers of the Soviet Union, and on the thuggish nullity of those who tried to break them. And this was prescient, as well as fine. (The only really stupid critique of Isaiah Berlin that I have ever read was by that recreational vulpicide Roger Scruton, who accused him of being soft on communism.) Nothing can spoil this memory. If Akhmatova was persecuted afresh as a result of the rendezvous, she had no illusions, and had not been trapped into anything. Berlin's Uncle Leo was later treated barbarously during the Jew-baiting that surrounded the Doctors' Plot, but Soviet antisemitism was sui generis. The only subsequent meeting between Berlin and Akhmatova was an anticlimax as, given her queenly manners, it more or less had to be. But without her vanity, an aspect of her irreducible courage and confidence after all, she would not have proved that an individual may outlast both a state and an ideology.

There was one moment of bathos during the Leningrad meeting, which was the fault of neither participant. As Berlin and Akhmatova talked, there came disconcerting bellows of "Isaiah" from the courtyard below. This was Randolph Churchill, puce and solipsistic, demanding that his friend come without loss of time to the Hotel Astoria, there to explain to the domestics of the famine-stricken city that Mr. Churchill's newly purchased caviar should be placed on ice. Berlin actually broke off conversation with Akhmatova to go and see to the matter. But then, poor dear Randolph was very much a part of that same package of Englishness which he had already bought.

If it is fair to say, as Ignatieff does, that Berlin never coined an epigram or aphorism, it is also fair to add that he never broke any really original ground in the field of ideas. He was a skilled ventriloquist for other thinkers. Still, even in proposing wobbly antitheses (positive v. negative, liberal v. romantic, Enlightenment v. Counter-Enlightenment, incomparable goals as distinct from incompatible or incommensurable ones) he turned over some mental baggage. The letters, too, promise to be a magnificent trove, even if they contain some rude shocks to his liberal fan club. Perhaps, then, to paraphrase Wilde, the real genius was in the life and not the work: "a real 20th-century life," as Margalit puts it. Fearing that English liberalism on its own was too diffuse and benign and insipid, he tried to inject it with a dose of passionate intensity, much of it necessarily borrowed from some rather illiberal sources. Convinced also that pluralism of values was inescapable—a "relative" commonplace—he helped to refresh the sometimes arid usage of irony which the English regard as their particular discourse. In our native terms, the ironic style is often compounded with the sardonic and the hard-boiled; even the effortlessly superior. But irony originates in the glance and the shrug of the loser, the outsider, the despised minority. It is a nuance that comes most effortlessly to the oppressed. Czeslaw Milosz, Berlin's non-Jewish Baltic contemporary, went so far in his poem "Not This Way" as to term irony "the glory of slaves." He did not, I am certain, intend to say that it was a servile quality. But Berlin's aptitude in this most subtle of idioms was conditioned in part by his long service to a multiplicity of masters.

Letters

10 December 1998

Christopher Hitchens, reviewing Michael Ignatieff's study of Sir Isaiah Berlin, claims that I accused Sir Isaiah of being soft on communism. This is not true. In the piece to which Hitchens refers (the only article I have ever written about Berlin), I praised Berlin for his hostility to communism. But I criticized him for being soft on communists and their fellow-travelers. Like many liberals, Berlin pursued a policy of *pas d'ennemi à gauche*. The wisdom of this policy, in a man not naturally given to feats of courage, is amply displayed by Hitchens's review: a collage of mischievous gossip, innuendo and self-righteous contempt, the only ground for which is the support Berlin offered to those who were prepared to defend liberal democracy against revolutionary communism. Were history called on to judge, would Berlin's name come higher or lower than that of Hitchens, I wonder, on the list of those who have sided with political crime?

Roger Scruton
Brinkworth, Wiltshire

---

21 January 1999

Roger Scruton, a remote and ineffectual don, takes up his quavering, corroded pen: "Were history called on to judge," he asks, "would Berlin's name come higher or lower than that of Hitchens, I wonder, on the list of those who have sided with political crime?" Can Scruton cite a single political crime with which Hitchens has "sided"? If not, would he care to apologize for this libel—and, in future, to consign his malodorous ruminations to their proper place in his Wiltshire cesspit?

Francis Wheen
Pleshey, Essex

---

18 February 1999

Francis Wheen challenges Roger Scruton to "cite a single political crime" with which Christopher Hitchens has sided. Well, "crime" is rather strong, but Hitchens is a self-confessed homophobe. When I was on the national executive of Liberty, then called NCCL, in the 1980s, I wrote to Hitchens about his homophobic sneerings in the *New Statesman*. His reply makes it clear that gay oppression is not to be seriously compared to other (then more fashionable) types of injustice. Specifically alluding to my complaint that he used terms of abuse in order to underline his contempt for gay people, he wrote: "I think that people's sexual preferences are a legitimate subject for humor, dirty humor if at all possible. Obviously, one of the comic things about the Cambridge spy ring is that all or most of its members were/are queer...Faggotry, in my judgment, is as good a metaphor for that little world as any other." When he appeared on Channel 4's *Face the Press* in October 1984, Hitchens's homophobic outbursts led Julian Barnes to say that "you'd certainly need a lot of karma not to reach for your baseball bat" after hearing Hitchens's remarks.

What interests me is left homophobia. It is one manifestation of "gay exceptionalism," whereby people who are progressive in relation to other social issues, draw a line at homosexuality. Many of the canonical texts of feminism are blemished in this way. Homosexuality "is spreading like a murky smog over the American scene," according to Betty Friedan in *The Feminine Mystique*. The hostility of Channel 4 producers to the gay community is well documented. Quite recently, a review in the *Guardian* of a collection of academic literary essays I edited appeared under the heading "Fairy Stories." Throughout Peter Preston's editorship of that paper, there was no coverage at all of lesbian issues, a ban on equal access for personal ads and a continuation of the paper's traditional support for supernaturalism. Alexander Chancellor is "not sure," on 19 July 1997, whether equality for gay people is a good idea. As late as 1996, in his review of *Kids*, Derek Malcolm is dividing AIDS sufferers into the "innocent" (infection by non-sexual means) and "guilty." Throughout the 1980s, the *Times Educational Supplement* refused to cover the subject of homophobic bullying in schools, on the grounds that it was "not on the agenda," though it is probably the main type of playground humiliation. The *Observer* carries a column by Richard Ingrams, who came third in a poll some years ago in *Gay Times* (after Norman Tebbit and Rabbi Jacobovits) as Homophobe of the Year. Had the same level of prejudice been directed against a racial minority, or the disabled, it would have been denounced with vigor and might well have led to criminal proceedings or civil litigation.

Mark Lilly
University of Tunis

4 March 1999

It's not possible to please everyone, and it can be unwise even to try, but I found on reading Mark Lilly's letter that I felt a sort of commitment to cheering him up. Anyone who has so resentfully treasured one of my frivolous notes from the dear dead days of twenty years ago, and who keeps it by him in a gazelle-infested exile at the University of Tunis, is entitled to such consolation as I can afford.

His case against me is one of latent and blatant homophobia, of the sort that if directed at another target might be "denounced with vigor and might well have led to criminal proceedings or civil litigation." By happy chance, I can refer him to a recent "outing," conducted by Alexander Cockburn in the tabloid *New York Press* of the first week of February: "Many's the time male friends have had to push Hitchens's mouth, fragrant with martinis, away, as, amid the welcomes and goodbyes, he seeks their cheek or lips." Some good critics regard this as one of Cockburn's more polished pieces, especially dealing as it does with the absolute and inflexible requirement never to rat on an old pal. I offer it, though, as an example of a badge of supposed shame that one may wear with pride.

I was at first puzzled by Lilly's other faded but faithfully preserved clipping, wherein he quotes Julian Barnes, then in his TV critic period, from October 1984. Apparently "Hitchens's homophobic outbursts led Julian Barnes to say that 'you'd certainly need a lot of karma not to reach for your baseball bat' " after my appearance on the tiny screen. A quick call to Julian and the fount of memory was unsealed. I had done a chat show with Norman Mailer, after the incautious publication of his book *Tough Guys Don't Dance*. And I had ragged him a bit about his literary obsession with the occasions of sodomy, to say nothing of his then interest in the karmic. "I was," recalled Barnes, "sort of handing the baseball bat to Mailer." This same notion had in fact occurred to Mailer himself. After the show, he berated me, and inscribed his copy of *Tough Guys* with an admonition to "see what I say about you." Nor had I long to wait. In a lengthy interview with the *Face* he attributed his bad notices to the fact that the London literary racket was run by a daisy chain of queens, led by Martin Amis, Ian Hamilton and myself. (Amis and I composed, but did not eventually send, a letter to the *Face* protesting that this was *very unfair* to Ian Hamilton.)

Mailer and I have since made it up. So could one leave it like this? I would never persecute or deride Lilly, and he in return should drop his lugubrious demand that gay-teasers should be prosecuted. Also, he might bear in mind our relative advantages. He lives in Tunis. I live in sodding Washington, DC. Was it so kind of him to rub this in? Need he have reminded me of the time when I could dash off a mocking letter to the likes of himself, and had not reached the state of decrepitude when only women would even consider going to bed with me?

Christopher Hitchens
Washington, DC

What a Lot of Parties
On Diana Mosley
1999

I N THE AUTUMN of 1980 I was leafing through the latest number of *Books and Bookmen* and came across a notice of Hans-Otto Meissner's biography of Magda Goebbels. The reviewer was Diana Mosley. Fair enough, I thought, she had at least known the woman. Indeed, as she put it herself: "I knew Magda and Dr. Goebbels quite well. She was charming and beautiful, he was clever and witty." Eschewing bleeding-heart compassion, yet unusually ready to put in a humane word for the unfit, she found the kindest context for the dwarfishness of her hero, whom she described as "a small man, not much smaller than Napoleon. He limped because of a club foot, as did Byron. Very clever, he got a scholarship to Heidelberg where he acquired his doctorate." Lady Mosley burbled on in this vein for a bit, spicing things up with references to Goebbels's "inspired oratory." Concerning Kristallnacht she was scrupulously non-judgmental, concluding that "his guilt must rest on supposition." I remember wondering how she would tackle the ticklish question of the immolation of the Goebbels *Kinder*. Here is how she grasped the nettle: "Everyone knows the tragic end. As the Russians surrounded Berlin, the Goebbels painlessly killed their children and then themselves. The dead children were described by people who saw them as looking 'peacefully asleep.' Those who condemn this appalling, Masada-like deed must consider the alternative facing the distraught Magda." At this point, I threw the mag to one side and seized a pen. It's true that the shaggy fundamentalists in the Josephus yarn did put their families to the sword before falling on their own, but still . . . So I wrote a piece for the old *New Statesman*, emptying the vials over *Books and Bookmen* and saying rather pompously that I wouldn't turn in my next review for it until the editor had repudiated the Mosley/Masada trope.

Then several things happened. The owner of *Books and Bookmen*, an operator by the name of Philip Dosse, took the opportunity of emulating the Masada faction and the Goebbelses, and committed suicide himself. I received a moist letter from the editor of the magazine, written in the tone of "I hope you're satisfied *now*." I was accused in print, by Auberon Waugh, of having more or less driven Dosse to his death by my vile polemics and of having cruelly lampooned his name as "Dose or Dosser." And I got letters from both Mosleys, on writing paper from their preposterous address in Orsay, Temple de la Gloire. I curse myself for having lost the one from Sir Oswald, containing his usual disclaimers about ever having been a Nazi or a traitor, because he had only weeks to live and it may have been among his last efforts. The one from his fragrant wife survives, and reads as follows:

> Mr. Hitchens, in his attack upon me, says that I regretted the defeat of Germany in the Second World War. On the contrary, in my view the greatest tragedy for us would have been the defeat of our own country. My opposition to the war in 1939 was based

on the fact, as obvious to many people then as it is to everyone now, that it was a war we could not "win." The winners were the Soviet Union and America: Europe was the loser.

This was a silly letter, containing the same essential contradiction (the Goebbelses' action at once "appalling" and entirely forgivable) as had the original silly review. In fact, the whole episode was rather petty and absurd, for all that it got people going for a week or two. (I was relieved in spite of everything when it came out that Dosse had killed himself over some more private misery, and before he could even have scanned my poor barbs.)

Reading Jan Dalley's very scrupulous if slightly solemn book, I was visited by the same sense of pervasive pointlessness.* Here again one encounters teak-headedness and conceit among the overdogs. Here again one learns how vulgar bigotry can be veneered with sophistication. And here again one encounters a Waugh. Auberon's father dedicated his novel *Vile Bodies* and his travel book *Labels* to Bryan and Diana Guinness. He was certainly in love with the latter and probably derived the scene in *A Handful of Dust* about the complaisant husband's fakery of a compromising situation in Brighton from Bryan Guinness's willingness to undergo the same indignity when the time came to hand on his wife to Sir Oswald Mosley. How amusing it now seems that this was all done, in the jargon of the day, so as to "avoid scandal." But then, how minuscule appear the self-evidently scandalous doings of any of this "set," compared to what we have since learned and understood.

---

* *Diana Mosley: A Biography* by Jan Dalley (Faber, 1999).

The book opens and closes in Holloway Prison, where in a princess-and-the-pea setting that by no means denies sympathy to its subject, a society beauty is immured among coarse and unfeeling types, and made to lie on a verminous mattress on a damp floor. Here, I feel, we should better consult *Decline and Fall*, where Paul Pennyfeather languishes in Dartmoor, taking the rap for the exquisite but evil Margot Beste-Chetwynde, and reflects on

> the undeniable cogency of Peter Beste-Chetwynde's "You can't see Mamma in prison, can you?" The more Paul considered this, the more he perceived it to be the statement of a natural law. He appreciated the assumption of comprehension with which Peter had delivered it. As he studied Margot's photograph, dubiously transmitted as it was, he was strengthened in his belief that there was, in fact, and should be, one law for her and another for himself, and that the raw little exertions of 19th-century Radicals were essentially base and trivial and misdirected. It was not simply that he *saw* the *impossibility* of Margot in prison; the bare connection of vocables associating the ideas was obscene.

Of course Peter Beste-Chetwynde was a promising adolescent, whereas Diana Mosley's breasts were swollen with milk for a newborn when she was abruptly interned in July 1940 and made to share limited sanitary facilities with the lower-class female members of the British Union of Fascists. (This being good old Blighty, some of the other internees were political refugees from the Third Reich, who had been locked up on what you might call general "better safe than sorry" principles.)

Dalley evokes the general unease felt by Churchill's government—after all, he was a friend and a sort of relative—the prurient interest taken by the popular press and the vindictiveness displayed by the communists, who had not by 1940 quite adopted Mosley's view that this was a patriotic war in which all good Blackshirts should enlist under the colors of empire. (After the Communist Party did adopt its red-shirt version of this line, the Mosleys were released, causing another storm in the *Daily Worker*'s chipped teacup.) The entire absurdity is well caught in the observation of a Holloway wardress named Miss Davies, who years later told a prison visitor: "Oh, we've never had such laughs since Lady Mosley left." ("Oh, Nina, what a lot of parties!") We are confronted, here, with the worst and not the least bright of the Bright Young Things: with a vile mind and a gorgeous carapace, and with a maddening class confidence allied to a tiny, repetitive tic of fanaticism. It's easy to see how Diana Mitford/Guinness/ Mosley attracted the obvious clichés about the huntress and the nymph. Anyone with her first name, and a pleasing profile to boot, can earn such leaden gallantries, as Earl Spencer, that other upper-class thug, not long ago demonstrated afresh to the gaping peasants of the tabloid press. Though she never went to the length of adopting a black toyboy, as the fictional Margot did with Chokey, la Mosley certainly attended her share of *bals nègres* at Nancy Cunard's. She kept a circle of gay male friends, from Gerald Berners to Cecil Beaton, at a time when homosexuals were being whacked to a pulp in German and Italian prisons. When occasion demanded, she could speak with conviction about the "old gang" of politicians, and about the woes of the unemployed. But something else made her different from dozens of other women and men of her class, who didn't share her Bloomsbury connections but did echo her enthusiasm for the New Order and the New Germany. Just this: she kept it up longer than most of them did and in more arduous conditions. In a fashion, she keeps it up still. It's always seemed very obvious to me, and I'm confirmed in my view by a number of Dalley's findings, that her core obsession must have been with the Jews.

Antisemitism is a prejudice that may sometimes be, but usually is not, lightly worn. It has great appeal to pseudo-intellectuals and pseudo-aesthetes, such as she was and is, because it has great gossipy power and can draw on history and mythology and concepts like blood and gold. It can seem to explain a lot. And it can form a bond between upper-crust types and the plebeians, a bond of sturdy race and nation against the clever and the tricky and the "hard to place": the very "socialism of fools" that August Bebel identified and that the Mosleys tried to carry into practice.

A dead giveaway, in distinguishing the obsessive or morbid antisemite from the garden variety, is an inability to stay off the subject. See above the way that Masada substitutes for King Charles's head. See also the testimony that Lady Mosley gave to those who were vetting her in 1940. She announced that she would like to see the German system installed in Britain though (also see her facing-both-ways letter to me above) without an invasion or a British defeat: i.e. as the only uncoerced following of the Nazi example. After uttering this absurdity she was asked whether such a manifesto might include emulating the Reich's policy toward Jews? "Yes, up to a point. I am not fond of Jews." Dalley tells us that after Lady Mosley (I find I can't adopt her convenience name of "Diana") first met the grotesque "Putzi" Hanfstaengl in 1933, he told her that Jews were only 1 percent of the German nation, that the Führer's critics never stopped talking about the 1 percent, but that Hitler was determined to get a better life for the "remaining" 99 percent. Apparently, this slobbering bit of fallacy so impressed the fair visitor that she keeps on repeating it to this day: a sure indicator of the real deep-seated infection since (all other considerations to one side) she could hardly not notice that the Nazis talked about this same 1 percent at least 99 percent of the time. The same tendency to bogus rationalization was manifested in her oddball son Jonathan Guinness, who was obviously trying his best when asked if it had been difficult at Eton in 1944, what with his mother imprisoned as a Hitler sympathizer and all. No, he replied. The stigma was "about on a par with being Jewish." I think this remark must have come from the maternal hearth and not the genes.

So it isn't quite accurate to say, as Dalley rather awkwardly phrases it, that "in her personal story there is an almost eerie absence of the horrors that underlie all our thinking about fascism, Nazism and the Second World War." Sir Oswald, for example, always tried very strenuously to distance himself from said horrors after 1945 and, though he was unconvincing in his rewriting, at least made the attempt. His widow has never bothered even to feign that effort, and is sometimes too languid and spiteful to conceal her prejudices even now. The subject clearly fatigues and irritates her. A part of her, like the ghastly girl in Patrick Hamilton's *Hangover Square*, was and is secretly gleeful about fascism. Dalley describes as "unusual" her attendance at a Hyde Park rally in 1935, where she threw up her right hand in a Nazi salute while Clement Attlee was addressing a mild-as-milk protest against Hitler's early barbarities. It's improbable that she just stumbled on such an opportunity, or simply found herself taking it. That's on a par with her claim that Adolf Hitler was chief guest at her wedding because he lived so handily nearby and chanced to drop in. The illicit thrill of evil is the point—a thrill indulged by someone whose own circumstances and life chances gave no evident cause for complaint.

I once spent some time with Sir Oswald Mosley, in a television green room. He chatted amiably enough, reminiscing away and turning on the charm, and recalling (an event actually mentioned in these pages) that the most disconcerting disruption of any of his speeches took place in Oxford, when some pinko students simply opened newspapers in the front row of the hall and read them calmly throughout his rantings. Then he got on the set, adjusted his mike, set his jaw and delivered (this was 1972) a hideous attack on the arrival of Ugandan Asian refugees. I remember thinking that I had seen both Mosleys—the lounge lizard and the street-corner demagogue—in one afternoon. One can perhaps forgive the dim socialites who only ever saw one version—the dashing Tom of the West End—and never saw the other: the snarling leader in the East End. But his wife would have had to know of the duality, and this one would have had to love it, too.

There are some nice new curiosities to paste into one's album. Visiting Goebbels at an early stage of what became the Abdication crisis, Lady Mosley gave him all the scoop about the Simpson business:

> Goebbels and Hitler seemed shocked, but they did not forget that, as Prince of Wales, Edward had spoken publicly in support

of Hitler's social program. From October onwards the newspapers of America and the rest of Europe were full of the scandal, while the British press kept silent, and Hitler and Goebbels decided to support the king in the same way—Goebbels put a total ban on any mention of the royal goings-on in the German media. After the abdication two months later, Nazi wiretappers intercepted a comment from one British Embassy official, to the effect that the former king would be sure to remember Hitler's decision with gratitude.

Worth knowing and, for the fans of privacy laws, worth noting. But then, the Mosleys' connection with the prince's Blackshirt chum "Fruity" Metcalfe and his wife, Baba (sister to Mosley's first wife), and their later propinquity to HRH and "Wallis" in France, only serve to emphasize how faded and remote all this stuff has become. I once asked the heavenly Jessica Mitford if she ever had any contact with the Temple de la Gloire branch of her sisterhood. "Rather not!" she snorted. "I bowed a bit icily to Diana at dear Nancy's funeral, but otherwise it's been *utter non-speakers* since at least Munich." She didn't seem to feel that she'd missed much and after finishing this book I'm bound to say that neither do I.

11 September 1973
Pinochet and Britain

2002

I HAVE a more or less fixed memory of the end of the "Sixties." In the autumn of 1970 I went to join a strike picket at the General Motors plant in Fremont, California. Handy for Berkeley and Oakland, the factory was one of the salients of a national labor shutdown that was scheduled to begin at 12 o'clock at night. In the ranks of supporters were hardened veterans of the battle against the Vietnam War, especially of the famous blockades of the military recruiting centers in the Bay Area. Sympathizers of the not yet discredited Black Panther Party were in evidence, as were those who had been beaten and tear-gassed alongside Cesar Chavez in his fight to unionize the near serfs of the Salinas Valley agribusiness empire. All the strands of the "movement" were still in some kind of alignment. Just before the deadline, the company cops tried to smuggle some scab trucks through the gates, and the resulting bonfire of overturned vehicles gave a lovely light. In the next edition of the *People's World*, the splash headline was a very 1960s one: "Fremont—In the Midnight Hour." It competed for space with another, smaller headline, which announced the victory of Salvador Allende's Popular Unity coalition in Chile.

The Nixon-Kissinger regime was then only in its opening years, but it had become clear to some of us that the long, withdrawing roar of the Vietnam crisis was at least half over. What nobody quite suspected was that Chile, a country far below the equator and seemingly well out of the line of fire, would have such a determining effect on what it meant to be left or right in the ensuing two decades. Andy Beckett was born a few months before the moment I have just described, and I am stirred and astonished at his brilliance, and by the imaginative sympathy with which he rekindles the arguments and emotions of a period he never knew.*

For many people including myself, 11 September has long been a date of mourning and rage. On that day in 1973, lethal aircraft flew low over a major city and destroyed a great symbolic building: the presidential palace in Santiago, known (because it had once been a mint) as La Moneda. Its constitutional occupant, Salvador Allende, could perhaps have bargained to save his own life, but elected not to do so. Instead, over a crackling radio, he made a speech that will bear comparison with the last broadcasts from Athens in 1941 and Budapest in 1956:

> This is certainly the last time I shall speak to you...History has given me a choice. I shall sacrifice my life in loyalty to my people, in the knowledge that the seeds we planted in the noble consciousness of thousands of Chileans can never be prevented from bearing fruit...Much sooner than later, the great avenues toward a new society will open again, and the march along that road will continue.

---

* *Pinochet in Piccadilly: Britain and Chile's Hidden History* by Andy Beckett (Faber, 2002).

There's also an echo here of some of the defiant speeches made in defense of the Spanish Republic and the Popular Front. And, as a young politician in prewar Chile, Allende had arranged to give refuge to many anti-Franco Spaniards and Catalans and Basques. Moreover, he had sent a delegation to the Bolivian frontier in late 1968, to rescue the cadaverous survivors of Che Guevara's doomed insurgency. If you visit the Bodeguita del Medio in Havana today, there to sample the bogus Hemingway-style mojito cocktail that the management offers to the new tourist trade, you can see where Allende once added his signature to those scrawled on the wall. "Viva Cuba Libre," it says. "Chile espera." That was on 28 June 1961. The inscription possesses an almost antique quality these days, like a graffito from a revolutionary Pompeii. Allende, in other words, was old left: a dedicated physician, an anti-clerical Freemason, a tireless campaigner and reformer and internationalist. But, unlike the Fidelistas of the 26 July movement who promised an election in Cuba and have still never got round to holding one, he was absolutely committed to the routines and even the rituals of what was once known as bourgeois democracy. His victory in 1970 was the coronation of innumerable previous attempts to assemble a coalition of the Chilean left, large enough to include the radical Christians and those of the middle class who wanted some say in how the country's natural resources were exploited, and by whom. Pablo Neruda may have been a dank Stalinist in his politics, and have allowed this to infect his poetry, but he was writing as a patriot when he composed the potent verses entitled "They Receive Instructions Against Chile" (translated here by Robert Bly):

But we have to see behind all these, there is something
behind the traitors and the gnawing rats,
an empire which sets the table,
and serves up the nourishment and the bullets.
They want to repeat their great success in Greece.
Greek playboys at the banquet, and bullets
for the people in the mountains...
the generals retire from the army and serve
as vice-presidents of the Chuquicamata Copper Firm,
and in the nitrate works the "Chilean" general
decides with his trailing sword how much the natives
may mention when they apply for a rise in wages.
In this way they decide from above, from the roll of dollars,
in this way the dwarf traitor receives his instructions,
and the generals act as the police force,
and the trunk of the tree of the country rots.

This warning was published in 1967, just after the CIA had abolished civilian rule in Athens. Allende's election was principally a test of the limits of Chilean independence, but it was also a laboratory experiment in what used to be termed "the peaceful road to socialism." Would oligarchy and empire permit an election result to stand if it went against their interests? A good number of people on the left, myself again included, were convinced that no such window would be allowed to stay open for long. Graham Greene made a visit to Chile in the early Allende years and spent a good deal of time with the supporters of the MIR (Movement of the Revolutionary Left), who kept on warning that there would be a violent confrontation, engineered by the ruling class and the *Yanquis* without respect for "the rules." Allende himself gave a series of interviews to Régis Debray, Guevara's former epigone, in which he maintained to the contrary that a democratic transition was possible. Reviewing Debray's book for the Times in 1971, I quoted Tawney's old dictum that while you could peel an onion layer by layer, you could not skin a live tiger claw by claw.

In truth, as we now know in annihilating detail, the principle was not allowed to be tested. Even before Allende had taken the oath of office in 1970, death squads paid for by Henry Kissinger had embarked on a campaign of murder and destabilization, and had shot down the chief of the Chilean general staff, René Schneider, in the street, for nothing more than his legalistic opposition to a coup. There was an initial revulsion at this, on the part of the center and even the right, and the sheer voting strength and level-headedness of Popular Unity enabled it to postpone the evil day for three years. But in the meantime Nixon yelled orders, which were obeyed by his corporate and intelligence allies, to "make the Chilean economy scream." (As Daniel Ellsberg's wife commented when she first saw the Pentagon Papers, the American authorities in those days were fond of using "the language of torturers.") So that when the Chilean armed forces came out of their barracks in September 1973, and began their hysterical mop-up, there were depressingly many who found harsh authority a respite from shortage and scarcity, and from the kind of socialist rhetoric that brings diminishing returns. This moment is captured with consummate skill in the Costa-Gavras movie Missing, where the conservative American father of the "disappeared" Charles Horman arrives in town just after the coup and hands his son's girlfriend a bag of goodies from the prosperous North. "Here are some things Charlie said were in short supply." The girl (Sissy Spacek) fixes Jack Lemmon with a pitying look. "Not any more," she says. The scarcities, like everything else, were politically conditioned.

In one way, this strangulation of Chilean democracy was a jewel in the crown of those successful Washington-inspired military coups and counter-revolutions that featured Iran in 1953, Guatemala in 1954, Brazil in 1964, went on through Indonesia in 1965 and Greece in 1967, and extended as far as Cyprus in 1974. (The slogan of the extreme right in Chile during the Allende years was the single ominous word "Jakarta": intuitive proof in itself that the poisoned apple did not fall far from the tree.) But, as a Chilean comrade of mine ruefully commented recently, he never expected that Pinochet could produce a revolution as well as a counter-revolution. The new model "free economy" created in Chile became an inspiration for the British and the American right, even as its police state provided a rallying point for the international left. Andy Beckett makes both points with great acuity, but he confines himself to the British scene. In my view, Chile in those years had a catalytic effect on the entire political discourse. In Western Europe, it helped create the conditions both for Euro-Communism and for the "historic compromise" by which important elements among the conservative order (especially in Italy) decided not to identify themselves with authoritarian rule. In Eastern Europe, meanwhile, the incessant communist propaganda about solidarity with Chile had an unintended consequence. The moral grandeur of Allende's death, which was simplistically employed to demonstrate the obvious barbarity of American imperialism, also derived from the fact that he had been murdered as a legitimate president in between two free elections. So perhaps there was some missing point to be made about political pluralism as well. The emblematic moment here was reached in 1975, when the Soviet Union swapped the conservative dissident Vladimir Bukovsky for the imprisoned Chilean communist leader Luís Corvalán. The party press reported only that Corvalán had been released as a consequence of international proletarian solidarity, but in Poland in the winter of 1975, there to report on the beginnings of the workers' movement, I found that everybody in Warsaw knew the true state of the case. Some of the comparisons between Dubček in 1968 and Allende in 1973 were facile. And some were obtuse—Corvalán had enthusiastically supported the Soviet invasion of Prague, while not even the Red Army went so far as to murder Dubček or massacre his sympathizers. Over time, however, the idea of a universal human rights ethic gained enormous traction from both crimes. And in the United States, the identification of the authorities with the junta principle, and not just in Chile, was a perpetual source of embarrassment and discredit. (The recent Inspector Clouseau-like performance of the Bush team over Venezuela shows, perhaps paradoxically, that establishment confidence in such methods has not yet been regained.)

To take the British microcosm of these events, as Beckett does, is to recognize a somewhat neglected and in many ways rather charming aspect of our history. There is an old latent connection between the two countries, extending back as far as Admiral Cochrane's opportunistic semi-freelance aid for the War of Chilean Independence against Spain. (Some distant booms and cannon shots from this episode may be found in the later novels of Patrick O'Brian.) Is it too fanciful to see a common and self-consciously phlegmatic character as well? Chile is divided almost as surely from its continental neighbors, by the spine of the Andes, as is Britain by the Channel. The outlook is maritime: the principal industry is, or was, mining. Gabriel García Márquez once described Chile as "a cornice of the Andes in a misty sea." One could push this too far, no doubt (the sheer quality of Chilean wine would be a counter-indicator), but it remains the case that the Chilean upper class is highly Anglophile, as are many of the liberals and leftists, and that it's a cause of local regret that, whereas the Chilean navy owes much to British traditions, the Chilean army was trained by Prussians—who used to rehearse counter-insurgency on the local Araucanian Indians until the supply of exemplary victims was exhausted. Even so, and in order to distinguish it from the grisly recurrence of juntas and *pronunciamentos* in adjacent countries such as Argentina, Chile became known sometimes as the Switzerland, and sometimes also the England, of Latin America.

Life in the British Labour movement in the mid to late 1970s was mediocre and uninspired. At the Wilson-Callaghan level of leadership, the main features were compromise, consensus and corruption. The future SDP was evolving within the cabinet; the Liberals and even the Orangemen were abjectly wooed in Parliament. The IMF could dictate terms, often not very politely. Meanwhile, the activist left was mired in arguments over the closed shop and the dull referendum on the Common Market. Not exactly the stuff of radical intoxication. The Chile Solidarity Campaign supplied a much needed infusion of dash and authenticity. Here was a flagrant example of a regime of steel helmets and dark glasses, riding like a juggernaut over the wreckage of the unions, the universities and the free press. Many brilliant Chilean exiles found refuge in Britain, and many of them could recite poems and play musical instruments. Joan Jara, the English-born widow of the composer and musician Victor Jara, could still a large hall with the story of how, before Pinochet's goons murdered her husband in the camp they had improvised in Santiago's National Stadium, they had taken particular care to smash his hands. Concerts and rallies for Chile possessed real elan. Beckett doesn't mention it, but I remember that a fluent young MP named Neil Kinnock became the darling of the constituency parties by his advocacy of the Chilean cause. A row over the sale of British frigates to the Chilean navy led to Eric Heffer's resignation from the Labour government. And—in an episode Beckett does revisit in some detail—the workers at the Rolls-Royce factory in East Kilbride refused to touch, or let anyone else touch, the jet engines that were being repaired for Chilean air force Hawker Hunters (the very planes that had bombed their own capital city on 11 September 1973). The boycott was kept up for almost five years. It is strangely moving to read his reconstruction of that episode of gritty working-class internationalism, even if the minutes of the union meetings now sound a bit like the last signals from a dying planet.

Very much less publicly, and in meetings of which we do not possess the minutes, a faction of the British right was drawing the exactly opposite conclusion. Commenting on the Pinochet bloodbath on the day it began, the *Times* outdid itself by saying that matters in Chile had deteriorated to the point where "a reasonable military man" might have decided to become the savior of his country. We have since been told, in the memoirs of Field Marshal Sir Michael Carver, that there was quite a lot of loose talk in the officers' mess in those days, about taking Britain by the scruff of the neck and generally cleaning things up. The public face of this sinister idiocy was represented by blimpish figures of fun like General Sir Walter Walker, who perhaps thought he had found a formula to negate one of the oldest maxims of the class war—that you cannot dig coal with bayonets. But there were other serving officers who clearly hoped that they might improve on the silent mutiny with which they had prevented Harold Wilson from using force against Ian Smith's racist settler rebellion in 1965. For such people, the workers of East Kilbride were "the enemy within," to be grouped with Irish Republicans and revolting students.

Much more significant in the long run were the policy intellectuals crystallizing around the Thatcher candidacy, who wanted to revive the free market doctrines of Hayek and Friedman. The paradox in their case was obvious: it might take a very strong state to impose these libertarian values. Milton Friedman himself, and others of the so-called Chicago School of political economy, had been engaged by the Pinochet regime as advisers. In 1976, Allende's former comrade Orlando Letelier, by then living in exile in Washington, wrote an extraordinary essay for the Nation entitled "The Chicago Boys in Chile." I remember getting the New Statesman to reprint it. It laid out the principle of the free economy/strong state equation: shock treatment number one being the application of electrodes to the recalcitrant, and shock treatment number two being the withdrawal of public subsidy for the unfit or the inefficient. A few months after publishing the article,

Orlando Letelier was torn to pieces by a car bomb in rush-hour Washington traffic, just a few blocks from where I am writing these words. The explosive device, which also murdered an American colleague and friend, was detonated by agents of the Chilean dictatorship who, until recently, had the distinction of being the first state-supported terrorists to dare an attack in the middle of an American city. This—the blowback from Kissinger's policy of giving Pinochet a fair wind and a green light—has now been fully investigated by the Justice Department and the FBI. Their finding, that Pinochet himself ordered the hit, awaits executive action at a moment when the U.S. is at least officially pledged to combat such outrages without pity or discrimination.

Beckett explores the filiations between the Chilean "experiment" and such Thatcherite figures as Sir Alan Walters and Robert Moss. In the course of his inquiries, he almost incidentally explodes one false claim, which is that Thatcher's tenderness for Pinochet arose from his "helpfulness" over the Falklands/Malvinas War. This is a canard, sometimes also given currency by those who thought that the battle against Galtieri and Videla was not worth fighting. In fact, Chilean opinion about Argentine expansionism and promiscuity is fairly solid across the political board. The long-running Beagle Channel dispute in the Magellan Straits makes sure of that. No government in Santiago would have been anything but pro-British in such a confrontation. How nice it might have been to see Prime Minister Michael Foot thanking President Salvador Allende for his help in bringing down the gang of torturers and kidnappers in Buenos Aires. But the left forbids itself such thoughts. And the right, at least in its

Baroness Thatcher incarnation, forgets to say that a free market that requires death squads may be to that extent somewhat unfit for human consumption.

At any rate, there was a certain symmetry to the arrest of Pinochet in London, during one of his many Savile Row–type gentleman's vacations. His subsequent confinement in a Surrey mansion—Surrey with a lunatic fringe—was hardly less apt. A weekly visit from the Thatchers may not have seemed cruel, but was undoubtedly unusual. And it had been on a thank you visit to Chile in 1994 that the unironic lady had experienced the first fainting fit and collapse that presaged her ultimate decline and rancorous retirement. The picture is completed by the absolute gutlessness of British Labour in its second incarnation, and by Jack Straw's decision to send the old brute back to Santiago. In the post-Milošević moral universe, and in the wake of a finding even by the House of Lords that universal jurisdiction must stand and "sovereign immunity" must fall, that counted as a spectacular abdication. Indeed, it made Pinochet's long confinement in England a violation of habeas corpus and of his human rights.

As an unintended consequence, however, it will also pass into history. Thanks to Straw's scuttle, Pinochet was to be indicted in Chile itself, but then treated with the compassion which he had denied to his numberless victims. The judge in the case, Juan Guzmán Tapia, had voted for the extreme right in the 1970 election, had welcomed the coup in 1973, and had voted to keep Pinochet as president in the semi-fixed plebiscite of 1988. His decision to put the general in the dock was a cathartic event for the whole society. And his current investigations, into the murder of Charles Horman and others in 1970, and into the nexus of the continent-wide Operation Condor assassination scheme, remind one of nothing so much as the incorruptible magistrate in Costa-Gavras's Z. We will very soon know some even more dreadful things about how our rulers behaved in that period of despotism and disappearance. (Those nostalgic for the Castro version of what might have been should take note, however: their beloved Fidel was one of the first to denounce Pinochet's arrest, on the grandiose grounds that it infringed Latin American dignity. This demonstrated the autumnal character of his own patriarchy, and the shift toward *caudillismo* that now infects the sympathizers of people like himself, and of his ally Milošević.)

Writing just after the coup in 1973, Gabriel García Márquez produced a minor masterpiece of quasi-Castroite prose, entitled "Why Allende Had to Die." I remember helping this essay, too, into the pages of the *New Statesman*. Its closing passage still has the power to make me quiver:

He would have been 64 years old next July. His greatest virtue was following through, but fate could grant him only that rare and tragic greatness of dying in armed defense of the anachronistic booby of the bourgeois law, defending a Supreme Court of Justice which had repudiated him but would legitimize his murderers, defending a miserable Congress which had declared him illegitimate but which was to bend complacently before the will of the usurpers, defending the freedom of opposition parties which had sold their soul to fascism, defending the whole moth-eaten paraphernalia of a shitty system which he had proposed abolishing, but without a shot being fired. The drama took place in Chile, to the greater woe of the Chileans, but it will pass into history as something that happened to us all, children of this age, and it will remain in our lives forever.

To reread this was like scenting a madeleine of the drama and struggle that once was. Allende had famously been given a present of a sub-machine gun by Fidel Castro, and he died wielding it—the first time he had ever taken up arms. Had he used that gun first, and mounted a pre-emptive strike of his own against the parasitic armed forces and their cold-eyed foreign patrons, he might well have been morally justified. But the subsequent regime would have become a stupid people's democracy and would have expired, or been overthrown, in discredit, within a decade or two. Allende chose instead to die for the values which García Márquez satirized, and it can safely be said that the long struggle of the Chilean people to depose and replace Pinochet did no dishonor to those principles, which are now being slowly and painfully internationalized.

By accident—indeed by an opportunistic and cowardly deportation—Britain has repaid a portion of the debt it owes to Chile. Today, the family of General René Schneider is bringing a lawsuit in Washington against Kissinger, every page of which consists of a U.S. government declassified document. The Chilean courts are conducting inquests and autopsies on the mutilated bodies that continue to surface. The gargoyles and goons are having to try to dodge inconvenient questions. Like some other small or faraway countries in our past, Chile is one of those which—to its glory and its misery—has produced more history than it can consume locally.

Index

Reich, Robert, 146
Reno, Janet, 119, 126
Rhodesia, 48, 51, 66, 117, 173
Ribicoff, Abraham, 211
Richards, Ann, 125
Richards, Ivor Armstrong, 144
Richardson, Cecil Antonio "Tony,"
    112
Richardson, John, 111
Ridley, Nicholas, 82
Rimington, Stella, 86–8
Robertson, Marion Gordon "Pat,"
    120, 127–9, 161
Rockefeller, Winthrop, 153
Rogers, Lela, 39
Romania, 213, 219–20
Roosevelt, Eleanor, 140
Roosevelt, Franklin Delano, 138,
    189, 238–9
Roosevelt, Theodore "Teddy," 132,
    138
Rosenstiel, Susan, 30–1
Rosselli, Johnny, 188
Rothschild family, 95, 97–8, 101,
    120, 127–9
Rovere, Richard, 143
Rucker, Arthur, 102
Ruffin, Marshall, 33
Rushdie, Salman, 55–63
Russell, Richard, 191
Russian Federation, 16

Said, Edward, xii, 259
Sakharov, Andrei, 248
Salinger, Pierre, 199
Salisbury, Robert Gascoyne-Cecil,
    5th Marquess, 173
Santayana, George, 141–2
Saudi Arabia, 18, 99
Scargill, Arthur, 79–80, 83–4, 86

Schlesinger, Arthur, 179–80, 187,
    199–203, 247
Schneer, Menachem, 235
Schneider, René, 293, 302
Schwarzenegger, Arnold, 107
Schwarzkopf, Norman, 15
Scruton, Roger, 269, 273–4
Shamir, Yitzhak, 160, 258
Shays, Daniel, 117
Shvets, Yuri, 91
Sidey, Hugh, 184
Simpson, Orenthal James, 109–10
Simpson, Wallis, 131, 176, 286
Sinclair, Upton, 131
Sithole, Ndabaningi, 51
Smith, Charles Aubrey, 23
Smith, Ian, 175, 298
Smith, John, 53
Snell, Richard Wayne, 116
Soames, Nicholas, xiv, 170
Sontag, Susan, 259
Sorensen, Theodore, 186
Soviet Union, 16, 186, 200, 212–3,
    259, 265, 269, 281, 295
  Chile, relations with, 295
  Cuba, relations with, 184–8,
    190–1, 198–200, 203, 217
  Czechoslovakia invasion, 93,
    139, 211, 213, 216–7
  Cambridge spy ring, 91–104, 274
  Gulf War and, 16–17
  Vietnam, relations with, 212–3
  World War II, 138–9, 280, 285
Spain, 92, 182, 223, 291, 295
spanking, xiii, 65–75, 209–10
Spellman, Francis, 31, 63
Stalin, Joseph, 36, 92, 95–8, 100,
    214, 217, 232, 267–8, 291
Stallone, Sylvester, 107
Steiner, George, 241

About the Author

Christopher Hitchens (1949–2011) was a contributing editor to *Vanity Fair* and a columnist for *Slate*. He was the author of numerous books, including works on Thomas Jefferson, George Orwell, Mother Teresa, Henry Kissinger, and Bill and Hillary Clinton, as well as his international bestseller and National Book Award nominee *God Is Not Great*. His memoir *Hitch-22* was nominated for the Orwell Prize and was a finalist for the National Book Critics Circle Award.